MW01254540

War and the Mind

Ford Madox Ford's *Parade's End*, Modernism, and Psychology

Edited by Ashley Chantler
and Rob Hawkes

EDINBURGH
University Press

© editorial matter and organisation Ashley Chantler
   and Rob Hawkes, 2015
© the chapters their several authors, 2015

Edinburgh University Press Ltd
The Tun - Holyrood Road, 12(2f) Jackson's Entry,
Edinburgh EH8 8PJ

www.euppublishing.com

Typeset in 10.5/13 Adobe Sabon by
Servis Filmsetting Ltd, Stockport, Cheshire,
and printed and bound in Great Britain by
CPI Group (UK) Ltd, Croydon CR0 4YY

A CIP record for this book is available from the British
Library

ISBN 978 0 7486 9426 6 (hardback)
ISBN 978 0 7486 9427 3 (webready PDF)
ISBN 978 1 4744 0457 0 (epub)

The right of Ashley Chantler and Rob Hawkes to be
identified as the editors of this work has been asserted
in accordance with the Copyright, Designs and Patents
Act 1988, and the Copyright and Related Rights
Regulations 2003 (SI No. 2498).

Contents

Acknowledgements

The idea for this volume was conceived at the international conference 'Ford Madox Ford's *Parade's End*: Modernism and the First World War', which we organised at the Institute of English Studies (IES), University of London, in September 2012. Our first thanks go to Jon Millington and all at the IES, along with everyone who attended and contributed to one of the most stimulating and convivial conferences we've had the fortune to be involved with. We are especially grateful to our special guests Susanna White, director of the BBC/HBO adaptation of *Parade's End*, and Rupert Edwards, writer/director/producer of the BBC's *Who On Earth Was Ford Madox Ford? A Culture Show Special*, both of which were first broadcast shortly before the conference. Alongside a number of specially commissioned pieces, several of the chapters included in this volume were inspired by papers delivered at the IES.

We are immensely grateful to the members of the Ford Madox Ford Society, the international community of scholars and enthusiasts that sustains and enriches Ford studies. In particular, we would like to thank Max Saunders, who helped refine our plans for the volume from its earliest stages and, later, contributed a chapter. Like Max, all of the contributors have been a pleasure to work with and to them we owe a great debt of gratitude.

We would like to thank Jackie Jones and Dhara Patel at Edinburgh University Press for their wonderful help and encouragement in bringing this project to fruition and the Imperial War Museum for permission to reproduce the cover image. Our colleagues at the universities of Chester and Teesside have provided supportive environments within which we've been able to complete our editorial work. Finally, we thank our families for their invaluable support, with our special thanks and love to Nanette and Ruth.

Introduction

Ashley Chantler and Rob Hawkes

Dust and corpses in the thistles
Where the gas-shells burst like snow,
And the shrapnel screams and whistles
On the Bécourt road below,
And the High Wood bursts and bristles
Where the mine-clouds foul the sky ...
But I'm with you up at Wyndcroft,
Over Tintern on the Wye.[1]

Ford and the War

Having enlisted in the summer of 1915, Ford Madox Ford, aged forty-
two, was sent to France on 13 July 1916 as a second lieutenant with
the Welch Regiment (Special Reserve). Attached to the 9th Battalion of
the Regiment at Rouen, he was then sent to the Somme, just behind the
Front Line.[2] Towards the end of July, things were okay with Ford, all
things considering:

> We are right up in the middle of the strafe, but only with the Ist line transport.
> We get shelled two or three times a day, otherwise it is fairly dull – indeed,
> being shelled is fairly dull, after the first once or twice. Otherwise it is all very
> interesting – filling in patches of one's knowledge & so on [. . .]. The noise
> of the bombardment is continuous – so continuous that one gets used to it,
> as one gets used to the noise in a train and the ear picks out the singing of
> innumerable larks. . . .[3]

That day or the next,[4] Ford was 'blown into the air by something'
and fell 'on [his] face',[5] causing concussion, damage to his mouth and
teeth, and subsequent memory loss.[6] 'It had been from some date in
August till about the 17th September that I had completely lost my
memory, so that [. . .] three weeks of my life are completely dead to
me.'[7] Sent to a casualty clearing station in Corbie, Ford's shell shock

went undiagnosed: 'nothing more romantic [. . .] happened than having my teeth fixed'.[8]

> [B]y the 1st of September I had managed to remember at least my name and, by the 17th, when Evans and I rejoined the battalion, which had come out of the line and gone in again to the G trenches in front of Kemmel Hill [in Ypres Salient], facing Wyndschaete [now Wijtschate], I could remember most army matters fairly well.[9]

In late August, he sent his mother a reassuring letter, stating: 'I got pretty well after my shaking up & got back to the B[n.] [. . .]. I am pretty well – indeed quite well & view life with considerable composure.'[10] And on 6 September: 'it is jolly to have been in the two greatest strafes of history – & I am perfectly well & in good spirits [. . .] & for the time, perfectly safe'.[11] However, in a more honest letter, probably written a few days before,[12] to his friend and former collaborator, Joseph Conrad, Ford writes of 'a *very* big artillery strafe':

> Well I was under the table & frightened out of my life – so indeed was the other man with me. There was shelling just overhead – apparently thousands of shells bursting for miles around & overhead. I was convinced that it was all up with the XIX Div[n]. because the Huns had got note of a new & absolutely devilish shell or gun.[13]

It is in this letter and the next to Conrad (6 September) that Ford first begins to consider, not just report, the effects of the war on the mind: 'I have been for six weeks – with the exception of 24 hours – continuously within reach of German missiles &, altho' one gets absolutely to ignore them, consciously, I imagine that subconsciously one is suffering.'[14] On 6 September, he writes of emotions, having 'no *emotion*' and 'Subconscious emotion'.[15]

On 13 September, regarding taking leave and going to Paris to revise and write an epilogue for his propaganda book *Entre Saint Denis et Saint George*, Ford wrote to C. F. G. Masterman:

> The writing rather exhausted me – and indeed I collapsed & was made to see the M. O. who said I was suffering from specific shell-shock & ought to go to hospital. However, I wdn't. & got back here [Ypres Salient].[16]

Diagnosed but not cured, on 15 September Ford wrote the essay 'Arms and the Mind', his first extended treatment of 'the psychology of war'[17] (see below).

Shortly after this, Ford 'was sent back to the 3rd Battalion's home base in North Wales, at Kinmel Park, near Rhyl', but he 'found his new posting a new waste of his abilities, and – without overseas pay – a strain on his financial resources'.[18] Ordered back to France at the end of December, Ford's time as a soldier abroad was soon to end:[19] his 'lungs intervened',[20] as did his mind – 'I wasn't so much wounded as blown up by a 4.2 and shaken into a nervous breakdown'[21] – and he was sent to No. II Red Cross Hospital in Rouen. Recovery was slow and on Christmas Eve he had a relapse:

> all night I lie awake & perceive the ward full of Huns of forbidding aspect – except when they give me a sleeping draft.
>   I am in short rather ill still & sometimes doubt my own sanity – indeed, quite frequently I do. I suppose that, really, the Somme was a pretty severe ordeal, though I wasn't conscious of it at the time. Now, however, I find myself waking up in a hell of a funk – and going on being in a hell of a funk till morning. And that is pretty well the condition of a number of men here. I wonder what the effect of it will be on us all, after the war – & on national life and the like.[22]

As Max Saunders observes, 'Ford's writing from 1916 onwards [. . .] bears the impress of that blind terror he later characterised as his "Corbie-phobia": above all, the terror of losing control of his mind.'[23] It is little wonder that Ford struggled to write about the war. During it, Ford pondered in 'Arms and the Mind' on 'why I can write nothing – why I cannot even think anything that to myself seems worth thinking! – about the psychology of that Active Service of which I have seen my share'.[24] The reason then was, presumably, the shell shock he was suffering after being 'blown into the air', but also because of what Ford had 'seen' and had been, consciously or perhaps 'subconsciously', affected by. In the manuscript 'That Same Poor Man', a revised typescript of his unpublished novel 'Mr Croyd', Ford writes of a soldier: 'The sights, sounds, psychologies and conditions of trench warfare had at first appalled, then disgusted and finally wearied him beyond the bounds of patience.'[25] In *The Marsden Case* (1923), this is rendered as: 'the eyes, the ears, the brain and the fibres of every soul [. . .] have been profoundly seared by those dreadful wickednesses of embattled humanity'.[26]

After the war, 'Heaven knows I, who saw something of that struggle, would willingly wipe out of my mind every sight that I saw, every sound that I heard, every memory in my brain.'[27] The mind can take only so much:

> No one could have come through that shattering experience and still view life and mankind with any normal vision. [. . .] Nay, it had been revealed to you that beneath Ordered Life itself was stretched, the merest film with, beneath it, the abysses of Chaos. One had to come from the frail shelters of the Line to a world that was more frail than any canvas hut.[28]

The post-war mind had to make 'readjustments';[29] Ford's post-war writer's mind also had to make others, and it was not until 14 October 1923 that Ford could tell H. G. Wells: 'I am as happy as it is decent to be [. . .]. I've got over the nerve tangle of the war and feel able at last really to write again – which I never thought I should do.'[30] Ford's 'really' should be emphasised. After the war, he had continued to write, and to write about the war, as we have seen,[31] but his war writing, he felt, had 'a touch of queerness'[32] about it: he had not been able to *really* write about the war in a way that really satisfied him, that really did justice to his and others' experiences, and which would, he hoped, prevent future wars.[33] At the time of his letter to Wells, however, over seven years since enlisting and over four since leaving the army, Ford had begun *Parade's End*, his modernist masterpiece that illuminates, with deep profundity and humanity, the war and the mind.[34]

Modernism and the Mind

Modernist literature has long been recognised for its acute interest in matters of psychology, in the development of new techniques for the representation of consciousness, and for implicitly (if not explicitly) registering the influence of Sigmund Freud. In 'Modern Fiction' (1919), Virginia Woolf memorably observes that:

> [the novelist] has to have the courage to say that what interests him is no longer 'this' but 'that': out of 'that' alone must he construct his work. For the moderns 'that', the point of interest, lies very likely in the dark places of psychology.[35]

Woolf's remarks help to establish the link often made by scholars between the development of key modernist stylistic innovations and the increasing awareness of new theories of the mind – especially those based on Freud's ideas – among modernist writers. For example, when Michael Bell points out that 'modernist literature is often concerned with the question of how to live within a new context of thought, or a new worldview', he cites Freud, alongside Marx and Nietzsche, as the founders of this 'new context'.[36] Perry Meisel refers to a 'shift from outside to inside',[37] which Astradur Eysteinsson links explicitly to Freud: 'in view of previous literary history, modernism is felt to signal a radical "inward turn" in literature, and often a more thorough exploration of the human psyche than is deemed to have been probable or even possible in pre-Freudian times'.[38] As is well known, the term 'stream of consciousness' originated in psychological discourse: in William James's

The Principles of Psychology (1890), where human consciousness is described as 'nothing jointed; it flows. A "river" or a "stream" are the metaphors by which it is most naturally described'.[39] It was May Sinclair who first applied the term to literature, in a 1918 review of Dorothy Richardson's novels.[40] Sinclair's use of the term, however, focuses on the contrast between conventional approaches to plot (beginning, middle, and end), situation and scene, and Richardson's radical departure from these frameworks:

> In this series there is no drama, no situation, no set scene. Nothing happens. It is just life going on and on. It is Miriam Henderson's stream of consciousness going on and on. And in neither is there any grossly discernible beginning or middle or end.[41]

Sinclair, then, in an important sense, presents 'Miriam Henderson's stream of consciousness' as Richardson's subject matter. Critical discourse since Sinclair has tended to refer to the stream of consciousness *technique* and, therefore, to foreground formal experimentation as opposed to the shift in emphasis or narrative attention away from scenery and plot and towards the mind. New ways of thinking about the mind, consciousness, and psychology were, of course, intimately bound up with technical and stylistic innovation during the modernist period. In other words, the 'inward turn' played out at both the level of content and of form.

Ford's recovery from the war, as we have seen, was inextricably tied to his ability to write about it. Discussing the development of *Parade's End* in *It Was the Nightingale* (1933),[42] Ford makes clear that the challenge of representing 'the world as it culminated in the war' was as much technical as emotional; specifically, since you 'cannot make the world your central character', there is a problem of perspective, of point of view.[43] The approach Ford eventually took, in keeping with the sweep of much modernist fiction, was to situate his 'immense novel' within the minds of his characters. Turning inward, in modernist writing more broadly, very often means turning *away* from the bewildering complexity of modern life. In *Ancient Lights* (1911), Ford remarks that 'the life of to-day is more and more becoming a life of little things. We are losing more and more the sense of a whole, the feeling of a grand design.'[44] As this observation makes clear, Ford's interest in the instabilities and uncertainties of modernity as well as in psychological responses to that very sense of insecurity began well before 1914. He suffered the first of a number of nervous breakdowns in 1904 and was treated in a series of sanatoria in Austria. As Sara Haslam notes: 'His sufferings poisoned his mind against mental specialists in general, including psychoanalysts.'[45] Nevertheless,

Ford's 1910 novel *A Call* features the character Katya Lascarides, who Max Saunders describes as 'one of the first psychotherapist-characters in English fiction'.[46] Despite the disclaimer, 'I don't know that analysis of my own psychology matters at all to this story',[47] Dowell's entire narrative in *The Good Soldier* has been interpreted in terms of the 'talking cure',[48] and he refers more than once to his 'dual personality' during the course of the novel.[49]

One way of responding to the life of little things, no longer graspable in its entirety, is to retreat into the limited perspective of the singular consciousness, and it is this very movement inwards that *Parade's End* dramatises: the sequence begins within the omniscient perspective that presents the reader with 'two young men' in a 'perfectly appointed railway carriage'[50] and ends with Mark Tietjens' extremely limited perspective in *Last Post* (1928).[51] Alongside this formal shift from exterior to interior, the mental life and, along with it, notions of mental health form an important aspect of the tetralogy's subject matter. When Tietjens returns from France suffering from amnesia in the second part of *Some Do Not . . .* (1924), he describes his memory loss as resulting from an impaired brain: 'It's half of it, an irregular piece of it, dead. Or rather pale. Without a proper blood supply. . . . So a great portion of it, in the shape of memory, has gone' (p. 207). The same sense of hesitation between physical and psychological causes for mental phenomena appears in *No More Parades* (1925), when Tietjens attributes his growing obsession with O Nine Morgan's death to 'a crack in his [. . .] brain. A lesion!'[52] Either way, Ford's concern remains to register the effect – both physical and psychological – of war on the mind. Indeed, it is only after the 'shattering experience'[53] of the war that the mind moves to centre stage in Ford's fiction, both in terms of content (with characters whose minds have been shaken, scarred, or damaged irrevocably by the war) and of style (with abrupt time-shifts which frequently enact mental as well as structural fragmentation, and extensive use of free indirect discourse).

The shadow cast by the war on the lives and minds of both veterans and civilians also looms large in Woolf's fiction. Jacob Flanders, whose name itself refers to the war, is a marked, traumatic absence when, at the end of *Jacob's Room* (1922), his mother holds out a pair of shoes and asks his friend: 'What am I to do with these, Mr. Bonamy?'[54] Andrew Ramsay's death is announced – to shocking effect – in parenthesis in the 'Time Passes' section of *To the Lighthouse* (1927).[55] However, it is *Mrs Dalloway* (1925), and the shell-shocked veteran Septimus Warren Smith who demonstrates most forcefully the psychological legacy of the war: Smith is haunted by visions of war throughout the novel, including the appearance of his dead friend and officer, Evans.[56] Despite both having responded to the war in their fiction and having done so during the same period of years, there is little evidence of Ford having engaged directly with Woolf's writing.[57] Nevertheless, both writers developed comparable techniques for representing the mind thinking. Both, too, responded to the example of James Joyce, who Woolf describes in 'Modern Fiction' as 'concerned at all costs to reveal the flickerings of that innermost flame which flashes its messages through the brain'.[58] Ford was one of the first to recognise the importance of *Ulysses*, writing in July 1922 that: '*Ulysses* contains the undiscovered mind of man; it is human consciousness analysed as it has never before been analysed. Certain books change the world. This, success or failure, *Ulysses* does.'[59] Ford went on to discuss Joyce's novel at length in the *English Review* in December 1922:

> The literary interest of [*Ulysses*], then, arises from the fact that, for the first time in literature on an extended scale, a writer has attempted to treat man as the complex creature that man – every man! – is. The novelist, poet, and playwright hitherto, and upon the whole, have contented themselves with rendering their characters on single planes. A man making a career is rendered simply in terms of that career, a woman in love as simply a woman in love, and so on. But it does not take a novelist to see that renderings of such unilateral beings are not renderings of life as we live it. Of that every human being is aware! You conduct a momentous business interview that will influence your whole future; all the while you are aware that your interlocutor has a bulbous, veined nose; that someone in the street has a drink-roughened voice and is proclaiming that someone has murdered someone; that your physical processes are continuing; that you have a headache; you have, even as a major motive, the worry that your wife is waiting for you at the railway terminus and that you may miss your train to your country home. Your mind makes a psychological analysis of the mind of your wife as she looks at the great clock in the station; you see that great clock; superimposed over the almanack behind the head of the bulbous-nosed man, you see the enormous hands jumping the minutes.
>
> And that rendering of a very uncomplex moment in the life of the most commonplace of men; for many, such a scene will be further complicated by associations from melodies humming in the ear; by associations sweeping across them with scents or conveyed through the eye by the colours and forms of wainscotings. . . . Or merely by pictures of the estates that you may buy or lands that you may travel in if the deal on which you are engaged goes through.[60]

We might compare this to Woolf's famous entreaty in 'Modern Fiction': 'Examine for a moment an ordinary mind on an ordinary day. The mind receives a myriad impressions – trivial, fantastic, evanescent, or engraved with the sharpness of steel.'[61] However, it also recalls one of the principles underpinning Ford's Impressionism: that 'we are almost always in one place with our minds somewhere quite other'.[62]

There are striking moments throughout *Parade's End* when just this sense is evoked of the mind in one place with the body in another. *No More Parades*, for example, concludes with a lengthy scene in which Tietjens is interviewed by General Campion while his mind continually wanders away from and then back to the present moment:

> He remembered once or twice – it must have been in September, '16 – having had the job of taking battalion transport down from Locre to B.H.Q., which were in the château of Kemmell village. . . . You muffled every bit of metal you could think of: bits, trace-chains, axles . . . and *yet*, whilst you hardly breathed, in the thick darkness some damn thing would always chink and jolt; beef tins made a noise of old iron. . . . And *bang*, after the long whine, would come the German shell [. . .] . . . . Imagine doing it with lorries, that could be heard five miles away! . . . [. . .] He exclaimed: 'By God! How my mind wanders! How long will it go on?' He said: 'I am at the end of my tether.' He had missed what the general had said for some time.
> The general said:
> 'Well. Has he?'
> Tietjens said:
> 'I didn't catch, sir!' (pp. 229–30)

This passage is characteristic of the way that Ford uses free indirect discourse throughout *Parade's End* to shift from the perspective of the third-person narrator to that of a character. Here, 'He remembered' at the start of the paragraph shifts, or rather merges, into 'You muffled' and 'Imagine', which are clearly Tietjens' thoughts. Furthermore, the extensive use of suspension dots, which is, again, characteristic of the novel, contribute to the sense of Tietjens' fragmented and fragmenting mind 'at the end of [its] tether'. Again, here, the novel's focus on the mind and mental strain concerns both thematic and formal levels so that style and content are rendered inseparable.

The development of literary techniques enabling writers to produce the effect of the mind thinking, giving a sense of direct access to the consciousness of characters, was one of the major innovations of the modernist age and one that Joyce, Woolf, and Ford each contributed to. In Ford's case, though, technical and stylistic inventiveness went hand in hand with the recovery of his ability to write at all and especially to write about the war and to register its effect on the mind. This volume seeks to demonstrate something of the complexity of Ford's achievement in *Parade's End* in terms of the wide-ranging ways in which it recalls and evokes the impact of the war on the minds of those who fought and those who stayed at home. In doing so, it also demonstrates just how rich the territory surrounding *Parade's End*, modernism, and psychology really is. As noted above, the modernist interest in psychology has often been linked back to Freud – and this runs the risk of presenting an overly simplified view – just as the literary techniques for representing the life of the mind can be framed, somewhat reductively, solely in terms of the stream of consciousness. In the chapters that follow, however, alongside Freud and alongside modernist technique, we will encounter questions of sadism and sexuality, trauma, empathy, discipline, self-analysis, insomnia, intermediality, shell shock, heroism, peace, and many more.

War and the Mind

Because of its focus and its scope, *War and the Mind: Ford Madox Ford's Parade's End, Modernism, and Psychology* proved complex to structure into discrete sections. (So much relating to Ford is complex.) All the chapters connect, being illuminations of Ford's masterpiece and their centring on and around various key issues: the war, war trauma, shell shock, the effects of the war on those who fought and those at home, contemporary psychological and psychoanalytical discourses, and Ford's awareness of the challenges posed to modes of representation, including literary Impressionism, by the mental states brought about by the war.

Several chapters have obvious connections, notably Eve Sorum's 'Empathy, Trauma, and the Space of War in *Parade's End*' and Meghan Marie Hammond's 'Fellow Feeling in Ford's *Last Post*: Modernist Empathy and the Eighteenth-Century Man'. Sorum considers Ford's insights into the problems with perspective-taking that underlie war writing in general, and trench-warfare writing in particular; in *Parade's End*, questions of perspective-taking are integrally connected both to the form of Ford's novels and to the possibilities for empathetic engagement. Throughout the tetralogy, Ford narrates the war as a series of erasures, defacements, and ellipses – gaps that not only speak to the traumas enacted upon both individual and social memory, but that also indicate the problems inherent in engaging with other's perspectives. With movements between subjective and cartographic modes of seeing, Ford finds a form to represent the violence done both to individual perception and to the ability to 'stand in someone else's shoes' (that familiar trope of empathetic engagement). Sorum brings into her chapter early twentieth-century theories of empathy, particularly as articulated in German art historian Wilhelm Worringer's seminal *Abstraction and Empathy* (1908).

Worringer is also present in 'Fellow Feeling in Ford's *Last Post*: Modernist Empathy and the Eighteenth-Century Man', where Hammond examines the role that empathy plays in the final novel of the tetralogy, *Last Post*. Like many other exemplars of high modernism, Ford's novel circulates between characters, revealing multiple inner monologues and idiosyncratic interiors. *Last Post* thus allows the reader to empathise with those characters by turn. Worringer is deeply critical of empathic forms of representation, and while *Last Post* practises empathic representation, it also asks us to challenge the legitimacy of such representation. Tietjens' disappearance from the last volume of *Parade's End*, Hammond suggests, might be read as a flight from the modernist era's new, specifically empathic, form of feeling with others. Empathy, the ability to 'think with' or 'feel with' another person, has deep roots in eighteenth-century discourses – it is the twentieth-century cousin of sympathy as laid out in the influential works of David Hume and Adam Smith. Hammond argues that our readerly engagement with the silent Mark is fundamentally empathic in nature. The text's way of introducing our minds to his mind circumvents the inference-based processes of sympathy, meaning we encounter in *Last Post* a clear break with eighteenth-century habits of mind.

Following Sorum's and Hammond's engagements with empathy, of looking out beyond the self, Barbara Farnworth, in 'The Self-Analysis of Christopher Tietjens', looks at the self-looking self, notably how Tietjens' consciousness reveals a constant concern with protecting his intelligence, emotional control and mental health. He has developed a set of rules for when and how he will allow his mind to confront traumatic events. Tietjens lives by the general principle of 'not talking', which includes repressing his feelings, protecting his wife's reputation and concealing his private life. He worries, however, that his repression of difficult events and emotions may eventually rebound upon him. Tietjens frequently refers to himself as an eighteenth-century man who feels out of place in the twentieth century and yearns to return to an earlier, feudal era. Despite this characterisation, Tietjens' constant self-conscious monitoring of his mental fitness reveals his engagement with contemporary psychological theories of the late nineteenth and early twentieth century as he negotiates the trauma of war.

Chapter 6, 'Composing the War and the Mind; Composing *Parade's End*', by Alexandra Becquet, considers how Ford, in 1923, finally found a way to write about the war. (As discussed above, Ford had not been able to *really* write about the war until then.) *Parade's End* is partly about disorder and disruption. It is also about how one can find a centre, a stable place for the self, the mind, the relationship, and the family beyond the expected (in a post-war world). And Becquet's chapter, with its engagement with Ford's drawing upon painting and music to create an 'intermedial' text that helps him write about the war, is in itself a centre: beyond that centre, the other chapters radiate.

Three chapters might seem to have been placed together because they just explicitly consider Ford alongside other writers about the war. However, there are fruitful connections to be made between 'The Work of Sleep: Insomnia and Discipline in Ford and Sassoon', by Sarah Kingston, 'Representing Shell Shock: A Return to Ford and Rebecca West', by Charlotte Jones, and '"I hate soldiering": Ford, May Sinclair, and War Heroism', by Leslie de Bont, relating to the effects of the war on the mind. Kingston discusses the descriptions and uses of insomnia and other sleep-related behaviours in *Parade's End* and Siegfried Sassoon's *Memoirs of an Infantry Officer* (1930) in order to illustrate the way in which these texts present evidence of and contribute to a contemporary discourse on insomnia as it is related to subjectivity and the functioning of power. Because of its connections with isolation (sleep-space unconsciousness), sleep is, in some respects, private; however, because of its implications for productivity, it also becomes subject to intervention and normalisation. Both texts feature characters who experience insomnia, and, when paired with contemporary medical texts, provide evidence of Edwardian society's interpretation of sleep habits and failures, as well as definitions and representations of the insomniac. *Parade's End* and *Memoirs of an Infantry Officer* also expose expectations regarding one's obligation to one's society, the society's dependence on complicity, causes of and reactions to anxiety created by the war and modernisation. They thus expose a discourse in which discipline is maintained through the prevention of independent thought and an emphasis on the (illusory) mastery of control over one's body and mind.

In 'Representing Shell Shock: A Return to Ford and Rebecca West', Charlotte Jones considers another discourse: reading *Parade's End* and West's *The Return of the Soldier* (1918) alongside one another, she traces the aetiology of shell shock as a socio-cultural discourse across the immediate post-war period. Jones argues that West furthered the redefinition of prevalent medical discourse surrounding shell shock in an attempt to recognise the psychological condition as a legitimate consequence of war trauma. Ford had recourse to West's formulation in his explorations of the dehumanisation and objectification of soldiers that was responsible for an experiential chasm between citizen and (former) soldier in the 1920s. Both novelists' representation of shell shock reflects and contributed to society's nascent understanding of the condition. Furthermore, both engage with other paradigms increasingly shaping society's response to shell shock at the same time: medical definitions; military classifications; and emergent psychoanalytic models of memory, trauma, and repression. Jones argues that, in working through the returns of their respective soldiers, Ford and West were 'rewriting' contemporary narratives of shell shock in their attempts to imagine and represent the reintegration of the mind after war. Leslie de Bont furthers Jones's discussion by considering the emphasis in Ford's and May Sinclair's war writing 'on the psychological issues faced by soldiers involving shell shock, the influence of war on the relationships between genders, the return to civilian life, fear of and fascination with death, the anxiety of loss, and the difficulty of articulating pre-war, war and post-war times'. Through the complex (and mutable) notion of 'heroism' (before and after the war), de Bont argues that Ford and Sinclair reveal a new heroism: one of the mind, with (perhaps paradoxically) its fears, neuroses, and dark unconscious.

Max Saunders' '"Sex ferocity" and "the sadic lusts of certain novelists": Sexuality, Sadomasochism, and Suppression in *Parade's End*' opens the volume, partly because its focus is initially on *Some Do Not . . .* and shows Tietjens before the war, partly because it lays the foundations for the ensuing chapters through four closely related topics: the omnipresence of sexual thoughts; the relationship between sexuality, madness and violence, particularly sex and the war; the idea of repression; and the concepts of sadism and masochism. These topics lay the foundation for Saunders' conclusion regarding how the war moves Tietjens from a pre-war world to a post-war world, and a tentative freedom. Saunders considers Ford's wariness about Freud, but argues that Ford's presentation of sexuality has much in common with a psychoanalytic view, probably influenced by British psychical researchers such as F. W. H. Myers and Oliver Lodge. In the volume's second chapter, 'Freud Madox Ford: Impressionism, Psychoanalytic Trauma Theory, and Ford's Wartime Writing', Karolyn Steffens reminds us that readers in the 1920s of Ford's work thought that there were various Freudian strains in his work, to the extent that Osbert Sitwell coined the cynical moniker 'Freud Madox Fraud'. Steffens employs Freud's theory of trauma established in *Beyond the Pleasure Principle* (1920) as a framework to understand how Ford's literary Impressionism, adapting to the historical particularities of the war, is heightened by and ultimately evolves into an aesthetic oscillating between Eros and Thanatos when rendering his war experience. By considering *Parade's End* and other wartime writing by Ford, Steffens argues that Ford's Impressionism becomes an aesthetic of duality, mirroring Tietjens who becomes the paradigmatic 'homo duplex' in the trenches: Ford's Impressionism evolves into one that defines traumatised consciousness as interpenetrated by both Eros and Thanatos, an aesthetic that illuminates the frequently overlooked intersections between sexuality and violence in Freud's theories of trauma.

Given what is going on in the world as we write this, it seems appropriate (Ford would no doubt have approved) to conclude the volume with Gene M. Moore's 'Peace of Mind in *Parade's End*'. Here, Moore examines both the psychological effects of war on the mind, as represented in *Parade's End*, and the various strategies developed by men suffering stress to preserve their sanity and self-control under wartime conditions. Tietjens, although severely tested by the trauma of war and the threat of insanity, emerges from the test with his values strengthened and clarified. As Moore argues, while *Parade's End* marks the end of parades, of ceremonies and fanfare, it also signals the possibility of a more humane and intimate peace than the one declared by the treaty at Versailles. The values that sustain Tietjens in the war – living simply, frugally, and with an abiding awareness of the natural world – are those through which he eventually finds his peace of mind. Things can be simple rather than complex.

Notes

1. Ford, 'The Iron Music', *On Heaven and Poems Written on Active Service*, p. 36. The poem is dated 22 July 1916.
2. Saunders, Introduction, *War Prose*, p. 3. See also Saunders, *Ford Madox Ford*, I, pp. 479–94; II, pp. 1–15. On 18 July 1916, Ford wrote to Lucy Masterman from Rouen: 'We leave here today to join our various units – presumably in the firing line: I don't know where. We are all scattered – wh. is disagreeable, but, as jollities go, we have had a jolly time till now, on the boat & so on': *Letters of Ford Madox Ford*, p. 66. On Ford's reasons for enlisting, see Ford to Catherine Hueffer (18 September 1915), *War Prose*, p. 218; Saunders, *Ford Madox Ford*, II, pp. 480–4.
3. Ford to Lucy Masterman (28 July 1916), *Letters of Ford Madox Ford*, pp. 66, 67.
4. Saunders, Introduction, p. 4.
5. Ford, *It Was the Nightingale*, p. 175.
6. Saunders, *Ford Madox Ford*, II, p. 2.
7. Ford, *It Was the Nightingale*, p. 175.
8. Ford, *It Was the Nightingale*, p. 175. 'Sir Charles Myers, a Cambridge academic who became consultant psychologist to the British Expeditionary Force in 1915, was the first to employ the term "shell shock" in an official capacity, although the term was already in popular usage': Reid, *Broken Men*, p. 26. On shell shock, amnesia and other symptoms, see also Babington, *Shell-Shock*; Binnevald, *From Shell Shock to Combat Stress*; Bonikowski, *Shell Shock and the Modernist Imagination*; Leese, *Shell Shock*; Shephard, *A War of Nerves*.

9. Ford, *It Was the Nightingale*, p. 175. Evans was a soldier in Ford's regiment: 'In September, 1916 we had both been rejoining the battalion after sick leave. He came from England, where he had been recovering after a wound in the thigh; I from a place called Corbie': *It Was the Nightingale*, p. 175. Saunders gives 23 August as the date when Ford rejoined the 9th Battalion: Introduction, p. 4. See also Ford to F. S. Flint (23 June 1920), *Letters of Ford Madox Ford*, p. 106: 'I am not done in and am gradually recovering physical fitness; and mental, too. The only thing that seems to have gone is my memory – and even that comes back slowly! You see, when I was in Corbie C. C. S. in July 1916, my memory went altogether. For thirty-six hours I did not even know my name.' Also *Mightier Than the Sword*, pp. 264–5: 'after I was blown up at Bécourt-Bécordel [now Bécordel-Bécourt] in '16 and, having lost my memory, lay in the Casualty Clearing Station in Corbie, with the enemy planes dropping bombs all over it and the dead Red Cross nurses being carried past my bed, I used to worry agonizedly about what my name could be – and have a day-nightmare. The night-nightmare was worse, but the day was as bad as was necessary.'
10. Ford to Catherine Hueffer (c. late August 1916), *War Prose*, p. 224.
11. Ford to Catherine Hueffer (6 September 1916), *War Prose*, pp. 4–5.
12. In a letter to Conrad dated 6 September 1916, Ford writes of continuing 'my notes upon sounds' 'for yr information': in Naumburg, 'A Collector Looks at Ford Again', p. 172. The letter and three others at that time to Conrad are also reprinted, with understandable variants (Ford's handwriting is at times illegible), in *Letters of Ford Madox Ford*, pp. 71–6, 78–80.
13. Ford to Joseph Conrad (September 1916), in 'A Collector Looks at Ford Again', p. 170.
14. Ford to Joseph Conrad (September 1916), p. 172.
15. Ford to Joseph Conrad (6 September 1916), pp. 173, 176.
16. Ford to C. F. G. Masterman (13 September 1916), *Letters of Ford Madox Ford*, p. 76. See also Ford, 'Trois Jours de Permission', 817–18; Saunders, *Ford Madox Ford*, II, p. 21. Ford's *Between St. Dennis and St. George: A Sketch of Three Civilisations* (London: Hodder & Stoughton, 1915) and the slightly earlier *When Blood Is Their Argument: An Analysis of Prussian Culture* (London: Hodder & Stoughton, 1915) were prompted by Masterman, who in September 1914 was head of the War Propaganda Bureau. See Jain, 'When Propaganda Is Your Argument', pp. 163–75.
17. Ford, 'Arms and the Mind', *War Prose*, p. 37. A companion essay, 'War and the Mind' (written in the summer of 1917), starts as a meditation on the soldier's 'division of the mind': the 'mind at rest' (the 'quiescent mind') and the active mind of 'the observant – as it were the official observer's mind': *War Prose*, pp. 43, 42.
18. Saunders, Introduction, p. 8.
19. For a fascinating record of Ford's time as a soldier back in England, see the letters from 26 October 1917 to 14 January 1919 in Ford, *The Correspondence of Ford Madox Ford and Stella Bowen*, pp. 3–55.
20. Ford to C. F. G. Masterman (5 January 1917), *Letters of Ford Madox Ford*, p. 81. Writing to Conrad (19 December 1916), Ford admitted: 'As for me, –

c'est fini de moi, I believe, at least as far as fighting is concerned – my lungs are all charred up and gone': 'A Collector Looks at Ford Again', p. 177.
21. Ford to Katherine Hueffer (10 December 1916), *War Prose*, p. 9.
22. Ford to C. F. G. Masterman (5 January 1917), p. 82.
23. Saunders, Introduction, p. 17. On 'Corbie-phobia', see *Mightier Than the Sword*, pp. 265–6.
24. Ford, 'Arms and the Mind', p. 36.
25. Ford, 'That Same Poor Man', *War Prose*, p. 265. The narrator also says that the soldier 'had, for long, been too much afraid, himself, of going mad' (p. 266).
26. Ford, *The Marsden Case*, quoted in *War Prose*, p. 144.
27. Ford, *The Marsden Case*, p. 263.
28. Ford, *It Was the Nightingale*, pp. 48, 49.
29. Ford, 'From a Paris Quay' (1924), quoted in *War Prose*, p. 17.
30. Ford to H. G. Wells (14 October 1923), *Letters of Ford Madox Ford*, p. 154.
31. See also *War Prose*; Harvey, *Ford Madox Ford*; Saunders, 'Ford Madox Ford: Further Bibliographies'.
32. Ford, 'From a Paris Quay', p. 18.
33. On Ford's hopes for *Parade's End*, see the dedicatory epistle 'To Gerald Duckworth' in *A Man Could Stand Up –*, pp. 3–5, and *It Was the Nightingale*, pp. 205–7.
34. Saunders, Introduction, pp. 14–15.
35. Woolf, 'Modern Fiction', p. 108.
36. Bell, 'The Metaphysics of Modernism', p. 10. See also Childs, *Modernism*, pp. 47–54; and Stevenson, *Modernist Fiction*, pp. 65–71.
37. Meisel, 'Psychology', p. 79.
38. Eysteinsson, *The Concept of Modernism*, p. 26.
39. James, *The Principles of Psychology*, I, p. 239.
40. For further discussion of the term 'stream of consciousness' and its origins, see Fernihough, 'Consciousness as a stream', pp. 65–81.
41. Sinclair, 'The Novels of Dorothy Richardson', pp. 5–6.
42. See Ford, *It Was the Nightingale*, pp. 172–207.
43. Ford, *It Was the Nightingale*, p. 195.
44. Ford, *Ancient Lights*, p. 62.
45. Haslam, *Fragmenting Modernism*, p. 24.
46. Saunders, *Ford Madox Ford*, I, p. 301.
47. Ford, *The Good Soldier*, ed. Martin Stannard, p. 75.
48. See Childs, *Modernism*, p. 52.
49. Ford, *The Good Soldier*, pp. 75, 86.
50. Ford, *Some Do Not . . .*, ed. Max Saunders, p. 3. All further references are to this edition.
51. For further discussion of this shift, see Rob Hawkes, *Ford Madox Ford and the Misfit Moderns*, pp. 147–52; and James Heldman, 'The Last Victorian Novel', pp. 271–84.
52. Ford, *No More Parades*, ed. Joseph Wiesenfarth, pp. 228–9. All further references are to this edition.
53. Ford, *It Was the Nightingale*, p. 48.
54. Woolf, *Jacob's Room*, p. 155.

55. '[A shell exploded. Twenty or thirty young men were blown up in France, among them Andrew Ramsay, whose death, mercifully, was instantaneous.]': Woolf, *To the Lighthouse*, p. 145.
56. See, for example, Woolf, *Mrs Dalloway*, p. 76.
57. Ford did review Woolf's *Night and Day* in the *Piccadilly Review* in October 1919: 'I. The Novel', *Critical Essays*, pp. 186–9; but he does not include Woof in his 'haughty and proud generation' alongside James Joyce, D. H. Lawrence, Wyndham Lewis, Katherine Mansfield and Dorothy Richardson: 'A Haughty and Proud Generation', *Critical Essays*, pp. 208–17.
58. Woolf, 'Modern Fiction', p. 107.
59. Ford, 'A Haughty and Proud Generation', p. 217.
60. Ford, '*Ulysses* and the Handling of Indecencies', *Critical Essays*. p. 219.
61. Woolf, 'Modern Fiction', p. 106.
62. Ford, 'On Impressionism', *Critical Writings of Ford Madox Ford*, p. 41.

Chapter 1

'Sex ferocity' and 'the sadic lusts of certain novelists': Sexuality, Sadomasochism, and Suppression in *Parade's End*

Max Saunders

> J'ai seul la clef de cette parade sauvage.[1]
> Arthur Rimbaud

What would it mean to take seriously Graham Greene's claim that Ford's Tietjens books (along with *The Good Soldier*) are 'almost the only adult novels dealing with the sexual life that have been written in English'?[2] What is it that he thought 'adult' about Ford's rendering of the sexual life? And why 'almost'? What comparable works might he have had in mind? The comment appeared in 1950, in the promotional pamphlet put together by Knopf when publishing *Parade's End* together for the first time in one volume. Greene's own novel that might be said to be his most adult dealing with the sexual life, *The End of the Affair* – and which (as Greene himself acknowledged) would have been virtually inconceivable without Ford's *The Good Soldier*[3] – was published the following year. Does that mean he had his own writing in mind?

Whichever specific novel or novels Greene may have meant, his point was that there weren't many of them. As a judgement on English fiction of the early twentieth century, this is curious. What about all those works David Trotter termed 'Edwardian Sex Novels',[4] written by figures such H. G. Wells or his friend and Ford's lover Violet Hunt? Or by Ford's friend and discovery, D. H. Lawrence, who carried on writing more adult and more explicit sex novels long after the Edwardian period. Don't *The Rainbow*, *Women in Love*, and *Lady Chatterley's Lover* deserve to be described as 'adult' works? Or Joyce's *Ulysses*? And what about the later generation of writers like Henry Miller or Christopher Isherwood? Perhaps Greene didn't think they were 'adult' either. Even thinking in terms of Ford's *oeuvre*, it doesn't make much sense to claim *Parade's End* as exceptional in its emphasis on sexuality.

Where Greene's claim is valuable, however, is in provoking us to confront the *ways* in which *Parade's End* deals with the sexual life. For, although written at too late a date to qualify as an Edwardian sex novel, *Parade's End* is certainly a novel representing Edwardian sex. While sexuality in the tetralogy has received attention from many critics, the topic has often been displaced by social history – the war, Tietjens as the 'last Tory', the Suffragettes – or by discussions of narrative technique. This is partly because, as Julian Barnes has argued in a valuable recent corrective: 'It is not at first obvious how saturated *Parade's End* is with sex – with memories of it, hopes for it, and rumours about it.'[5] The sexual theme isn't exactly concealed. As Barnes continues: 'the central emotional and sexual vortex is that involving Sylvia, Christopher and Valentine'.[6] But its pervasiveness is surprising. In Barnes's words again: 'the lives of lesser characters, even those who are specks at the periphery of the reader's vision, are also endlessly disrupted and twisted by sex'.[7] Those 'specks at the periphery of the reader's vision' hint punningly at how it is sex which is always in the reader's peripheral vision. That is perhaps one reason why one might find Ford's treatment of sexuality 'adult'. He is able to approach the topic obliquely, getting sex in in subliminal ways, so that the novels *are* saturated, but not obviously so.[8] Soon after finishing *Parade's End*, Ford wrote:

> The trouble is that, at any rate in Anglo-Saxondom, the moment a man of distinction gets hold of an unorthodox idea – be it connected with politics or religion or sex – straight-way he loses most of his sense of proportion and nearly all his power of putting things.[9]

That 'sense of proportion' is also a writer's sense of the proportion of a novel; its form: the discipline he thought lacking in a writer like Lawrence – whose genius Ford was nevertheless the first to proclaim.

This chapter concentrates on the ways in which, in *Parade's End*, Ford 'gets hold of' ideas of sexuality that – if they scarcely seem unorthodox now, and had entered metapsychological discourse in the decade before the war – were certainly uncommon in the fiction of the time. I shall focus on how sexuality is represented in four central characters: Christopher Tietjens and the three main women, Sylvia, Valentine, and Edith Ethel Duchemin; though Macmaster and Reverend Duchemin will also be considered. If I concentrate on *Some Do Not . . .* for brevity's sake, the argument could be extended throughout the tetralogy: that, for all Ford's wariness about Freud, his presentation of sexuality has much in common with the emerging psychoanalytic view (though he probably arrived at it by other routes), especially with respect to four closely related topics:

1. the omnipresence of sexual thoughts;
2. the connection between sexuality and madness and violence;
3. the idea of repression;
4. the concepts of sadism and masochism.

Barnes gives a good account of the pervasiveness of sexual thoughts in *Parade's End*, making it unnecessary to elaborate upon it here, except to add that it is brilliantly rendered in the subtexts of conversation in much of Ford's work. To choose just one example: it is perceptible in General Campion's rage with Tietjens over the car crash that closes the first half of *Some Do Not . . .*, which is also rage over what he presumes is Tietjens' affair with Valentine – a rage which is partly motivated by his own infatuation with Sylvia. But such thoughts are very much at the periphery of our attention to the scene. What dominates is the extraordinary, contradictory mix of Campion's responses. He is suspicious – he just assumes that because Tietjens is in a cart with Valentine they must already be lovers – then he indulges in what is tantamount to a form of paternalistic collusion, as he immediately switches into male solidarity mode, trying not to let his sister in his car see who Tietjens is with, so that the assumed affair can be hushed up. And he is angry, not just because his grand car has been damaged, but because he has been rattled by the shock of crash, the fear of almost killing someone, and further shock of discovering that the person he nearly killed was the godson for whom he feels such affection.

This episode is also a palpable example of the second topic: the connection between sexuality and madness and violence (and therefore, of course, war). In this case, the combination has been anticipated in the extraordinary breakfast scene at the Duchemins, during which Edith Ethel's husband, the vicar with a remote connection to the Pre-Raphaelites, has an insane outburst of obscenities, until Macmaster instructs Duchemin's prize-fighter minder to punch him agonisingly in the kidney to keep him quiet. Duchemin's taunts seem insane in the violence they do to the good manners and decorum of the social occasion. Yet from another point of view he is simply articulating the sexual undercurrents of the scene, in which Macmaster, who had ostensibly come to interview Duchemin about the Pre-Raphaelites, has been distracted by his wife, and the two of them are flirting under the guise of a Pre-Raphaelite literary sensibility. Meanwhile Tietjens has recognised Valentine as the lead Suffragette whose protest had ended in sexual violence the previous day; and the air is thick with sexual tension as the two of them begin to get to know each other better. As Barnes says: 'the emotional level of the novel is high, and often close to hysteria'.[10]

Ford shows Valentine, too, to be concerned about the possible connection between sexuality and violence: a connection that is always in the air during wartime, but arguably had remained current since the 'Jack the Ripper' Whitechapel murders of prostitutes of the late 1880s and early 1890s. Seeing Tietjens again, on Armistice Day, Valentine worries that, clearly deranged by the war, he might do her violence: 'A madness caused by sex obsessions is not infrequently homicidal', she thinks, though immediately doubts the diagnosis: 'But perhaps he had not got sex-obsessions.'[11] And perhaps someone wondering whether someone else does or doesn't have 'sex-obsessions' may have them herself?

We shall return to this question of the relationship between sexuality and violence, and especially between sex and war. First, let us consider the remaining two topics, so as to tease out how Ford's presentation of sexuality differs from Barnes's description. The idea of repression is as pervasive as the idea of sex; and it too is an important component of the crash scene. Tietjens and Valentine figure as those capable of holding such feelings of sexual or aggressive impulses in check, at least up to a point; as being some of those who 'do not . . .' (the question of ellipses and suppression dots is crucial throughout the tetralogy). Take the marvellous detail of Valentine's petticoat in the scene just after the car accident. The petticoat brings together all these ideas. All they've done is talk, yet he can order her to take off her petticoat as unembarrassedly as if he were asking her to post a letter, as if they both understand that the needs of the injured horse must override any proprieties. There is even a suggestion that there is nothing improper about it, as if both are able to suppress the sexual connotations. The fact Tietjens thinks at once of her petticoat indicates his unsentimental resourcefulness. And yet: doesn't it also suggest he might have been thinking about her undergarments already? Indeed, petticoats already had come to his mind, associated with violence, during his earlier walk with Valentine back from the Duchemins:

> Tietjens paused and aimed with his hazel stick an immense blow at a tall spike of yellow mullein with its undecided, furry, glaucous leaves and its undecided, buttony, unripe lemon-coloured flower. The structure collapsed, gracefully, like a woman killed among crinolines!
> 'Now I'm a bloody murderer!' Tietjens said. 'Not gory! Green-stained with vital fluid of innocent plant . . . And by God! Not a woman in the country who won't let you rape her after an hour's acquaintance!' He slew two more mulleins and a sow-thistle! A shadow, but not from the sun, a gloom, lay across the sixty acres of purple grass bloom and marguerites, white: like petticoats of lace over the grass![12]

Doesn't Tietjens' thinking of Valentine's petticoat even suggest too that he has associated the blood of the horse with female sexuality? Violence with sex; and sex with rape and murder? Though the story of the tetralogy is of how Valentine's kind of sexuality is the cure for the violence he has suffered as a result of Sylvia's kind (as we shall see). And then, just as Campion is arguing with Tietjens, Valentine throws a bundle of rolled-up strips of torn petticoat over the hedge towards them. This socially incriminating material fact not only rolls to their feet, but Tietjens tells Campion: 'Pick up that thing and give it me' (p. 176). It's a wonderfully judged moment, in which neither of them comment on what the 'thing' is; and Ford leaves it open whether this is because Campion doesn't know – isn't paying attention to it, because he's concentrating on Tietjens and the wounded horse – or because he does, but is pretending he doesn't for form's sake, or is repressing the knowledge for his own sake.

Petticoats were a familiar synecdoche for women, especially for the kind of complications of femininity that men of action don't want bothering them in a crisis. For example, James said of Stevenson: 'His books are for the most part without women, and it is not women who fall most in love with them. But Mr. Stevenson does not need, as we may say, a petticoat to inflame him.'[13] If Valentine's petticoat is partly what inflames the argument between Tietjens and Campion, its sexual implications are repressed. It's because Tietjens and Valentine are free-thinkers, and can speak directly about sex without the repression of euphemism, that they can also ignore it when the situation requires. Tietjens' instructions imply that under these circumstances the petticoat is just a petticoat, and her removing it will not have any suggestion of intimacy or impropriety. You can't imagine Macmaster telling Edith Ethel to get her underwear off, in so many words, to do something practical like administer first aid. (Of course such social constraints can't be negated this simply; and also, the fact that they think so alike through this episode signifies their intimacy.) The petticoat is a wonderfully ambivalent symbol, which puts Valentine's femininity in the forefront under the guise of divesting her of it.

Macmaster and Edith Ethel also appear to stand for repression. Their Pre-Raphaelite aestheticism is a kind of sublime renunciation: a sublimation of sex into beauty; as when Valentine thinks of love as 'the beautiful inclination' (p. 281). The word 'circumspect' keeps attaching itself to them. They might value it as a form of vigilant self-control. But to Tietjens it seems a form of hypocrisy, which he has already attacked in his discussion about Rossetti on the train to Rye. For him, such a pose of moral superiority is merely an alibi, for, as he puts it, 'committing adultery [. . .] with the name of Heaven on our lips' (p. 27). Tietjens interrupts Macmaster and Mrs Duchemin having their first kiss at the end of Part I, Chapter V. It's just after that that he has the thought about there being: 'Not a woman in the country who won't let you rape her after an hour's acquaintance!'

Parade's End is often discussed as if its centre is the change in Tietjens from being one of the ones who 'do not' to someone who can accept happiness for himself despite social convention. But that's also Valentine's story. Even more so, since she starts from a less cynical place than Tietjens. She takes Edith Ethel Duchemin's self-presentation at face value, because it fits with her view of the world as a 'place of renunciations, of high endeavour and sacrifice' (p. 279). But when the war breaks out, Edith Ethel loses her self-possession. She's been staying surreptitiously with Macmaster in a hotel in Scotland. They can't travel back to London together, so Macmaster asks Tietjens to escort her; but they are seen by General Campion and his party who are also rushing back to London in the war-panic. She is thus suddenly the subject of scandal. It's assumed that she's Tietjens' mistress. But also she thinks Macmaster has got her pregnant. The implication is that this is a hysterical reaction. She summons Valentine, supposedly her friend, over to the rectory as soon as she's back, and Ford writes:

> By the light of candles in tall silver sticks, against oak panelling she had seemed like a mad block of marble, with staring, dark eyes and mad hair. She had exclaimed in a voice as hard as a machine's:
> 'How do you get rid of a baby? You've been a servant. You ought to know!'
> That had been the great shock, the turning-point, of Valentine Wannop's life. (p. 279)

This violent snobbishness from someone she thought was her friend is shocking enough. But Edith Ethel's outburst means Valentine has to adjust her vision of the world too: 'Mrs. Duchemin had revealed the fact that her circumspect, continent and suavely aesthetic personality was doubled by another at least as coarse as, and infinitely more incisive in expression than, that of the drunken cook' (p. 320). This episode also feeds into Valentine's subliminal concern that Tietjens too may have had an affair with Edith Ethel. It makes it all the more plausible, when Sylvia tells her over the phone: 'Young woman! You'd better keep off the grass. Mrs. Duchemin is already my husband's mistress' (p. 326). Sylvia may believe it herself, since she has seen Edith Ethel sneak into Macmaster's rooms and has heard the rumours about Tietjens being seen with her on the train down from Scotland, so suspects the two men might share her. But whether she does believe it or not, there's a wonderful comedy in the idea that she should be protecting one mistress against a potential rival.

The complexity and unconventionality of such moments are characteristic of Ford's writing about sex. Barnes is astute about Tietjens' unconventionality:

> Tietjens's notions of love and sex – which you would not expect to be con-
> ventional – are summed up, at one point, as follows: 'You seduced a young
> woman in order to be able to finish your talks to her'. Which is the exact
> opposite of one conventional male view, in which 'chatting up', with luck,
> leads to sex, and afterwards you wonder what to talk about.[14]

It is the book's presentation of sadism and masochism, though (the
fourth and last of our topics), that is where it is perhaps most unconven-
tional. There are three references to sadism in the manuscript of *Some
Do Not . . .*: two of them in relation to Edith Ethel and one in relation
to Tietjens and Valentine. But in each case something untoward happened to the word in the publication process – which goes some way to
account for why it is that readers have been less attentive to how sadism
is associated with the other characters than they have to Sylvia's sadistic
tendencies. Though *Parade's End* doesn't label Sylvia as sadistic, there is
no doubt that she relishes the pain she inflicts on others: psychological
pain in Tietjens' case; physical in the case of his white bulldog, which
clearly stands in for him in her mind as she whips it fatally: 'There's a
pleasure in lashing into a naked white beast. . . . Obese and silent. . . .
Like Christopher.'[15] Recollecting this pleasure later, she connects it with
sex:

> As Christopher is the last stud-white hope of the Groby Tory breed. . . .
> Modelling himself on our Lord. . . . But our Lord was never married. He
> never touched on topics of sex. Good for Him. . . . (p. 154)

The first instance of the explicit references to sadism in the manuscript is Tietjens' musings on what brought Edith Ethel and Macmaster
together:

> She had become Macmaster's mistress, as far as Tietjens knew, after a dread-
> ful scene in the rectory, Duchemin having mauled his wife like a savage dog,
> and Macmaster in the house. . . . It was natural: a Sadic reaction as it were.
> (*Some Do Not . . .*, p. 232)

The entire manuscript of *Some Do Not . . .* (apart from a discarded
variant ending discussed in my critical edition) is in Ford's holograph.
Though this is one of his more legible autograph manuscripts, his hand
is often hard to decipher, but it looks to my eyes as if Ford clearly wrote
'Sadic' here – an alternative at the time to 'sadistic', which is what
we'd almost certainly say now. 'Sadic' was certainly current at the time
Ford was writing. The *Oxford English Dictionary* cites an instance in

T. E. Lawrence's *Seven Pillars of Wisdom* from 1926. The Marquis de Sade had been dead for about 100 years by the time the novel is set; and there was nothing new about the idea of 'Sadism'. (The first *OED* citation is from 1818.) But terms such as sadism and masochism had a greater currency after the war, in the wake of Freud's writing and its appearance in English translation. For example, in *Three Essays on the Theory of Sexuality* (1905; first translated into English in 1910), he argued that the inflicting or receiving of pain during sexual intercourse was 'the most common and the most significant of all the perversions', and that both tend to occur in the same person.[16]

I take it what Tietjens means is that Edith Ethel was aroused – in a subconscious way – by her husband's violence towards her (and perhaps Macmaster was aroused by the idea of it too) and that arousal was enough to overcome any circumspection or restraint. It might be sadism on Macmaster's part, but it would be masochism on Edith Ethel's (though perhaps also counter-sadistic revenge on her husband). Perhaps Tietjens has the excuse that such terms were less familiar before the war than after. Yet Ford is careful to show intellectuals bandying psychoanalytic terms about at Macmaster's salon:

> A Mr. Jegg and a Mrs. Haviland were sitting close together in the far window-seat. They were talking in low tones. From time to time Mr. Jegg used the word 'inhibition.' Tietjens rose from the fire-seat on which he had been sitting and came to her. (p. 284)

Again, it's wonderful how Ford implies a sort of subconscious reaction here too, as if hearing the term 'inhibition' is enough to *dis*inhibit Tietjens, who immediately rises up and goes over to Valentine, his love for whom he's been trying to inhibit.

If Ford means to show us Tietjens' confusion between sadism and masochism here, it may be attributable to Tietjens' shell shock and memory loss. But the compositor and Duckworth's editor probably didn't have the same excuse. Somehow 'Sadic' got perverted in the British first edition to 'Sadix', which was followed by the US first edition. (The 1950 Knopf edition emended it to 'Sadic'.) But 'Sadix' appears otherwise unknown. So however familiar the term 'sadic' may have been to the author or characters, it appears unknown to the publishing staff familiar with contemporary literature who saw the book through production – though more suspicious critics might suspect a Freudian slip rather than a mere typographical error, made not because compositor or editor didn't realise it meant something sexual, but because they did.

Either way, something very similar happens in the second instance. After Tietjens comes over to sit with Valentine at this salon, they start

Sexuality, Sadomasochism, and Suppression

talking – for the first time since the car accident several years before: '"Well, Miss Wannop. What have you been doing?" and they drifted into talking of the war. You couldn't not' (p. 284). 'You couldn't not' is typical Ford. It sounds conversational, in this book of brilliantly mercurial conversation: idiomatic, in the kind of clipped, accentuated backchat that all three main characters specialise in. But it's also potentially awkward. How many creative writing tutors have advised against double negatives? But of course Ford's use is anything but clumsy, even if its apparent redundance causes a moment of unease. But that moment is enough to make the connection with the book's title phrase (which echoes through the text too): some do not. The story of Christopher and Valentine is of some who 'do not', gradually getting to the stage where they 'couldn't not' any longer, though they haven't quite reached it at this point.

As Tietjens talks about the war, Valentine is surprised to find that he's not the stereotypical soldier her pacifist friends have led her to abhor. Ford writes: 'she had an automatic feeling that all manly men were lust-filled devils, desiring nothing better than to stride over battlefields, stabbing the wounded with long daggers in frenzies of sadism' (p. 284). And he adds: 'She knew that this view of Tietjens was wrong, but she cherished it.' Why would you cherish a view of a man you cared for as killing helpless, wounded victims 'in frenzies of sadism'? Why is she attracted to the imagining of him as violent? Perhaps because cherishing this view helps her fight against cherishing the man, because she needs to turn him into an ogre so as *not* to love him so unbearably. Yet that word 'cherished' here is curiously unsettling. If Ford had meant just that she consciously determined to think of him as a brute, wouldn't he have said just that? Whereas the word 'cherished' can't help intimating that what she cherishes is not her strategically false image of Tietjens, but the man himself. But in that case, she would be doing a kind of violence to his integrity: mixing up her desire with violence in a sadistic manner. There's another degree of sadism that might be implied. If she's distorting his image to hold it at bay, isn't that a sign of anger against him (anger for making her love him even though he's married, and therefore determined not to make any advances towards another woman)? In other words, the frustration of her love for him results in a form of violence (albeit considerably controlled and sublimated). Alternatively, Ford might be suggesting that for all her attempts to see Edith Ethel's outburst as a mark of difference between them, Valentine's feelings for Tietjens actually operate along similar lines. She and Tietjens are also aroused to passion by violence; though in their case, the background violence of the war, rather than the domestic of the Reverend Duchemin.

Sylvia thinks of war in similar terms, but applied to men: 'This whole war was an agapemone. . . . You went to war when you desired to rape innumerable women' (*No More Parades*, p. 131) – though there is perhaps a dissonance between the Greek term *agapemone* – a place of orgies – and the image of countless assaults. Ford's ideas seem closer to those of his friend – and friend of D. H. Lawrence – Richard Aldington, that violence can arouse both sexes. Aldington's 1929 novel *Death of a Hero* scandalously took the idea even further, in the opening sequence in which the hero's mother is sexually aroused on hearing the news of the death of her son.[17]

The passage about 'frenzies of sadism' is clear in the manuscript. But, again, it wasn't what was first published. In this case the Duckworth first British edition garbled 'sadism' to read 'radism'. Here, too, the idea seems to be causing the compositor problems. The US first edition, which was almost certainly set from the Duckworth edition, corrects to 'sadism', so that term might seem less problematic, at least to American eyes, in 1924.

The third instance is also from Valentine's point of view and is again about Mrs Duchemin (whom she views more sympathetically than does Tietjens):

> Valentine knew that Edith Ethel really loved beauty, circumspection, urbanity. It was no hypocrisy that made her advocate the Atalanta race of chastity. But, also, as Valentine Wannop saw it, humanity has these doublings of strong natures; just as the urbane and grave Spanish nation must find its outlet in the shrieking lusts of the bull-ring or the circumspect, laborious and admirable city typist must find her derivative in the sadic lusts of certain novelists, so Edith Ethel must break down into physical sexualities – and into shrieked coarseness of fishwives. (*Some Do Not . . .*, p. 324)

But though Ford appears to have written 'the sadic lusts of certain novelists' in the manuscript, that wasn't how it came out in print. In the Duckworth edition, 'sadic' has been changed again, but this time to 'cruder'. This may simply have been another misreading by a compositor, perhaps by the same one who had made the earlier errors over 'Sadic' and 'sadism'. Yet – hard to read though the word is in Ford's cramped holograph – 'cruder' is further removed from 'sadic' than 'Sadix' is from 'Sadic' or 'radism' is from 'sadism'. It could be a wilder misreading, one which Ford, rarely a careful proofreader, didn't catch in the proofs. But it could also be, and perhaps more probably, an authorial revision (possibly to avoid the term coming to sound repetitive). We don't have surviving proofs for any but the first chapter of the novel, so we can't be sure. But where the other examples have to be errors, this one is at least plausible as an authorial change of mind.[18]

It is nevertheless striking that not one of these occurrences in the man-uscript of 'sadism' and its cognates survives into the British first editions. What is the significance of these wrinkles in the text? As suggested, the fact these words give trouble may indicate not only their potential to disturb, but also their unfamiliarity, especially to British readers. And the fact that the word 'sadic' seems to give particular trouble may indi-cate (as I suggest in my introduction to the Carcanet Press edition) that it was too early for there to be a consensus about whether the adjective should be 'sadic', 'sadist' or 'sadistic'.

If so, Ford's use of such terms would position him as a more avant-garde writer about sexuality than he's usually seen as being – someone in the company of writers such as Lawrence, Joyce, and Aldington, rather than James and Conrad – and this would lend support to the claims of Greene and Barnes about *Parade's End*. As Barnes says: 'The name Freud occurs only once, on Sylvia's lips: "I . . . pin my faith on Mrs Vanderdecken [a society role model]. And Freud".'[19] He wonders what this amounts to, proposing that Freud might afford 'some theoretical justification for what Tietjens calls "her high-handed divagations from fidelity"'. Barnes continues:

> But Freud is more widely present, if – since this is a very English novel – in a subtle, anglicised form: 'In every man there are two minds that work side by side, the one checking the other.' The word 'subconscious' is never used; instead, Tietjens at one point has been 'thinking with his undermind'. Later, Valentine had always known something 'under her mind'; Tietjens refers to 'something behind his mind'; while General Campion 'was for the moment in high good humour on the surface, though his subordinate minds [*sic*] were puzzled and depressed'. Ford moves between these levels of the mind as he moves between fact and memory, certainty and impression.[20]

The description of how Ford registers the mental multiplicity of his characters is well observed, and absolutely crucial to *Parade's End*. But though I agree about the presence of Freudian ideas in the tetralogy, I'm less convinced that Ford's language of two minds or an undermind is a sign of that presence. There was a 'very English' alternative lineage for Ford to draw upon in rendering subconscious thought processes. The 1911 *Encyclopaedia Britannica* – possibly the one Tietjens reads first to tabulate its errors before the war, then to restock his memory during it – has an article on the 'Subliminal Self':

> The phrase subliminal self, which is one that has figured largely of recent years in discussions of the problems of Psychical Research, owes its wide cur-rency to the writings of F. W. H. Myers, especially to his posthumous work *Human Personality and its Survival of Bodily Death*.[21]

Human Personality and its Survival of Bodily Death appeared in 1903 –
its posthumousness like an uncanny affirmation of its claim. Myers was
a strong influence on William James and his desire to prove the existence
of an afterlife, and may thus have indirectly influenced his brother Henry
James's ghostly tales. The intersections of 'psychical' research in this
period, and the kind of analysis of the psyche that Freud was to found,
are well known. When Myers died in 1901, Oliver Lodge took over the
Presidency of the London-based Society for Psychical Research. Lodge's
book *The Survival of Man* (1909) was reissued in an expanded volume
in 1920 – doubtless to satisfy a post-war demand for consolation for the
war-dead. And a chapter was added for this edition, discussing Myers'
theme of the 'subliminal self'.[22] So the term was definitely in public circulation just before Ford left England and began *Parade's End*. There's
no evidence Ford read Myers or Lodge, but he certainly knew Lodge
in 1909 and he certainly used phrases such the 'subliminal self'.[23] And,
pace Barnes, the words 'subconscious', along with 'subconsciously', *are*
used in *Parade's End*, ten times. In other words, Ford didn't need to
know Freud, only Henry James and Oliver Lodge.

   Though Myers' 'subliminal self' corresponds in some respects to
what we now call the unconscious, it is closer to the Jungian than the
Freudian version of it, in its mystical sense of a collective spirituality.
Where Myers and William James (and Jung) were more interested in
paranormal phenomena, it is the association of the unconscious and
sexuality that makes one want to ally Ford with Freud. Barnes is on
firmer ground where he shrewdly stresses the importance of ideas of
sadism and masochism to *Parade's End* – though of course these too
may have come to Ford from other sources than Freud: if not directly
from de Sade's or Sacher-Masoch's books, then from the German
nerve cures he describes in *Return to Yesterday*, from reading D. H.
Lawrence, say, or from his fraught and sometimes violent relationship
with Violet Hunt.

> Christopher is a mixture of chivalry and masochism (if it hurts, I must be
> doing the right thing); Sylvia a mixture of recklessness and sadism (if it hurts
> him, I must be doing the right thing).[24]

Barnes's distinction here has French elegance, but is too diagrammatic,
missing what seems to me the most original (if also the most Freudian)
aspect of Ford's representation of sexuality in *Parade's End*: its elaboration of the *combination* of sadism and masochism, of what we'd now
call sadomasochism.[25] This sadomasochistic combination is clearest in
Sylvia, who appears to get some kind of horrified pleasure not only from
sadism – from inflicting pain on others – but also from her memories of

violent sexual encounters with her lover Drake, which she accompanies with a haunting masochistic gesture:

> she had only involuntarily to think of that night and she would stop dead, speaking or walking, drive her nails into her palms and groan slightly. . . . She had to invent a chronic stitch in her heart to account for this groan, which ended in a mumble and seemed to herself to degrade her. . . .
>
> The miserable memory would come, ghost-like, at any time, anywhere. She would see Drake's face, dark against the white things; she would feel the thin night-gown ripping off her shoulder; but most of all she would seem, in darkness that excluded the light of any room in which she might be, to be transfused by the mental agony that there she had felt: the longing for the brute who had mangled her: the dreadful pain of the mind. The odd thing was that the sight of Drake himself, whom she had seen several times since the outbreak of the war, left her completely without emotion. She had no aversion, but no longing for him. . . . She had, nevertheless, longing, but she knew it was longing merely to experience again that dreadful feeling. And not with Drake. . . . (*Some Do Not . . .*, pp. 185–6)

Sylvia is driven here by masochism rather than sadism. It is a disturbing passage from many points of view; not least, that it might appear to deflect my argument, which started out as an attempt to consider Ford as an advanced, 'adult', novelist of sexuality, into making him seem even more of a nightmare to feminists than Lawrence, in the suggestion here that women desire assault (and the suggestion, following from that, that when Sylvia says men go to war to rape, that expresses her desire as much as theirs). Ford isn't explicit about how Drake 'mangled' Sylvia, but the term implies violence, and the situation is clearly sexual. If Sylvia's response suggests something more complex than rape, her subsequent conduct can be seen – as Janet Soskice has argued[26] – as like that of many rape victims. Ford, that is to say, isn't peddling fantasies of female desire, so much as bearing witness to the fact of male brutality and its psychological aftermath. Such an interpretation offers a less demoniacal account of Sylvia's character than it often receives. Rather than a diabolical sadist, we might see her as someone whose sadism is a frustrated masochism: she keeps goading others because she is compelled to repeat the experience of being the victim of attack.

But couldn't that equally stand as a description of Christopher? And doesn't his masochism also imply a bit of sadism? Is there a point at which his extreme virtuousness becomes aggression: a desire to cut others down to size by comparison? And in his relationship with Sylvia, isn't his categorical pursuit of honour an attack on her as dishonourable? Doesn't he know that it's the course guaranteed to drive her the most mad? Barnes sees this, and sees that it is Sylvia's continuing 'sexual passion' for Tietjens that accounts both for the hold he still has over her and for her rage at him: 'She still desires him, still wants to "torment and allure" him; but one of the Anglican saint's conditions for her return to the marriage is that he will not sleep with her – a torment in return.'[27] Such perceptions are evidence, as Barnes says, for Ford's subtle and complex psychological insight. He uses them to advance a more humanised version of Sylvia: tormented lover rather than bitch goddess or wicked witch:

> Their relationship is not just about the infliction and the bearing of pain. Key to an understanding of Sylvia are those rare moments when Ford, a profound psychologist, allows us to consider that she is more than just a vengeful spirit possessed by evil. However infuriating Tietjens might be, however 'immoral' his views, he is the only truly mature man she has been with, the only one whose conversation can hold her: 'As beside him, other men simply did not seem ever to have grown up.' So he has spoiled her for all other men, and must be punished for it. The more so because he is the only one who can still move her.[28]

As a fellow-novelist's appreciation of what motivates a character, this is compelling. But it pulls back from the darker conclusion to its own logic. The very love that provides a sympathetic, humanising account of her vengefulness could itself provide evidence of a sadomasochistic orientation. That is, rather than being tormented because she loves Tietjens, mightn't she love him because he torments her? Of course this is humanising in another way: from a more Freudian perspective which attributes affect to unconscious motivations. But it indicates how Ford's psychological profundity can be a double-edged weapon.

Similarly, our account of Tietjens' psychology might be susceptible of another twist of the mind. If he has an intuitive sense that what she wants is to be manhandled, isn't his principled refusal of physical contact an aggressive act or one that he knows she will feel as such? This is getting perilously close to the joke about the masochist who says 'Hit me' and the sadist who answers with cruel relish: 'Nooooah'. But Ford's point is, more seriously, that sadism and masochism can take many forms. And indeed, such ideas are everywhere in the novels – from the golfing party at Rye thinking it would be a good sport to hit the objectionably vulgar city men with their golfing shots to the conduct of the war itself. As Barnes puts it:

> The middle two volumes of the novel are spent at the Western Front. Other, more conventional novelists might have set the madness of war against the calm and balm of love and sex; Ford knows more and sees deeper. War and sexual passion are not opposites: they are in the same business, two parts of the same pincer attack on the sanity of the individual.[29]

That is one of the major sources of Ford's originality in *Parade's End*, and its treatment of sexuality. As Charles Hoffmann understood nearly half a century ago, it is 'essentially a psychological novel in which the causes of war are traced back to psychological causes for conflict in man'.[30] Sondra Stang, too, in her fine 1977 study, wrote shrewdly about how 'the relation between the sexes is seen as a condition of warfare' in the tetralogy, but that the struggle between Christopher and Sylvia 'is neither simple nor one-sided and [. . .] they are two antagonists of considerable subtlety, whose antagonism is made all the more subtle by the similarities between them'.[31] She picked out quotations about Sylvia's 'sex viciousness' and 'sex cruelty', as substantiating Greene's praise of the books as 'almost the only adult novels dealing with the sexual life', yet stops short of describing this sexual life in terms of sadism or masochism. Barnes comments on the phrase given to Mark Tietjens, as he lies outside, awake at night, listening to 'nightingales producing not their normal, beautiful sound, but something much coarser, which seems to him to contain abuse of other males, and boastfulness to their own sitting hens'.[32] Mark thinks of this as an example of 'sex ferocity' (*Last Post*, p. 197) – that is, not just the violent force of sexuality but the violence sex can arouse.

The 'conflict' model might seem to lead to a tragic account of *Parade's End* in which humanity is doomed to endure external violence (whether in the 'sex war' or the World War) as the inevitable expression of internal conflict – as, for example, when Tietjens says, in *Some Do Not . . .*: 'war is as inevitable as divorce' (p. 28). Yet, ultimately, the tetralogy does not tell a tragic story, though it countenances individual and collective disasters. Rather, it allows Tietjens and Sylvia to extricate themselves from their sadomasochistic bind, making a peace of a kind. It allows him to enter a new relationship, with the pacifist Valentine, which, if not free from anxiety, appears free from conflict; and which ushers in a phase of regeneration and reconstruction; new love and new life. Such release could be understood as still locked into a mimetic relationship between sexuality and war: the rhythms of dissension and happiness within relationships mirroring those of war and peace between nations. Yet the structure of *Parade's End* offers another possibility. The war doesn't merely reflect internal conflict, but, in doing so, externalises it: makes it visible and intelligible. In doing that, it allows such conflicts to be addressed and worked through. From a religious perspective this would be understood as a matter of violent urges being chastened by being subjected to purgatorial fires. But in my view Ford presents it as a more secular and psychological process: the subject being forced to confront both the sexual and aggressive urges in itself that it has hitherto repressed; a process of enactment, insight, recognition, and acceptance. The war takes Tietjens physically out of the marriage that has become a trap. That physical extrication is the prelude to his psychological liberation; not because the physical distance loosens Sylvia's hold over him – after all, she pursues him to the army base in France as if to prove that false – but because war's devastation blasts away the debris of their past lives. Nowhere is this clearer than when, in the third volume, *A Man Could Stand Up –*, Tietjens is momentarily buried in the earth disturbed by a high explosive shell. Theologically inclined critics are wont to read this as a resurrection moment, confirming Tietjens as Christ-like, and after which he attempts to 'save' some of his men. Certainly the symbolism of rebirth and the language of salvation are there. The question is; what are they doing there? It seems to me to make more sense of *Parade's End* to see this as a moment of secular renewal, as precisely the moment when Tietjens stops 'Modelling himself on our Lord', having arrived at a more chthonic sense of his own bodily strengths and desires. As Sylvia says in *No More Parades*: 'But our Lord was never married. He never touched on topics of sex' (p. 154). Tietjens has done both. And now the war has exploded and burnt away the codes and parades of Victorian and Edwardian propriety, and left him with the knowledge that what he ought to do is commit adultery – something even the most determined advocate of a neo-Christian reading would have to acknowledge represents something of a departure from the supposed role model. 'Well, he could never be a country parson. He was going to live with Valentine Wannop!' (*A Man Could Stand Up –*, p. 164). Some do not . . . You couldn't not. A man could . . .

Notes

1. Rimbaud, 'Parade', p. 264: 'I alone have the key to this wild parade' (p. 265).
2. Greene quoted in Strauss, *Ford Madox Ford*, inside front cover: quoted in Young, *Ford Madox Ford*, p. 30.
3. In *Ways of Escape*, Greene says apropos *The End of the Affair*: 'I had learned something from my continual rereading of that remarkable novel *The Good Soldier* by Ford Madox Ford' (p. 136).
4. Trotter, 'Edwardian Sex Novels', pp. 197–213. See also see his *The English Novel in History: 1895–1920*.
5. Barnes, Introduction to *Parade's End*, p. xii.
6. Ibid. p. xii.
7. Ibid. pp. xii–xiii.
8. For example, writing in the *Observer* in June 1924, Gould lists a number of contemporaries, saying: 'As for Mr. Ford Madox Ford, he is the jolliest

and subtlest of *les jeunes*, though nearly in his thirtieth year of authorship': 'The English Novel of Today', p. 9. Yet two months earlier, and in the same month that *Some Do Not . . .* was published, he wrote a piece for the same column on Lawrence and Joyce, headed 'Sex Obsession'.

9. Ford, 'Declined with Thanks', p. 6. Compare Ford, 'On the Functions of the Arts in the Republic', *The Critical Attitude*, p. 33: 'what we so very much need to-day is a picture of the life we live. It is only the imaginative writer who can supply this, because no collection of facts, and no tabulation of figures, can give us any sense of proportion'.

10. Barnes, Introduction, p. xii.

11. Ford, *A Man Could Stand Up –*, ed. Sara Haslam, p. 186. All further references are to this edition. Compare Sylvia's (and probably Christopher's) son wondering: 'But wasn't sex a terrible thing': Ford, *Last Post*, ed. Paul Skinner, p. 56. All further references are to this edition. See also Tatar, *Lustmord*.

12. Ford, *Some Do Not . . .*, ed. Max Saunders, p. 133. All further references are to this edition.

13. James, 'Robert Louis Stevenson', p. 141.

14. Barnes, Introduction, p. ix.

15. Ford, *No More Parades*, ed. Joseph Wiesenfarth, p. 154. All further references are to this edition.

16. Freud, *Three Essays on the Theory of Sexuality*, p. 157.

17. Aldington, *Death of a Hero*, pp. 10–14.

18. Either way, the US first edition followed the UK first.

19. Barnes, Introduction, p. xiv. It is perhaps worth noting that this sole mention of Freud appears to have caused a comparable hiccup in the text of the *transatlantic review*, in which 'to Mrs. Vanderdecken. And, of course, Freud' gets garbled into: 'to Mrs. Freud Vanderdecken. / And, of course,': see *Some Do Not . . .*, pp. 49, 359. The three occurrences of 'sadism' and its cognates all appear in Part II of the novel, which was not serialised in the review.

20. Barnes, Introduction, pp. xiv–xv.

21. *Encyclopaedia Britannica*, XXV, pp. 1062–4 (p. 1062). The *Encyclopaedia* also has a brief entry on 'Sade, De', which notes rather misleadingly: 'The word Sadism, meaning a form of sexual perversion, is derived from his name' (XXIII, p. 990).

22. Lodge, 'On the Subliminal Self and on the Book *Human Personality*', pp. 358–67.

23. See Saunders, *Ford Madox Ford*, I, p. 276, for evidence of Ford knowing Lodge. See Ford, *The Marsden Case* on the 'subconscious self', 'subliminal self' or 'underself' as opposed to the 'surface self' or 'conscious mind' (pp. 20, 57, 56, 20, 56 respectively). See also Ford, *No Enemy*, pp. 21, 42, and *Return to Yesterday*, p. 228, for 'subconscious mind'; and *Some Do Not . . .*, p. 226, for 'under mind'.

24. Barnes, Introduction, pp. ix–x.

25. Ford's presentation of sadomasochism as a cause of anguish it would be better to escape contrasts with the *fin-de-siècle* investment in it analysed by Romana Byrne. Byrne tracks sadomasochism at different periods where it is 'constructed as a form of art, a chosen means of social communication

and self-creation whose meaning is located in its aesthetic value – at surface level – rather than in any presumed underlying cause': Byrne, *Aesthetic Sexuality*, p. 16.

26. In conversation.
27. Barnes, Introduction, p. xi.
28. Ibid. p. xi.
29. Ibid. p. xii.
30. Macauley, 'The Good Ford', p. 283; Hoffmann, *Ford Madox Ford*, p. 106.
31. Stang, *Ford Madox Ford*, p. 110.
32. Barnes, Introduction, pp. xiii–xiv.

Chapter 2

Freud Madox Ford: Impressionism, Psychoanalytic Trauma Theory, and Ford's Wartime Writing

Karolyn Steffens

Parade's End is not a typical war narrative, its unconventionality apparent at the level of both form and content. Not only was it published earlier than the 1929–30 boom in Great War narratives (*Some Do Not . . .* was first published in 1924),[1] but the tetralogy also differs from this canon of war literature in its unique Fordian Impressionism that is explicitly preoccupied with consciousness and subjectivity at the expense of the action, drama, and disillusionment of the battlefield. For example, Ford recounts the daily experience of the war as follows:

> But, had you taken part actually in those hostilities, you would know how infinitely little part the actual fighting itself took in your mentality. You would be lying on your stomach, in a beast of a funk, with an immense, horrid German barrage going on all over and round you and with hell and all let loose. But, apart from the occasional, petulant question: 'When the deuce will our fellows get going and shut 'em up?' your thoughts were really concentrated on something quite distant: on your daughter Millicent's hair, on the fall of the Asquith Ministry, on your financial predicament, on why your regimental ferrets kept dying, on whether Latin is really necessary to an education [. . .]. You were there, but great shafts of thought from the outside, distant and unattainable world infinitely for the greater part occupied your mind.[2]

The Fordian mind at war focuses not on present danger but on things 'quite distant' such as worries about one's children, finances, government, and the men in one's battalion. Thus, Ford devotes the vast majority of the tetralogy not to impressions of the trenches but to domestic disturbances in the form of adultery, divorce, repressed sexual passion, and the battle between the sexes. Ford reiterates these sentiments in his dedicatory letter to the second volume, *No More Parades*, stating that the predominant emotion during the war was a 'never-ending sense of worry', a worry 'that applied not merely to the bases, but to the whole field of military operations. Unceasing worry!'[3] Such 'unceasing worry' causes one to become what Ford dubs '*homo duplex*' or 'a poor fellow whose body is tied in one place, but whose mind and personality brood eternally over another distant locality',[4] a condition dramatised throughout his *oeuvre* but one that is particularly heightened in wartime. Not only is the *homo duplex* the exemplary Fordian soldier, he is also the paradigmatic Impressionist subject. One of the defining formal features of Impressionism, as Ford theorises it, is immersion into a character's mind which wanders while the reader follows the many detours through memory and association. In addition to being representative of the Fordian soldier and the Impressionist subject, Ford himself embodies the *homo duplex*, as Max Saunders illustrates in his biography in which the war and Ford's subsequent name change are hallmarks of his 'dual life'.[5] Thus, the *homo duplex* is the chief figure within Ford's work and life, and when transported to the trenches, Tietjens becomes the *homo duplex* par excellence, one who was 'there, but great shafts of thought from the outside, distant and unattainable world infinitely for the greater part occupied your mind'.[6]

Ford had mastered the Impressionist technique encapsulated by the *homo duplex* earlier in *The Good Soldier* (1915) but had yet to translate it to representing what Valentine Wannop calls the 'immense miles and miles of anguish in darkened minds' that remained when 'Men might stand up on hills, but the mental torture could not be expelled.'[7] Valentine's observation about the overwhelmingly psychological nature of the war has come to dominate critical discussions and literary representations of the event, as evident in Elaine Showalter's *The Female Malady* (1985) and Pat Barker's *Regeneration* trilogy (1991–5). Ford's statement via Valentine that mental suffering epitomises the trauma of the Great War predates such re-imaginings and critical studies and is tied to his tireless advocacy and use of the Impressionist aesthetic. A pattern of juxtaposition between sexual and trench warfare emerges in *Parade's End* when viewing these 'great shafts of thought' from the world outside the battlefield. Recall, for example, how O Nine Morgan's blood in *No More Parades* transports Tietjens back to the climactic scene at the end of the first part of *Some Do Not . . .* in which General Campion's car crashes into Tietjens and Valentine's dog-cart. As Tietjens stares at O Nine Morgan's body, he was 'astonished [. . .] to see that a human body could be so lavish of blood' (pp. 28–9) and his mind jumps to the following reflection: 'He felt as he did when you patch up a horse that has been badly hurt. He remembered the horse from a cut on whose chest the blood had streamed down over the off foreleg like a stocking. A girl had lent him her petticoat to bandage it' (p. 29). The time shift at the moment of Morgan's death recalls this earlier violent scene and Tietjens substitutes his repressed passion for contemplating Morgan's shocking death. In another pivotal scene from the trenches, Tietjens' mind superimposes Valentine's face over Lance-Corporal Duckett's after the slow motion shell explosion in *A Man Could Stand Up –*, Duckett's lifeless face, black with dirt, appearing asleep, as if 'Valentine Wannop had been reposing in an ash-bin' (p. 180). In both cases, Eros erupts into scenes of violence, Tietjens' mind trading repression of the traumatic for sexual repression. Similarly, violence erupts into scenes of Eros, Sylvia herself embodying this tension between violence and sexuality in her famous sadistic impulses that proliferate throughout *Parade's End*.[8] More than the recurring worry of a wandering mind, the tetralogy repeatedly presents sexuality as the shaft of thought that pierces the violent representations of war. While Eros dominates his earlier masterpiece, *The Good Soldier*, when Ford turns to representing his experiences in the trenches, his Impressionism must adapt to rendering mass trauma, the Thanatos of warfare.

Although Ford and his unique aesthetic innovations are frequently studied in relation to Impressionism, analysing Impressionism itself in terms of the challenge of rendering a collective, historical trauma has not received the same critical attention. Literary Impressionism is primarily understood as responding to epistemological problems. Jesse Matz contends that the Impressionists work between phenomenology and empiricism since the impression is neither pure sensation nor pure reason. According to Matz, the literary Impressionist, as differentiated from Impressionism in the visual arts, grapples with philosophical questions of subjectivity and embodied consciousness by occupying a middle ground between these two philosophical discourses. This middle ground takes the form of collaboration, Matz citing Ford's uneducated cabman in 'On Impressionism' as an example of how the Impressionist must invent a figure (often working class, female, or a colonial other) to embody the corporeal and sensational world and thus retain his or her authorial rationality.[9] Michael Valdez Moses contributes to this redefinition of literary Impressionism as distinct from visual Impressionism by interpreting it as stemming not only from the epistemological problem Matz outlines but also from historical phenomena such as colonialism and imperialism. Moses suggests that Conrad, in *Heart of Darkness* (1899), 'attempts to generate in the reader a cognitive and emotional dissonance that is the experiential "aesthetic" correlative of the shock felt by [his] characters when confronted with the unsavory realities of Western imperialism'.[10] Such dissonance mimicking shock resonates with both Ford's experiences in the war and Sigmund Freud's founding description of trauma as a breach in the conscious mind, trauma springing from the experience of being unprepared both emotionally and cognitively for the event. Furthermore, Moses crucially resituates the origins of Conradian Impressionism from a philosophical and epistemological concern to an historical problem of rendering lived experiences and collective, often traumatic, events.[11]

If we agree with Moses and view Conrad's Impressionism in *Heart of Darkness* as emerging from the historical context of imperialism in the Congo, we can interpret Ford's later Impressionism as similarly responding to historical events rather than solely to epistemological problems. In other words, the trenches are to Ford what the Congo is to Conrad, both historical sites of violence pressuring the Impressionist to respond to lived experiences in addition to epistemological challenges. With this framework in mind, I argue that Ford revises his previous Impressionist aesthetic when representing the historical trauma of the Great War, much as Conrad did earlier after his encounter with Belgian imperialism. Just as the soldier in the trenches becomes an extreme example of *homo duplex*, Ford's Impressionism, under the pressure of rendering the Great War, becomes a dual entity characterised by both Eros and Thanatos since the thoughts that continually break through the impressions of violence are those of sexuality and vice versa. Through a comparison of *Parade's End*, *No Enemy* (1929) and the manuscript 'True Love & a GCM' (written 1918–19), Ford's Impressionism emerges as an aesthetic depicting traumatised consciousness as Janus-faced, torn between Eros and Thanatos.

My description of a Janus-faced traumatic consciousness is deliberately laden with psychoanalytic overtones and, indeed, it is not far from Freud's own conception of the mind as torn between conflicting instinctual drives of which Eros and Thanatos are the most commanding. Although Ford never records having been influenced by psychoanalysis, he certainly knew of Freud, particularly in the 1920s when the latter's influence was pervasive among the modernists.[12] The Freudian strains within Ford's work were so obvious to readers in the 1920s that Osbert Sitwell coined the cynical moniker 'Freud Madox Fraud'.[13] Just as World War I was a turning point in Ford's personal life and career, the war also figures prominently in Freud's career and biography, arguably as an equally monumental watershed.[14] After World War I, explicitly discussed in *Beyond the Pleasure Principle* (1920), Freud revises his theory of the mind to make room for the death drive and those events that override the pleasure principle, as in the case of the traumatic neuroses. Thus, from 1918 on, Freud's theory of the mind remains one of duality, but whereas in his earlier work he pits libidinal and egoistic drives against one another, in his later work during and after the war he replaces these drives 'with a new, more dramatic pair of contestants: life against death'.[15] Apart from notable exceptions such as Sara Haslam in *Fragmenting Modernism* (2002), Ford critics have not, as a rule, paired Ford with Freud's work in the broader context of contemporary trauma theory.[16] In the following pages, I juxtapose Freud's *Beyond the Pleasure Principle* with Ford's wartime writing in order to explicate the intersections between World War I, Impressionism, and trauma. Ultimately, I show how Freud's theory highlights new aspects of the evolution Ford's Impressionism underwent when rendering his war experience.

The role sexuality can play within the broader field of trauma studies also becomes apparent when pairing Ford and Freud, a dynamic that is overlooked by the majority of contemporary trauma theorists who focus exclusively on Freud's late work.[17] Tietjens, as *homo duplex,* comes to embody the tension between Eros and Thanatos that is constitutive of the trauma of the Great War for Ford. Although the war signals the shift in Freud's thinking toward the death drive, what Freud does not discuss in *Beyond the Pleasure Principle* is the role sexuality plays in a psychoanalytic conception of trauma.[18] In the earlier seduction theory published in *Studies on Hysteria* (1895), however, Freud proposes a direct link between an external sexually traumatic event and hysteria, a position he eventually renounces in order to privilege wish-fulfilment, dreams, and the imagination as the root cause of neuroses. While I do not intend to resurrect Freud's seduction theory, his initial hypothesis concerning external traumatic events and sexuality provides the starting point for a fuller theorisation of Ford's depiction of trauma as defined by both Eros and Thanatos. In other words, although Freud abandons the link between external, sexually traumatic events and hysteria, Ford pursues this line of inquiry, substituting sexually traumatic events for the external events of the Great War as they are inflected with Eros. Indeed, a conception of trauma including Eros is crucial to understanding how Ford and others represent the war. Many wartime poets, such as Wilfred Owen, and more recent authors such as Pat Barker, depict a pervasive disillusionment with nineteenth-century masculine ideals like heroism, valour, and courage, and the overwhelming assault and revision to masculinity caused by shell shock, which transformed soldiers into hysterical and 'feminized' patients.[19] By focusing on these earlier historical and textual events, the necessity of re-evaluating the psychoanalytically inflected foundations of trauma theory to include sexuality emerges. Instead of relying exclusively on theories originating in the Holocaust or the clinical symptoms of post-traumatic stress disorder, the historical specificity of the First World War as represented by Ford challenges us to arrive at a fuller conception of traumatic consciousness, one accounting for not only moments of shock and intense bombardment but also the 'unceasing worry' often linked to issues of gender and sexuality.

Apart from sexuality, Ford and Freud both theorise belatedness as central to their theories of Impressionism and traumatic consciousness, respectively. Ford, in the chapter 'On the Functions of the Arts in the Republic' in *The Critical Attitude* (1911), argues that in modern life, due to increased bureaucracy and the speed of interpersonal relationships, 'it is impossible to see [life] whole' and thus one must always experience it vicariously through the arts. In the case of literature: 'it is only in the pages of naturalistic novels that we can hope nowadays to get any experience of modern life, save that individual and personal experience of our own which comes always too late'.[20] This individual and personal experience is precisely what the Impressionist attempts to capture by rendering the consciousness of the characters on the page, an experience that, as Ford describes it, is always belated since one doesn't register the experience as worthy of representation until it has already passed. Such belatedness echoes Ford's famous statement in 'On Impressionism' that: 'Impressionism is a thing altogether momentary'; an Impressionist work being: 'the record of the recollection in your mind of a set of circumstances that happened ten years ago – or ten minutes. It might even be the impression of the moment – but it is the impression, not the corrected chronicle.'[21] Thus, the Impressionist is always belatedly reconstructing experiences and impressions for the reader, rendering remembered stimuli filtered through memory and language. Significantly, this belated reconstruction of life appears to the reader with all the vividness and force of the event itself – it cannot appear belated or read like the 'corrected chronicle'. When applied to the war, an event signalling the culmination of the effects of modernity in Europe, the Impressionist struggles even more to grasp an image of the whole since life, especially in the trenches, has become fragmented and is only experienced belatedly on a daily basis.

Belatedness also figures prominently in Freud's theory of trauma, not as an image of modernity per se, but as the way in which a traumatic experience is registered in consciousness. In *Beyond the Pleasure Principle*, he describes the traumatic neurosis as temporarily disabling the pleasure principle in that:

> there is no longer any possibility of preventing the mental apparatus from being flooded with large amounts of stimulus, and another problem arises instead – the problem of mastering the amounts of stimulus which have broken in and of binding them, in the psychical sense, so they can then be disposed of.[22]

Such a description sounds much like the challenges facing the Impressionist who tries to translate all the stimuli around him into language. The individual suffering from the traumatic neurosis is haunted by the event in nightmares and flashbacks, with Freud hypothesising that traumatic dreams are 'endeavoring to master the stimulus retrospectively, by developing the anxiety whose omission was the cause of the traumatic neurosis'.[23] This 'retrospective' attempt to master all the stimuli of the event is the source of the belatedness fundamental to traumatic experience. The mind never experiences the event fully the first time since it is overwhelmed by stimuli and thus must revisit it in dreams and flashbacks to get an image of the whole, much like Ford's modern observer who only experiences the whole vicariously and belatedly in the pages of the novel.[24] The psychoanalyst therefore could be said to function like the Impressionist: he must interpret the stimuli and the repetitions the patient describes, piecing them together into a narrative of the event or, in Ford's case, an impression of modern life.

Indeed, Freud sounds much like Ford when describing his method in *Beyond the Pleasure Principle*, repeatedly asserting that the pages of his book contain 'speculation, often far-fetched speculation' as to the inner workings of consciousness.[25] He continues, stating that 'Psycho-analytic speculation takes as its point of departure the *impression*, derived from examining unconscious processes, that consciousness may be, not the most universal attribute of mental processes, but only a particular function of them.'[26] Thus, the psychoanalyst deals in 'impressions' of how the mind functions and what consciousness looks like, particularly since consciousness is not subject to visible proof like many of the cellular processes Freud refers to throughout the text. Since dealing in impressions, the psychoanalyst must admit that his theory is open to debate given the non-empirical nature of his observations. Freud notes that the hypotheses are 'a direct translation of observation into theory' and that his theory of the instincts 'rests upon observed material – namely on the facts of the compulsion to repeat'.[27] Just as the Impressionist deals in observations about the world and translates them into language, attempting to render the workings of individual consciousness, the Freudian psychoanalyst translates impressions of consciousness based on observations from life (the example of the veterans suffering from war neuroses and the *fort-da* game of his grandson being his primary 'case studies'). Such observations appear throughout Freud's case studies that, it is often noted, read more like short stories than empirical science. In translating these observations into theory, Freud resorts to the medium of 'the figurative language, peculiar to psychology'[28] just as the Impressionist renders in the figurative language peculiar to the novelist.

The point of these observations is neither to make an Impressionist of Freud nor to make a psychoanalyst of Ford. Instead, I am suggesting that such an intersection between the methodologies of Ford and Freud is illuminated by their writing about trauma – Freud resorting to impressions and padding his theory with admissions of speculation in the text that most fully investigates trauma and Ford's method of Impressionism most strongly challenged by rendering the impressions of a massive, collective experience like a World War. Trauma is fundamentally an experience of an overwhelming impression: the impression of violence imprinted on consciousness. Freud makes a comment to this effect in *Reflections on War and Death* (1918), stating that 'caught in the whirlwind of these war times' we 'become confused as to the meaning of impressions which crowd in upon us or of the value of the judgments we are forming'.[29] The psychoanalyst must render the traumatic impression into a coherent narrative that reintegrates such an experience into the patient's consciousness so the traumatic neurosis can be 'disposed of'.[30] Similarly, the Impressionist must render the impression of the trauma of the Great War into a narrative that reconstitutes a subject and allows the reader and author to vicariously experience an image of the whole. Belatedness is therefore a key point of intersection between psychoanalysis and Impressionism, both methods depending upon observations taken from life and then belatedly translating those observations into theories that end up carrying traces of their composition.

In returning to *Parade's End*, this convergence between psychoanalysis and Impressionism appears most explicitly in *A Man Could Stand Up –*. As mentioned above, belatedness literally occurs in Tietjens' recurring hallucination of O Nine Morgan's death, a pivotal example of how his consciousness belatedly tries to work through the traumatic event (alongside its attempted working through of his sexual repression). Belatedness occurs at another level, however, in that the tetralogy is peppered with examples of writings and rewritings of Ford's own experience of the war. In the passages analysed below, Ford rewrites the anecdotes in the tetralogy after previously presenting them in other works in an effort to work through his traumatic memories. Ford's Impressionist writing carries the traces of repeated attempts at working through the traumatic experience in language. Thus, *Parade's End* displays its composition history as one of traumatic remembrance, undercutting Ford's own emphasis on rendering the immediacy of the sensory experience. Clearly, Ford revises all of his Impressionist work, not just the work dealing with trauma. As Sara Haslam observes, one of the hallmarks of Ford's aesthetic is that he 'is writing the processes of memory, establishing a multiplicity of narrative personae: Ford as narrator, Ford as implied author, Ford as subject, Ford as child'.[31] In conjunction with this interpretation, I contend that this process of writing memory and the history of that composition is heightened when representing his wartime experiences, forcing the Impressionist goal of immediacy to bear the traces of traumatic working through.

An episode with a skylark that first appears in Ford's incomplete war novel 'True Love & a GCM'[32] provides an illustration of this Impressionistic working through. In the manuscript, the first piece of writing Ford attempted after the war, the narrator recalls a particularly traumatic memory in which, to avoid the shrapnel of a shell burst, he dropped to his hands and knees 'and he had stuck his hand right into a dead, putrid Hun's ribs'.[33] During his current occupation watching No Man's Land on a rainy night in the trenches, he recalls this earlier episode and fears the same thing happening. Using a technique akin to delayed decoding, Ford describes the action in the present immediately after the soldier remembers this earlier experience as follows:

> He jumped to his feet and said: 'Hell! Oh Hell!' and his heart beat fifty to the minute and he felt sick. It was because there had been a loud rustle just under his invisible left hand. A bird had got up from a tuft in the darkness and flut-tered away. He caught a glimpse of it against the pale sky [. . .]. You could see a bird; you could recognise the form – like the lower half of an iron cross. It had been a skylark. What the devil was a skylark doing there; frightening you out of your wits.[34]

The juxtaposition of the two moments of fear due to surprise empha-sises the point of the passage that warfare and shelling are no longer frightening but routine, the surprise of the skylark and encountering a German corpse scaring the soldier more than bombardments. In *A Man Could Stand Up* –, Tietjens also contemplates the mundane nature of the war and the boredom that besets him and his men when he is fright-ened by a skylark in a strikingly similar fashion. The scene unfolds as follows:

> He stepped once more on to the rifle-step and on to the bully-beef-case. He elevated his head cautiously: grey desolation sloped down and away F.R.R.R.r.r.r.! A gentle purring sound!
>
> He was automatically back, on the duckboard, his breakfast hurting his chest. He said:
>
> 'By Jove! I got the fright of my life!' A laugh was called for; he managed it, his whole stomach shaking. And cold! (p. 62)

When Tietjens realises that what flew by him was not a sniper's bullet but a skylark, a sergeant-major empathises, recounting a similar shock that happened to him when he was on:

a raid in the dark, crawling on 'is 'ands 'n knees wen 'e put 'is 'and on a skylark on its nest. Never left 'is nest till 'is 'and was on 'im! Then it went up and fair scared the wind out of 'im. (p. 62)

In the tetralogy, Ford displaces the trauma of the original anecdote as it appears in 'True Love & a GCM' onto two different characters: Tietjens experiences the fright in the present (in the relative safety of the trench, not in the middle of No Man's Land) and the memory of the sergeant-major comes closest to that of the soldier in 'True Love & a GCM' who puts his hand into the corpse. Ford further dilutes the shock of the scene by erasing the corpse entirely and transforming it into a skylark's nest in the sergeant-major's story. Similarly, the thick dialect of the sergeant-major also displaces the force of the anecdote, the reader working to interpret the story in contrast to the soldier's clear prose. Thus, only the overall point about how fright in the trenches comes not from shells but from unexpected surprises like skylarks remains in *Parade's End*.

Ford makes a similar turn to fictionalisation and an amplification of rich Impressionistic rendition at the expense of direct description of death and trauma in an episode with swallows in *A Man Could Stand Up – and No Enemy*. The scene that ends part two of the third volume, in which Tietjens and his men are hit directly by a shell, parallels the death of O Nine Morgan that opens *No More Parades*. These scenes bookend the two novels and are the most famous depictions of warfare in the tetralogy, both dealing explicitly with Tietjens' experience at the Front. After the shell bursts, Tietjens and his men, Duckett and Aranjuez, are buried in mud. Duckett, whose face continually reminds Tietjens of Valentine Wannop's throughout the scene, ends up being buried alive and Tietjens cannot uncover him in time to save him. Several critics read this scene as Tietjens' rebirth: the man of *Last Post* who commits himself to being with Valentine emerging after literally being buried in the mud of the trenches with his memory erased.[35] Instead of a rebirth, I read this scene in terms of revisitation, the prelude to the bombing being a rewriting of an earlier traumatic scene in *No Enemy*.[36] Leading up to the strafe, Tietjens contemplates topics ranging from the end of the war to his battalion to Valentine Wannop to skylarks. He recalls an earlier moment during the war in which he had been walking down a hill after escaping the German guns feeling elated for surviving and resolving to write to Valentine to declare his love:

He went down with long strides, the tops of thistles brushing his hips. Obviously the thistles contained things that attracted flies. They were apt to after a famous victory. So myriads of swallows pursued him, swirling round and round him, their wings touching; for a matter of twenty yards all round and their wings brushing him and the tops of the thistles. And as the blue sky was reflected in the blue of their backs – for their backs were below his eyes – he had felt like a Greek God striding through the sea. . . . (*A Man Could Stand Up –*, p. 167)

After recalling this memory, Duckett joins him and the strafe begins, the shell hitting the earth that turns 'like a weary hippopotamus' and settles over the men in a 'slow wave' that was 'like a slowed down movie' (p. 167). Such a rich Impressionistic description of the earth after the shell burst echoes and depends on the earlier description of Tietjens' feeling like a Greek god, no less poignant for the uncertainty as to whether or not Tietjens will be able to experience such jubilation again after this current brush with death.

In *No Enemy*, Gringoire, the fictional veteran narrator Ford constructs to relay his memories of the war, recounts a strikingly similar experience of feeling like a Greek god. Gringoire believes he has escaped death when he falls asleep in a hut and a passing lorry lifts the tin roof and bangs it back down, making him think he is being bombed. When he realises what has happened and that he is not in danger, Gringoire walks down a hill and contemplates how his 'subsequent exultation' was due to it just being 'so good to be alive after that'.[37] He notes:

> I remember thinking on the other occasion that there were a good many dead amongst the thistles and that I must be putting up a huge number of flies. But that, again, was the thought of my subconscious mind. On the surface I just felt myself to be a Greek god, immortal, young forever, forever buoyant, amongst the eddies of a dark blue and eternal sea. (pp. 24–5)

Clearly the repetition of one's escape from death inspiring one to feel like a Greek god aligns these scenes. Underneath this jubilant tone in both versions, the repression of the death that permeates such a landscape is striking. In the tetralogy, Ford suppresses the explicit naming of the dead, noting that 'obviously' the thistles contain 'things' that attract flies. The observation in the tetralogy that: 'They were apt to after a famous victory' also hints at the presence of death and the downside to military victory for both sides. Compared to the 'good many dead' in *No Enemy*, however, in the tetralogy Ford deliberately avoids the explicit mention of the corpses lying just out of sight under the thistles.

These hints at the death surrounding Tietjens are sublimated by the lavish description in the tetralogy of the visual spectacle of the swallows, a spectacle heightened by the repetition of the blueness of their backs and the waving thistles that give the impression of striding through a sea. Similarly, he omits the psychological terminology used in *No Enemy* such as the 'surface' and 'subconscious mind' that perceives the corpses. Such compositional differences between the two texts illuminate how Impressionism, through its aesthetic elaborateness that creates lush images and sensory immediacy before the reader's eyes, represses the traumatic content underlying such a vision. In other words, Ford's Impressionism represses the trauma of death in these passages and rather highlights the visual experiences that impart a tone of jubilation, not trauma. Thus, the response to the sensory overload caused by the dissonance between the beauty of the field of swallows and the distressing presence of decaying corpses lying just under the thistles becomes one of focusing on the pleasures of the French countryside, despite the death permeating it. Furthermore, the passage in *Parade's End* is also deliberately fictionalised in its aestheticisation, a move that distances Ford from the memory of the scene he describes in the first person through his alter-ego Gringoire. Impressionism in the tetralogy, therefore, acts to displace the compositional and biographical working through that appears much more clearly in the less aesthetically polished *No Enemy*.

Such scenes illustrate what kind of war narrative Ford composes – a chronicle not of facts and dates but of sensory experiences heightened by Impressionism. Indeed, he refers to his war writings as a chronicle several times, in *No Enemy* stating that he is not 'writing a military treatise' but rather is 'only chronicling the psychology of an Infantry officer as he was affected by certain circumstances' (p. 101). In recalling the genesis of the tetralogy in *It Was the Nightingale*, he states that with Proust's death no one was doing a 'certain literary work' and he thus saw himself as a novelist who would act 'as historian of his own time'.[38] In the interpretations above I am not arguing that Ford's story is less true or valid because he has artistically embellished it to make its visual and aesthetic impact greater. Instead, I suggest that under the pressure of rendering trauma, Ford's Impressionism forces him to turn away from a literal rendition of the traumatic event and instead elaborate the visual impact of these traumatic experiences on a conscious mind. The final Fordian chronicle of his time in the war either takes the form of amplifying figurative language, as in the revisions analysed above, or of using the *homo duplex* to interrupt scenes of violence with memories of sexual desire, as occurs during O Nine Morgan's death and the bombing in which Valentine's face is superimposed on Duckett's. Thus Fordian Impressionism deals in psychoanalytic terms – always repressing either Eros or Thanatos in order to more effectively render and amplify the sensory impact of the other.

In his dedicatory letter to *No More Parades*, Ford reflects on the problem of narrating trauma directly, stating that: 'If you overstate horrors you induce in your reader a state of mind such as, by reaction, causes the horrors to become matters of indifference' (p. 4). The first attempt at rendering trauma in 'True Love & a GCM' parallels horrific descriptions of the trenches in Great War novels such as Remarque's *All Quiet on the Western Front* (1929) and Barbusse's *Under Fire* (1916), both of which contain scenes relating the shock of accidentally touching or encountering corpses. In his revisions, Ford ends up using Impressionism and its highly aestheticised language not to narrate these traumas directly but rather to displace them onto multiple fictional narrators and refract the horror of the trenches through devices like delayed decoding and the time shift. Such revisions reveal his belated working through of his own war experience. Impressionistic techniques thus allow Ford to find a medium between these two extremes of writing a novel that glorifies war and one that desensitises readers to violence. The final form in the tetralogy, after the experiments in 'True Love & a GCM' and *No Enemy*, is one that hints at traumas but refuses to narrate them explicitly, rather emphasising Eros and the life instinct by suppressing Thanatos just under the surface. In moving from more direct, explicit prose to what I'm calling the amplified Impressionism in the tetralogy, the tension between immediacy and recollection is high-lighted. Such passages show that a belated Fordian working through is a process of amplifying Impressionism, not amplifying the violence of war. Ultimately, theorising traumatic consciousness in conjunction with Eros allows us to see healing not as a cathartic forgetting of the event, but rather as a productive working through that is continuous and necessary and will always bear the traces of that process. I would like to end by suggesting that Ford's Impressionism, when applied to the trauma of the Great War, provides added nuance to the crisis of representation discussed in contemporary trauma theory. Ford makes a unique intervention in what Cathy Caruth calls the 'doubling telling' central to narratives of trauma that oscillate between 'the story of the unbearable nature of an event and the story of the unbearable nature of its survival'.[39] Ultimately, through his portrayal of a Janus-faced trau-matic consciousness, Ford makes his traumatic past bearable by ampli-fying his Impressionistic aesthetic yet not overstating such unspeakable horrors.

Notes

1. War narratives published between 1929–30 include: Remarque, *All Quiet in the Western Front* (1929); Graves, *Goodbye to All That* (1929); Hemingway, *A Farewell to Arms* (1929); and Sassoon, *Memoirs of an Infantry Officer* (1930).

2. Ford, *Joseph Conrad*, p. 192.
3. Ford, 'To William Bird' (dedicatory letter), *No More Parades,* ed. Joseph Wiesenfarth, pp. 3–4. All further references are to this edition.
4. Ford, *It Was the Nightingale*, p. 197.
5. See Saunders, *Ford Madox Ford.*
6. Ford, *Joseph Conrad,* p. 192.
7. Ford, *A Man Could Stand Up –*, ed. Sara Haslam, p. 200. All further references are to this edition.
8. See Max Saunders' chapter in this volume for a fuller discussion of sadism in *Parade's End.*
9. Matz, *Literary Impressionism and Modernist Aesthetics*, pp. 33–5.
10. Moses, 'Disorientalism', p. 47.
11. Ibid. p. 52.
12. Although Saunders notes: 'There is no evidence that [Ford] read Freud', he observes during his discussion of *The Good Soldier* that Ford had 'known about – and disapproved of – *The Interpretation of Dreams*' and that 'the influence of Freud's ideas about the Oedipus complex is probable' on the novel: Saunders, *Ford Madox Ford*, I, pp. 186, 425.
13. Gordon, *The Invisible Tent*, pp. 108–9.
14. Peter Gay observes that *Beyond the Pleasure Principle* marks Freud's turn toward the opposition between aggression and Eros and the introduction of the death drive to psychoanalytic theory. Although psychoanalytic critics also note the death of Freud's daughter, Sophie, as a biographical justification for his preoccupation with death in his later works, as Gay argues, the nearly complete manuscript of *Beyond* exists well before Sophie's illness and thus we should view the turn to the death drive as 'not an exercise in autobiography, but as a turning point in theory': *The Freud Reader*, p. 594.
15. Gay, *Freud*, p. 594.
16. For an overview of violence in *Parade's End* but without reference to psychoanalytic trauma theory, see Gordon, *The Invisible Tent*. For interpretations employing contemporary memory studies, see Meyer, 'Ford's War and (Post)Modern Memory'; and Erll, 'The Great War Remembered'. On trauma in *No Enemy*, see Boulter, '"After . . . Armageddon"'.
17. For example, Cathy Caruth, in her now canonical work for trauma theorists, *Unclaimed Experience*, focuses exclusively on Freud's late work including *Beyond the Pleasure Principle* and *Moses and Monotheism*. Although he mentions *Interpretation of Dreams*, Dominick LaCapra similarly concentrates on Freud's late work in *Writing History, Writing Trauma*. Shoshana Felman and Dori Laub in *Testimony* present an extensive discussion of trauma in relation to *Interpretation of Dreams*, focusing not on sexuality but on dream interpretation as a mode of confession and testimony.
18. Of course, some trauma theorists do discuss gender but typically through analyses of child abuse, rape, and incest. See Kalí Tal, *Worlds of Hurt* for a theorisation of trauma explicitly in these terms. For the purposes of this article, I discuss sexuality more broadly as an instinctual drive that defines consciousness and the experience of trauma in the Great War. Unlike other theorists who focus on testimony, memoir, and identity politics at play when depicting child abuse, sexual assault, and incest, I theorise Ford's

representation of trauma as divided between instinctual drives such as Eros and Thanatos.

19. See Cole, *Modernism, Male Friendship, and the First World War* for a discussion of intimacy but not in terms of Freud or trauma theory. See also Bourke, *Dismembering the Male*.
20. Ford, 'On the Functions of the Arts in the Republic', *The Critical Attitude*, p. 28.
21. Ford, 'On Impressionism', *Critical Writings of Ford Madox Ford*, pp. 40, 41.
22. Freud, *Beyond the Pleasure Principle*, pp. 33–4.
23. Ibid. p. 37.
24. The notion of trauma's belatedness is central to Caruth's interpretation of both Freud and her subsequent theory of trauma in *Unclaimed Experience*. She argues that 'trauma is not locatable in the simple violent or original event in an individual's past, but rather in the way that its very unassimilated nature – the way it was precisely *not known* in the first instance – returns to haunt the survivor later on' (p. 4). Such a notion of haunting is common within trauma theory and memory studies.
25. Freud, *Beyond the Pleasure Principle*, p. 26.
26. Ibid. p. 26. Emphasis mine.
27. Ibid. p. 71.
28. Ibid. p. 72.
29. Freud, *Reflections on War and Death*, p. 1.
30. Freud, *Beyond the Pleasure Principle*, p. 34.
31. Haslam, *Fragmenting Modernism*, p. 23.
32. As Max Saunders observes, the manuscript, written in 1918–19 and left unfinished by Ford, is a testing ground for *Parade's End*: 'True Love & a CGM', *War Prose*, p. 77.
33. Ford, 'True Love & a GCM', p. 109.
34. Ibid. p. 109.
35. See Conroy, 'A Map of Tory Misreading in *Parade's End*'; and Snitow, *Ford Madox Ford and the Voice of Uncertainty*.
36. Although published in 1929, after the publication of *A Man Could Stand Up* – in 1926, as Paul Skinner notes in his introduction to the Carcanet edition, Ford wrote the majority of *No Enemy* in 1919 'between his two acknowledged masterpieces, *The Good Soldier* (1915) and *Parade's End* (1924–8)': Skinner, Introduction to *No Enemy*, p. vii. According to Skinner, *No Enemy* is a necessary precursor to *Parade's End* since it is 'about a writer's rediscovery of his ability to write – about something even more than ability, the will, the necessity, the *duty* to write' (p. xix).
37. Ford, *No Enemy*, p. 24.
38. Ford, *It Was the Nightingale*, p. 180.
39. Caruth, *Unclaimed Experience*, p. 7.

Chapter 3

Empathy, Trauma, and the Space of War in *Parade's End*

Eve Sorum

In 'Arms and the Mind', written while in Ypres in 1916, Ford claims that he 'can write nothing – why I cannot even think anything that to myself seems worth thinking'.[1] This problem with finding an appropriate literary form – 'we have no method of approach to any of these problems',[2] Ford moans in a posthumously published essay that was found in Ezra Pound's papers – becomes an issue of perspective or, rather, the lack of a proper perspective. 'One is always too close or too remote',[3] Ford writes, and the challenge of the writer is to somehow find a form that reveals both the details and the broader picture of the war. Yet it also appears that this dilemma is something that should *not* be resolved, since it is a sensation central to the habitual state of the soldier in the trenches, whose perspective is circumscribed by the limits of a rifle sight. Ford describes:

> Dimly, but very tyrannically, there lurk in your mind the precepts of the musketry instructors at Splott or at Veryd ranges. The precepts that the sights must be upright, the tip of the foresight in line with the shoulders of the ˉVˉ of the backsight are always there, even when the ˉVˉ of the backsight has assumed its air of being a loophole between yourself and the sun and wind and when the blade of the foresight is like a bar across that loophole. And the dark, smallish, potlike object upon whose 'six o'clock' you must align both bar and loophole has none of the aspects of a man's head. It is just a pot.[4]

The limits on one's ability to see other perspectives are what enable survival in war, Ford argues, even as they are also what disable narrative.

Not only does this tension about perspective-taking define the shifting points of view in *Parade's End* and, more broadly, in modernist war literature, but it also indicates the challenges of empathetic engagement in a war world. I argue that, perhaps counter-intuitively, *Parade's End* frustrates attempts at connection and empathy in order to then allow for them, collapsing the easy distinctions between categories of orientation and disorientation. These are the very categories, I posit, that are central to empathetic engagement. Over the course of the tetralogy, Ford explores the possibility of empathy in a war-traumatised world in which the failure and fear of empathy are at the forefront, and the characters may only be able to experience emotion just at the moment when they think all has been lost. Yet, through their emphasis on moments of disconnection and on the various barriers to perspective-taking, Ford's novels paradoxically reveal a robust desire to enhance communication and understand other points of view.

In this chapter I focus on the spatial basis of empathy and the role perspective-taking plays in experiencing and promoting acts of empathetic imagination. Empathy has been defined on cognitive, emotional, and physical levels since the term was first coined in the early part of the twentieth century. It was introduced to the British reading public by critics such as Vernon Lee (Violet Paget) and T. E. Hulme through their translation of the German word *Einfühlung* from the texts of Theodor Lipps and Wilhelm Worringer, to name two of the most influential theorists of empathy and art.[5] In his 1908 book *Abstraction and Empathy*, Worringer claims that art is governed by two opposing urges: the urge to empathy, which results in realist or naturalist representation, and the urge to abstraction, which suppresses spatial representation in favour of abstract forms. The production of this non-representational art springs, Worringer writes, from a fear of space; the aesthetic pleasure one gets from it is akin to an almost desperate act of sense-making in a disorderly world. He argues that the:

> happiness [Eastern abstract artists] sought from art did not consist in the possibility of projecting themselves into the things of the outer world [. . .] but in the possibility of taking the individual thing of the external world out of its arbitrariness and seeming fortuitousness, of eternalizing it by approximation to abstract forms and, in this manner, of finding a point of tranquillity and a refuge from appearances.[6]

The difference between the abstract and the realist here, as Worringer describes it, involves the relationship between the artist and the surrounding world; the realist artist is 'projecting' himself into the exterior world, creating an identifiable and reciprocally defining space in the artwork; the abstract artist, on the other hand, wishes to retreat from the chaos of the surrounding environment. This process involves a distillation of the 'thing' from the outside world into an 'abstract form', thereby rendering it orderly and under control. In both of these definitions, Worringer locates artistic production as a psychological act – what he describes as 'the psychic attitude toward the cosmos'.[7]

Unlike Theodor Lipps, who saw empathetic engagement with art as central to what constitutes beauty, Worringer does not favour realist art.

In fact, he posits that abstraction is the only 'and the highest' possible aesthetic response to a world in which people's relationship to nature has lost its sense of ease. Empathetic engagement is linked to the psychological state in which one has a sense of locatedness in the 'external world'.[8] This resonates with our familiar trope of empathy as 'standing in someone else's shoes': a spatial metaphor for imagining oneself in another's place in order to 'share' cognitive, affective, and volitional states. It thus seems, at first, that empathy in Worringer's formulation is the more balanced of the two aesthetic and psychological states, for it is a sign of an easy relationship between viewer and world, artist and society. Yet, though I will adhere to Worringer's general distinction, I want to highlight that a very literal *dis*orientation and *re*orientation occurs when experiencing empathy, for standing in someone else's shoes requires a shift in perspective – a shift that can be more or less challenging depending on the 'distance' that one has to traverse. Empathy can involve, therefore, both hard cognitive and emotional work, as well as discomfort.

Arguing this, I hope to provoke thought about the labour involved in empathetic imagining, as well as highlight the threat to the idea of the autonomous individual that is implicit in an act of perspective-taking. As Max Saunders has written in his comprehensive biography, Ford's choice to narrate the war through the perspective of a character who was based on his late friend, Arthur Marwood, 'has too often been discussed as if it were an easy thing to do' because it is 'a self-effacing device, which can be confused with a mere appropriation of the *déja vu* and the *déja dit*', as opposed to the 'extraordinary act of imagination' that it actually manifests.[9] While I am less concerned with the authorial empathy at work in this novel, and more with readerly empathy and the representations of empathy between characters, Saunders' comment points to one of the dangers of empathy – the potential loss of the self in the act of imagining other perspectives – as well as to the effort involved in crossing the boundaries of one's individual experience. Perhaps counter-intuitively, the stylistic difficulty of Ford's narrative turns out to be central to the project of perspective-taking. As Suzanne Keen describes it in her seminal analysis of narrative empathy, research by David S. Miall suggests that potential formal barriers to perspective-taking like those found in 'difficult and discontinuous texts' may in fact enable readerly empathy *because* of the interpretive work that they ask readers to do.[10] Stylistically disorienting narratives do not necessarily engage in a 'refusal of empathy' like the one Sianne Ngai locates in a text such Herman Melville's *The Confidence-Man* (1857), which is a result of a proliferation of characters and the foreclosure of 'sympathetic identification at all levels by foregrounding "objectified emotion"'.[11] Even though the idea of objectified emotion is pertinent to a discussion of *Parade's End,* as we will see most vividly with the map image in *No More Parades,* such moments of objectification fascinate and horrify the characters. Indeed, unlike with Melville's Bartleby or the characters in *The Confidence-Man,* who present surfaces that resist identification, I argue that the characters in *Parade's End,* through their own alienation from their experiences and sense of disorientation with the emotional and experiential terrain, actually invite the reader into a world that might otherwise be inaccessible.

This focus on alienation and disorientation as much as on connection and orientation is one central aspect of what I call 'modernist empathy'. The loss and confusion are as important to the process as is the gain of a new perspective. They do not signal a failure of empathy; instead, they are an inevitable and integral part of the empathetic experience. From this standpoint, the seemingly alienating experience of war trauma emerges as centrally linked to the production of empathetic experiences. In arguing this I am following in the footsteps of Vincent Sherry's discussion of the 'interrupted functions of imaginative reason and poetic statement' that define the change between the pre-war and the post-war writing of central modernists such Ezra Pound, T. S. Eliot, and Virginia Woolf.[12] Sherry only touches upon Ford briefly in his book, but he locates *Parade's End* as a fiction 'that witnesses the true difficulty of the disruption' posed by the war to narrative 'models of progressive time'.[13] He categorises Ford as not quite modernist: as having the desire to adhere to more traditional modes of narration, even when he recognises the need for innovation. While it is true that Ford's protagonist, Christopher Tietjens, repeatedly attempts to transform the disorder into something more orderly, I argue that the novels' narrative gaps and elisions perform, rather than elide, those stresses.

The problem of entering other perspectives is foregrounded in Ford's dedicatory letter to *No More Parades,* as he discusses the question of how to write a war novel that will bring 'about such a state of mind as should end wars as possibilities'.[14] The solution, Ford recounts, was to 'use my friend's eyes as a medium' (p. 5); this choice of a guiding perspective would allow him, Ford hoped, to represent the emotional side of war without being emotional. In many ways, as Saunders has reminded us, interest in the very 'act of perception' was the cornerstone of Ford's aesthetic project, first articulated through his theory of Impressionism during and after his collaboration with Joseph Conrad. Thus from the early stages of his writing career, '[c]onsciousness is his subject, rather than the objects of consciousness'.[15] And this consciousness is, we see, also rooted in spatialised memories. Describing his decision to narrate from the perspective of his dead friend Arthur Marwood (whom he calls 'X' in the preface), Ford writes: 'I remember the very spot where the idea came to me' (*No More Parades*, p. 4).

This project takes on new resonances, of course, when faced with the damaged consciousnesses and spaces that emerge as casualties of war. We can immediately see in the first lines of *No More Parades* how problematic the issue of perspective-taking will be in this war world:

> When you came in the space was desultory, rectangular, warm after the drip of the winter night, and transfused with a brown-orange dust that was light. It was shaped like the house a child draws. Three groups of brown limbs spotted with brass took dim high-lights from shafts that came from a bucket pierced with holes. (p. 9)

Here, we get a scene in which the intuitive and normal modes of understanding identity and location are immediately disrupted. Everything here is atomised: the space is broken up into lines and planes – 'rectangular', with a 'parallelogram of black that was the doorway' and men who are first simply 'Three groups of brown limbs'. The question of how the readers are supposed to parse these images is the primary dilemma (what can we make of dust that *is* light?); our disorientation is only heightened by the introduction of objects that speak with disconcerting violence – the 'tea-tray' whose 'voice' fills the air and the 'sheet-iron' that 'said, "Pack. Pack. Pack"' (p. 9).

The second word of the book has already alerted the reader that we need to think about *our* placement in the scene: 'When *you* came in, the space was desultory, rectangular, warm' (p. 9). It takes several pages before we can figure out who our focalising narrative consciousness may and should be; though we hear of an 'elder officer', he is not identified by name until a quarter of the way into the chapter, and only then do we move into his (it is Tietjens, it turns out) perspective. Yet Tietjens is a complicated figure when thinking about empathetic engagement. A seemingly expressionless and even emotionally obtuse figure, he is described by his notoriously unsympathetic wife Sylvia as having a face that was 'simply gazing over the heads of all things and created beings into a world too distant for them to enter' (p. 114). With Tietjens and Sylvia as the two centres of narrative knowledge and consciousness in the second novel, we see more of the injuries, rather than the benefits of being able to see from another's perspective. Their masochistic/ sadistic relationship thereby reveals some of the risks associated with seeing from another perspective: it allows one to wound, as well as help, another. These risks are coupled with the difficulty of finding a social and a narrative structure within this war-torn world that can enable empathetic engagement.

Despite Sylvia's characterisation and his own seeming obtuseness, Tietjens displays an understanding of both the limits to and the possibilities of stepping outside oneself. As he writes out a sonnet and waits for soldiers to come to him to make out their wills, Tietjens thinks it 'suddenly extraordinary how shut in on oneself one was in this life' (p. 42). 'This life' is the world of the Western Front in particular, and of the modern war machine in general. It is a world that disables insight as well as more literal forms of sight. Tietjens proves adept at entering into other perspectives, however, and his world is thus thrown into disarray when he realises that he might have misinterpreted something that Sylvia said before he left for the Front. Sylvia's appearance at his camp, in conjunction with the death of O Nine Morgan, sends him off into an emotional and cognitive tailspin; Tietjens suddenly reflects that he has been basing his assumption that their marriage was over on hearing Sylvia call out 'Paddington' as she headed off in a taxi, presumably for the station that would bring her to a 'convent at Birkenhead', a retreat that signified, he had thought, the end to their marriage (p. 20). Tietjens describes it thus: 'In the complete stillness of dawn he had heard her voice say very clearly "Paddington" to the chauffeur' (p. 38), and then soon after he reflects: 'Obviously his mind until now had regarded his wife's "*Paddington*" as the definite farewell between his life and hers' (p. 39). Sylvia's reappearance forces him to evaluate his previous interpretation, even going so far as to question whether it was she or her maid who had spoken the word.

The irony here is that Tietjens *had* been right, in terms of both identifying the voice as Sylvia's and hearing it as a sign of the end of their marriage. We learn this from Sylvia as she reflects on her change of mind:

> She had certainly meant their parting to be for good. She had certainly raised her voice in giving the name of her station to the taxi-man with the pretty firm conviction that he would hear her; and she had been pretty well certain that he would take it as a sign that the breath had gone out of their union. . . . Pretty certain! But not quite!' (p. 117)

The repetition of 'certain' is striking not only because of its construction in the past tense (such understandings are no longer certain in the present moment of war), but also because it highlights Sylvia's assumption that Tietjens *would* understand that a single, overheard word could function as the epilogue to their marriage. At the same time Sylvia's musings reveal the fragility of the material on which that certainty is based. Yet empathetic understanding is assumed, even at a moment of emotional and social separation.

Then Sylvia changes her mind – an eventuality that Tietjens had not imagined – and thus throws his understanding of the world into disarray. In the face of this reversal we see him engage in a characteristic form of activity as he tries to recalibrate his understanding of the situation: he attempts to order and schematise his own response and fit the events and characters into a set structure. The language of adopting an overarching perspective comes into play; as Tietjens begins to write out his memories of their parting, his mind moves to a scene of survey: 'On the Somme, in the summer, when stand-to had been at four in the morning, you would come out of your dug-out and survey, with a complete outfit of pessimistic thoughts, a dim, grey, repulsive landscape over a dull and much too thin parapet' (p. 72). The dangers of adopting this viewpoint are apparent in the description; rather than providing an enlightening contrast, the landscape mirrors his depression and the parapet provides little protection from the dangers of shells and bullets. Yet Tietjens persists, and his writing out of the events, too, takes on an instrumentalising and omniscient perspective, as he 'said to himself that he must put, in exact language, as if he were making a report for the use of garrison headquarters, the history of himself in relationship to his wife' (p. 73). In doing so, Tietjens moves into a version of perspective-taking that provides a counterpoint to an empathetic perspective; rather than trying to enter into an individual viewpoint, he attempts to step back in order to describe and comprehend the scene from a bird's-eye view. In the face of trauma, the first response seems to be to shut down empathetic engagement and to achieve a psychological distance through the imagined physical distance.

The solution is more complicated than it would at first seem, however, since neither looking down on the scene of battle nor writing out a narrative survey elucidates the problem of perspectives. Indeed, as Jeffrey McCarthy has argued, we can see an 'anxiety about instrumentalizing relations' and a critique of 'the industrial, bureaucratic society behind the war' at the centre of the tetralogy.[16] This political focus aligns with the perspectival one that Ford presents in the impulse to map the battlefield. In *A Man Could Stand Up* –, for example, the characters voice their desire for a commanding perspective and the inability to find one in the war: 'Imagine standing up on a hill! It was the unthinkable thing there!'[17]

This idea of an over-arching perspective that shuts down, rather than opens up, interpretation is most evocatively explored, however, through the bloodstained map that appears to Tietjens in a moment of profound stress. At the end of the long twenty-four hours, which start with the death of O Nine Morgan and culminate with Tietjens' slip of the tongue revealing Sylvia's infidelity, Tietjens imagines that 'The whole map of the embattled world ran out in front of him – as large as a field. An embossed map in greenish *papier mâché* – a ten-acre field of embossed *papier mâché*, with the blood of O Nine Morgan blurring luminously over it' (*No More Parades*, p. 239). As he goes on to recall a moment in which he was being asked to survey the space for 'a fat home general who had never come', Tietjens' shell-shocked memory abstracts and obscures the horror of his own experience, and he thinks with resignation, 'Now, having lost so much emotion, he saw the embattled world as a map' (p. 239). As a map, the particulars of the landscape are smoothed over, allowing it to become an abstracted representational system of a uniform colour and material; Tietjens correctly identifies this cognitive retreat from the experience as something to distrust, for it is the sort of objectifying perspective that perpetuates the violence that has caused trauma in the first place. Thus Tietjens' fear about the effect of the trauma on the mind – that his own loss of emotion would make him withdraw, only able to see the world as a map and unable to relate to the emotions of others – is linked not only to his own individual experience of the war and of social relations, but also to the larger political and psychological issue of what allows nations and men to go to war in the first place.

Yet the map Tietjens imagines offers a variation on the rectilinear grid that we might first assume when thinking about cartographic representation. As the novel's final metaphor for how to order one's perspective in this war world, this variation presents a way to make emotion and trauma visible and shows us how to understand a perspective that has *become* other. What we see Tietjens experiencing here is the most terrifying form of disorientation yet: the need to figure out how to move into one's *own* mind, which has become estranged in the face of trauma. Tietjens' map facilitates this on several levels, both in its messy three-dimensionality – 'greenish *papier mâché*', as large as a 'ten-acre field' – and, in particular, in the blood that stains and defaces its surface. The novel presents a double movement: on the one hand, Tietjens attempts to escape from strong emotions and terrifying experiences with this turn to the map ('having lost so much emotion, he saw the embattled world as a map'). On the other, his map vividly manifests trauma through 'the blood of O Nine Morgan blurring luminously over it'.

With this map image, Ford complicates our assumptions about the forms and representational strategies that enable or create empathetic engagement, whether with other people or with one's self (for that 'other' perspective is here his own, radically severed by shell shock, war trauma, and marital strife). Ford's use of this defaced map also suggests the need for an elaboration and revision of Worringer's thesis about realist art as the source of empathetic engagement. Gilles Deleuze and Felix Guattari provide one such insightful rereading of Worringer, arguing that abstraction is not always a function of distance and alienation. In essence, they propose that we must expand the definition of abstract art from the one used by Worringer, who only examined abstraction as a manifestation of the 'geometrical imperial Egyptian form' that works in a 'rectilinear' fashion.[18] Thinking through the question of whether abstract art can promote an urge to empathy rather than an urge to alienation, Deleuze and Guattari use the terms 'smooth' versus 'striated' for the forms of art and the types of spaces that embody, respectively, connective versus cartographic modes of being in the world. Within smooth or what they also call 'nomad' art, a single orientation and con-sistency in representation is not important, because the art represents the experiences of embedded individuals (it is from the perspective of the nomad rather than that of the cartographer). Contrastingly, striated or cartographic art and spaces are defined by their need for a coherent ori-entation and a sense of a central, defining perspective; the modern map can function as an exemplar of this. While Worringer was only looking at the organisational and cartographic modes of abstraction exemplified by geometric art, Deleuze and Guattari claim that we must think about a nomad and connective visual art that is 'abstract in an entirely different sense, precisely because it has a multiple orientation and passes *between* points, figures, and contours: it is positively motivated by the smooth space it draws, not by any striation it might perform to ward off anxiety and subordinate the smooth'.[19] Abstract art, in this reading, *can* facili-tate empathy because it creates new connections via the nomad lines that move through different spaces, objects, and perspectives. As our eyes follow the lines, we quite literally explore the effects of occupying other perspectives, not allowing one viewpoint to dominate. While nomad art does not enable empathy through identification with recognisable representations, it does create connections by manifesting the very act and idea of forming relationships. As Deleuze and Guattari define it, the '*abstract* in modern art' is a 'line of variable direction that describes no contour and delimits no form'.[20] Tellingly, they use ellipses to punctu-ate this claim; their ellipses function as a grammatical version of this absence of delimitation, and we will see how they perform powerfully in similar ways in Ford's narrative.

Thinking about this version of abstraction and its relationship to empathetic engagement helps uncover why the novels might work *for-mally* and why Tietjens' map image works *metaphorically* to promote not simply disorientation but also orientation. Thus, even in the middle of a scene in which the characters experience profound alienation from the minds of others, *No More Parades* itself might be promoting an urge to empathy. If we return to the first scene we can see how the narrative 'abstraction' of that opening and the oddly distanced perspective, while it disrupts our understanding of how to align our connections and affections, also forces the reader to establish new methods of connection within the event of war; our readerly alienation from the description puts us in a place that is similar to the disjunctive encounters of the soldiers. A later moment in *A Man Could Stand Up –* revisits this urge to connect in light of military tactics: Tietjens reflects on what he calls his 'mania' for 'communication drill' when he takes over, mid-battle, a battalion of which he had been second in command (p. 150). Appropriately, given the problems that always emerge, in Tietjens' battalion communications turn out to be the 'heel of Achilles' (p. 150). Yet for Tietjens 'It was perhaps the dominant idea [. . .], perhaps the main idea that he got out of warfare – that at all costs you must keep in touch with your neighbouring troops' (p. 159). What we learn is that, while Tietjens is right in his desire to connect, the only ethical method of doing so will be haphazard and enacted on the ground. While a 'single command' is what the Allies need in order to win the war, organisational systems and bureaucratic perspectives are always suspect in these novels. The true crime in Ford's tetralogy is how the individual suffering of soldiers can become simply part of a game of war; reflecting on the inhumanity of it all, Tietjens thinks about how even the 'war of attrition' could be 'not an uninteresting occupation if you considered it as a struggle of various minds spread out all over the broad landscape in the sunlight' (p. 152). Because the war had been put 'into the hands of the applied scientist' (p. 152), individuals can only function as part of a larger equation.

Yet even if the abstraction at work in the war machine is ultimately alienating in relation to the actual experience of the men, Ford's formal experiments in the novels offer a way to create a nomad art that brings us into the individual minds of the characters. In particular, we can turn to one of the other most striking characteristics of all of the *Parade's End* novels: the extensive use of ellipses within the text.[21] Tietjens' thoughts become perforated by ellipses at moments of trauma. When O Nine Morgan dies on top of him, for example, he even realises that 'It was impossible to think in this row. . . . His very thick soles moved gluily and came up after suction. . . .'. As he tries to keep a hold of himself at this stressful moment, when he is literally standing in blood, his 'thoughts seemed to have to shout to him between earthquake shocks' (*No More Parades*, p. 30). The ellipses emerge here as Tietjens frets about his inability to understand how Valentine might react to the scene, thus signalling, on the one hand, the very literal gaps in his under-standing and his mind's inability to move organically between different perspectives.

Yet there might also be a way in which these ellipses *enable* movement between perspectives, even in moments of trauma. Sylvia's mind also becomes punctuated by ellipses at a moment of sexual and emotional tension, as she gambles on whether she will let Christopher go or try to lure him back. She remembers whipping a bulldog that, it turned out, had been poisoned:

> And [I] got the rhinoceros whip and lashed into it. . . . There's a pleasure in lashing a naked white beast. . . . Obese and silent. . . . Like Christopher. . . . I thought Christopher might. . . . That night. . . . It went through my head. . . . It hung down its head. . . .' (*No More Parades*, p. 154)

These leaps and gaps bring the singularly self-centred Sylvia into a state where both Christopher's martyrdom and her own pain at his lack of interest in her ('It went through my head') become connected to the dog's suffering ('It hung down its head'). The ellipses here and elsewhere in the novel emphasise movements of the mind and the attempts to leap between perspectives, moments, and places. They are about connections and the disruption of a dominant perspective as much as they are about signalling erasures and gaps. As manifestations of syntactic erasure – a blotting of narrative, a shedding of words – the ellipses call attention to the very *idea* of movement between ideas, thoughts, and minds by sig-nalling of the missing links between those shifts.

Indeed, Tietjens' shell shock (which, we learn in an elliptical fashion, has taken place in the gap between the first and second parts of *Some Do Not . . .*) proves a form of psychological ellipses that jolts Tietjens out of his sometimes infuriating omniscience (he can no longer correct the encyclopaedia). Thus he reaches a state in *A Man Could Stand Up –* in which he cannot abstract himself from the tiresome and often terrifying business of the war: the question of whether or not an attack would come at his point in the line 'was wearisome nowadays, though once it would have delighted him to dwell on it and work it out with nice figures and calculations of stresses' (pp. 156–7). This is a form of redemption in *Parade's End*: Tietjens emerges as a character who can move outside of the instrumentalising perspective that views the world from a distance. Instead, he embodies the connective abstraction of the elliptical narra-tive, which allows the reader to enter into the mindsets and experiences of the characters, and the characters to break out of their limited per-spectives and imagine the experiences of others. Thus Tietjens ends up appearing as the Christ-like figure that Sylvia, in her attempt to sabotage his standing with General Campion, his godfather and superior, has declared he wants to be: "'He desires", Sylvia said, and she had no idea when she said it, "to model himself upon our Lord. . . ."' (*No More Parades*, p. 148). While Sylvia says this out of a half-insightful maliciousness, and while General Campion takes it as a sign of Tietjens' instability, the image works, not simply because Tietjens sacrifices his own reputation and wealth for others, but because he moves away from instrumentalisation and towards a more empathetic mode of being.

We therefore get in *No More Parades* and the other volumes some insight into how experimental, abstract, and defaced literary and visual forms might enable movement into other perspectives. Though Tietjens first appears as an exemplar of the statistical thinker who abstracts himself from the messy realm of empathetic engagement, the novels chart his painful emergence from this mode of being. Moreover, Ford does more than represent an individual movement into empathetic perspectives; in addition, he offers a narrative form – punctuated by syntactical and narrative ellipses, defined by disorienting shifts in perspective, and populated with central metaphoric images like the bloodstained map – that suggests how narrative forms of abstraction might work to engage empathy in the same way that visual forms do in Deleuze and Guattari's formulation. Yet Ford's narrative empathy is defined by and emerges from war trauma; it also highlights, therefore, the difficulties and the dangers of moving outside one's own perspective. His tetralogy might thereby provide an illuminating case study of a 'modernist empathy' that is defined by David S. Miall's idea of the 'dehabituating power of literary forms'.[22] If art's strength is in its representation of the affective and subjective realm of the individual, it struggles with what Margot Norris calls its 'epistemological inability to totalize' when faced with the mass horror of war.[23] In his movements between the nomadic and the cartographic, the empathetic and the instrumental, Ford questions the systems by which we normally try to move beyond our own perspective, suggesting that they are simply forms of shorthand that become almost criminally negligent when faced with trying to understand mass trauma. We can only stand in someone else's shoes, in this war world, if we understand how dangerous the act of standing in one's own shoes may be.

Notes

1. Ford, 'A Day of Battle', *War Prose*, p. 36.
2. Ford, 'Epilogue', *War Prose*, p. 59.

3. Ibid. p. 59.
4. Ford, 'A Day of Battle', pp. 38–9.
5. For further discussion of Worringer's analysis of empathy and representation, see Chapter 4 in this volume.
6. Worringer, *Abstraction and Empathy*, p. 16.
7. Ibid. p. 15.
8. Ibid. pp. 19, 15.
9. Saunders, *Ford Madox Ford*, II, p. 210. One could say the same thing about Saunders' own act in his astoundingly thorough and empathetic biography of Ford, which clearly required some serious work of the sympathetic imagination to create.
10. Keen, *Empathy and the Novel*, p. 87. Keen is quick to point out that the studies show only a very general link between difficulty and empathetic engagement.
11. Ngai, *Ugly Feelings*, pp. 49, 52.
12. Sherry, *The Great War and the Language of Modernism*, p. 13.
13. Ibid. p. 226.
14. Ford, *No More Parades*, ed. Joseph Wiesenfarth, p. 4. All further references are to this edition.
15. Saunders, *Ford Madox Ford*, I, p. 5.
16. McCarthy, '"The Foul System"', p. 178.
17. Ford, *A Man Could Stand Up –*, ed. Sara Haslam, p. 90. All further references are to this edition.
18. Deleuze and Guattari, *A Thousand Plateaus*, p. 496.
19. Ibid. p. 496.
20. Ibid. p. 499.
21. For a discussion of the connections between ellipses and the kinds of silences that occur as mourning mechanisms in the tetralogy, see Sorum, 'Mourning and Moving On'.
22. Quoted in Keen, *Empathy and the Novel*, p. 87.
23. Norris, *Writing War in the Twentieth Century*, p. 20.

Chapter 4

Fellow Feeling in Ford's *Last Post*: Modernist Empathy and the Eighteenth-Century Man

Meghan Marie Hammond

In this chapter, I examine the role that fellow feeling plays in Ford Madox Ford's final Tietjens novel, *Last Post* (1928). Like many other exemplars of high modernism, Ford's novel circulates between various characters' minds, revealing multiple inner monologues and idiosyncratic interiors. *Last Post* thus encourages the reader to think and feel with those characters by turn. What sets the last volume of *Parade's End* apart from other such novels of its era is the way it cuts off our access to one particular character: its protagonist, Christopher Tietjens. My analysis of Ford's novel focuses on both Christopher, who is away for almost the entirety of the novel, and his brother Mark, who remains motionless and outwardly mute until the novel's final pages. Christopher's conspicuous absence and Mark's conspicuous presence, I argue, press us to consider the traumatic effects of war on the mind. I am particularly interested here in the interaction between body and mind, and in the ways bodies mediate the reader's experience of characters' minds. For it is in the dying Mark, who seems to exist simultaneously at the extremes of both corporeality and mental activity, that we find the culmination of *Parade's End*'s sustained treatment of fellow feeling.

Throughout the *Parade's End* novels, Christopher understands himself as a man with an eighteenth-century mind and temperament caught in the twentieth century, a remnant of a dead past.[1] At the same time, he lives in an era that is trying to reinvent one of the fundamental moral concepts of eighteenth-century Britain: fellow feeling. Empathy, the ability to 'feel with' or 'think with' another person, has deep conceptual roots in eighteenth-century discourses – it is the twentieth-century cousin of the moral sympathy that David Hume and Adam Smith theorised in their influential philosophical works. Both eighteenth-century sympathy and twentieth-century empathy offer us powerful ways of understanding what is at stake in the *Last Post*, a text that has suffered considerable neglect and has been understood by some as a non-essential part of the series.[2] Yet if we think about *Parade's End* as a record of the First World War and the marks that conflict left on the minds of those who survived it, it becomes nearly impossible to imagine the series without its fourth volume. If we accept that war is often deeply traumatic, we must surely consider that like all traumatic experience, war lingers in individual minds and in the relationships that connect them. It is only in *Last Post* that we see the aftermath of the war and the lasting effects it has had on intersubjective thought and feeling. This is a novel that asks, in short, if it is possible to feel with others in a post-war world.

   Parade's End as a whole is governed by principles of fellow feeling. Christopher and Valentine Wannop, for instance, offer a prime example of sympathetic minds. From their first meeting in *Some Do Not . . .* they understand each other readily. Like the characters in Mrs Wannop's Victorian books, they form a union 'of the mind or of sympathy'[3] and mutually conclude that they should refrain from becoming lovers because they are 'the sort that . . . *do not!*'[4] Despite long separations, their minds remain tethered by reciprocal thoughts. All the while, each novel in the series features more interior monologue than the last, helping the reader 'feel into' the minds of the central characters.[5] Yet *Parade's End* is also haunted by constant failures of fellow feeling. During the war, Christopher and Valentine continue their individual lives while completely out of sympathy with the rest of the world. Christopher fights the psychological attacks of his wife Sylvia and the mental stress of the warfront while the pacifist Valentine suffers social disapproval and the ill treatment of Edith Ethel. The third volume, *A Man Could Stand Up –*, ends with Christopher and Valentine reunited on the Armistice, vacillating between fear of each other and a shared belief that their minds 'march together' (p. 192). But although they have become the kind of people who 'do', there is still a lingering psychological distance between them. Christopher's war experience makes his mind, more than ever, a 'grey Eminence' (p. 201) that Valentine's own mind cannot penetrate. She displays a veritable well of feeling and pity, but she has only the barest understanding of his war years. In her combination of concern and lack of knowledge, she is representative of what Rob Hawkes has called *Parade's End*'s 'preoccupation with the problem of shaping the seemingly incomprehensible experiences of the trenches into a coherent narrative'.[6] The coherence of that narrative, which is one of broken and mended intersubjective links, depends on *Last Post*. As Sara Haslam writes: 'when it comes to pity, empathy and comprehension, as generous a part of Ford's vision as we may feel them to have been throughout volumes 1–3, it is perhaps *Last Post* that pushes them to their limits'.[7] Indeed, *Last Post* might even push us *beyond* the limits of empathy in some instances.

Sympathy and Empathy

It is significant that Christopher is an eighteenth-century man caught in the first great conflict of the twentieth century. Through him, we see sympathy, that great eighteenth-century virtue, adapting to the cultural and emotional landscape of the modern world. The first major theoriser of sympathy in the British tradition was David Hume, whose *A Treatise on Human Nature* (1739) names the propensity to sympathise the most 'remarkable' human quality.[8] Hume writes that in the act of sympathy, 'the mind passes easily from the idea of ourselves to that of any other object related to us'.[9] The sympathy we experience with our fellows in daily life, as Hume understands it, is largely dependent on our acts of observation and imagination:

> When I see the *effects* of passion in the voice and gesture of any person, my mind immediately passes from these effects to their causes, and forms such a lively idea of the passion, as is presently converted into the passion itself.[10]

Our minds, then, have a potent ability to let us experience the passions of others. One thing that is important to note here is the direction in which sympathy operates. It starts with what Hume calls the effects of a passion or 'external signs in the countenance and conversation'[11] and moves 'inward' to consider the causes of those effects. In sympathy, we imaginatively move into another person's mind, the source of their passions. Our own mind creates an 'impression' of their passion that in turn 'produce[s] an equal emotion'.[12] Sympathy is thus a process of getting closer, of shrinking the distance between self and external object. It is not simply a matter of shared emotions or pity; it is an epistemological tool.

For Adam Smith, whose *The Theory of Moral Sentiments* (1759) also had a deep and lasting effect on the discourse of fellow feeling, sympathy is a constitutional component of human identity and moral life. Even the 'greatest ruffian', according to Smith, can feel compassion or suffer when others suffer.[13] From this perspective, failures of sympathy are serious social lapses, for he 'whose hard and obdurate heart feels for himself only' brings pain to others with his presence.[14] Smith even goes so far as to say, 'to feel much for others and little for ourselves [. . .] to restrain our selfish, and to indulge our benevolent affections, constitutes the perfection of human nature'.[15] It is easy to see how far from this mark of perfection the more unlikeable characters in *Parade's End* fall – the hard and obdurate hearts of Sylvia and General Campion, for example, bring considerable pain to those who suffer their presence. But even our protagonist, Christopher, often feels little for others. As Hawkes and Haslam both imply, it is the experience of war that teaches Christopher how to imagine and value other interiors.[16]

Like Hume, Smith understands sympathy as a product of our prodigious imaginations. Our fellow feeling, he explains, comes from 'changing places in fancy with the sufferer'.[17] In his most vivid treatment of sympathetic imagination, Smith explains how our mind proceeds when we see our fellow man being tortured on the rack:

> By the imagination we place ourselves in his situation, we conceive ourselves enduring all the same torments, we enter as it were into his body and become in some measure him, and thence form some idea of his sensations and even feel something which, though weaker in degree, is not altogether unlike them.[18]

Notably, Smith concedes here that our understanding, what Hume would call our 'impression', is weaker than the passion experienced by the subject of our sympathy. This weaker passion, an echo of our friend's original one, is as close as we can get to other minds, for as Smith points out, 'we have no immediate experience of what other men feel'.[19] But Smith is also very sure that sympathy does not mean simply observing a fellow person and imagining how we would feel if we were in his place. Rather, he explains, 'I consider what I should suffer if I was really you, and I not only change circumstances with you, but I change persons and characters.'[20] What we need to note here is that this sympathy acknowledges a fundamental distance between individual minds. It is an imagined experience of otherness, not an experience of being together with another.

Such being together with another, a confusion of subjectivities, is more in line with specifically *empathic* fellow feeling. The particular empathy with which I am concerned here derives from the German concept of *Einfühlung*, or 'feeling oneself into', put forth in the aesthetic theory of Robert Vischer in 1873. That concept made its way into psychology and phenomenology primarily through the turn-of-the-century work of Theodor Lipps, who, as a translator of Hume, was also familiar with the eighteenth-century understanding of sympathy from the British tradition. Vernon Lee (Violet Paget) and T. E. Hulme, contemporaries of Ford with connections to his social circle, were largely responsible for introducing the British reading public to empathy in the years just before the First World War.

While sympathy and empathy, as two related forms of fellow feeling, are not completely discrete concepts, they are also not synonymous. Certainly, early twentieth-century theorisers of empathy wanted to set up a distinction between the two. In order to differentiate the two forms of fellow feeling, Edith Stein, author of the influential 1917 work *Zum Problem der Einfühlung*, placed heavy emphasis on the sympathetic distance that Smith admitted in his work. During acts of sympathy, she writes, we 'concede to the foreign "I" its place and ascribe [an] experience to him'.[21] In empathy, especially in the earliest notions of empathy introduced to the British public by Lee and Hulme, we make no such concession. Rather, we push ourselves into the foreign 'I' and join it, bringing the force of our own life to it.

Lee understood empathy as 'the tendency to merge the *activities* of the perceiving subject with the qualities of the perceived object'.[22] For Lee, this could mean that when I observe a mountain, I find my body stiffening and rising up to match the qualities I perceive in that mountain. This is a particularly useful way to consider the fellow feeling that occurs in modernist literature. Such fellow feeling does not necessarily depend on being able to imagine what it would feel like to be another person. It depends on the text's ability to trick us, if only momentarily, into forgetting the psychological distance that separates us from a character. The text must induce readerly activity that merges with the qualities of a perceived object. Such readerly activity arises especially from narrative forms that, as Ford would say, 'do not narrate'.[23] When we read stream-of-consciousness narration, for example, our cognitive activity matches that of the perceived object, a mind in the act of thinking. For its own part, *Parade's End* is particularly good at getting us to merge our readerly activity with the qualities of Christopher's mind at war.

Lee's work on empathy started with the aesthetic investigations she carried out with Clementina Anstruther-Thomson. But she was also deeply influenced by the ideas of Lipps and Karl Groos. Hulme, on the other hand, got his understanding of empathy almost exclusively from Wilhelm Worringer, who claimed that there are two main drives behind artistic expression – the drive to abstraction and the drive to *Einfühlung*. Our desire for *Einfühlung* finds gratification in the beauty of the organic, while our desire for abstraction finds gratification in the beauty of 'the life-denying inorganic'.[24] In Worringer's work, we should note, '*Einfühlung*' tends to stand for all forms of fellow feeling. He believed that because European culture has long been one in which 'feeling into' is the primary aesthetic drive, we tend uncritically to value it over abstraction. In *Abstraktion und Einfühlung*, Worringer identifies realism and naturalism with the empathic drive, which is toward 'the most intimate union between ego and work of art'.[25] The ego needs something it can feel itself into in order to experience a gratifying oneness. In abstraction, on the other hand, the viewer seeks tranquillity by separating his mind from the 'entangled inter-relationship and flux of the phenomena of the outer world'.[26] Worringer's central problem with empathy is that it provides, in Lipps's words, 'objectified self-enjoyment',[27] or, as Lee elaborates, 'we feel activity and life, because our own activity, our own life, have been brought into play'.[28] For Worringer, the tension between *Einfühlung* and abstraction means that aesthetic experience is inherently dual. This duality is something that Ford deals with throughout his career, particularly in *Parade's End*, which culminates in *Last Post*'s simultaneous cultivation and rejection of fellow feeling.

The Absent Object

The mind that we know best in *Parade's End* before we open *Last Post* and find Mark lying motionless in an outdoor hut is that of Christopher. As Toby Henry Loeffler writes: 'it is [Christopher] Tietjens who most often focalizes the narrative; it is Tietjens who sees; it is Tietjens who feels'.[29] Paul Skinner points out the complications inherent in Christopher's role as our focaliser: 'while his *not* talking actually brings about many of the events detailed in the novel, he has also, despite all references to the tradition of "keeping mum", talked a great deal or, let's say, is often overheard by the reader'.[30] Christopher is an opaque mind for everybody around him (although, as I have noted, he and Valentine do experience a powerful connection). His large body, more than once described as a lumpy collection of meal sacks, seems to hide his thoughts and feelings. Throughout *Parade's End*, we watch character after character misunderstand Christopher's anachronistic mind and utterly fail to imagine, as Smith says, what it would be like to 'change persons' with him. Instead, those characters merely imagine that they are, themselves, in his circumstance. Hence Edith Ethel assumes Christopher will seek to ruin her and Macmaster because they owe him money – which is exactly what she would do given such power.

But all the while the eighteenth-century Christopher suffers from this lack of sympathy from his friends and family, the reader is experiencing fellow feeling with him. This is a process that deepens as the series continues, for at the beginning of *Some Do Not . . .* Christopher barely has a sense of his *own* interiority. Our initially distant narrator explains: 'For the basis of Christopher Tietjens' emotional existence was a complete taciturnity – at any rate as to his emotions. As Tietjens saw the world, you didn't "talk." Perhaps you didn't even think about how you felt' (p. 8). With time he will begin to think about how he feels and, as Haslam implies, value his own inner world: 'Tietjens is opened out, existentially speaking; he is made to be self-aware in his journey through warfare.'[31] That opening out also makes space for the reader to 'feel with' Christopher. The narrative perspective, which is decidedly external to Christopher as *Parade's End* opens, starts to align with his point of view as his emotional and imaginative life expands.

Christopher may indeed be an eighteenth-century man and the 'last Tory', but as an object of our fellow feeling, he becomes decidedly modern. By the start of *No More Parades*, the otherness of his mind starts to break down; he is not only the primary focaliser, but also the source of proliferating free direct thoughts that cultivate the illusion that the reader is 'thinking with' him (pp. 29–31). He becomes, in fact, the object of a distinctly new empathy that differs significantly from sympathy as Hume and Smith understood it. The reader's activity brings Christopher into the twentieth century via an empathic cognitive overlap that culminates in *A Man Could Stand Up –*. In that third volume, the reader is very much 'with' Christopher's mental activity as he is 'blown up' and decides to live with Valentine. The more 'unmediated' our experience of his mind appears, the closer he comes to acknowledging and answering his desires. But just when the series has convinced us that he has internally matured into his own young century, we are exiled from his post-Armistice interiority.

In *Last Post* we find that our empathic bridge to Christopher has disappeared. He has flown to Groby in Yorkshire, in an attempt to save Groby Great Tree. We 'overhear' nothing he thinks and see only a glimpse of his recognisably amorphous body. When he does show up, he speaks only three sentences and misses his brother's dying words by a matter of seconds. Instead of encountering Christopher's inner workings, we find only those of the other characters, whose relationships with him are marked by profound epistemological discomfort. Until the final pages of *Last Post*, Christopher is present only as a preoccupation of the others: Mark's thoughts continually return to their arguments about Groby and his mistaken beliefs about Christopher; Valentine wonders how he will manage to care for their unborn child; Sylvia descends on the Tietjens home to harass him yet further; and young Michael Mark wonders about the father he barely knows but greatly admires. Indeed, the young man's curiosity as he winds his way to Mark's hut mirrors our own: 'He kept his eyes fascinatedly fixed on the stone porch of the cottage whilst he stumbled up the great stone slabs to the path. [. . .] No form filled the porch' (p. 60). The space where we might expect to find Christopher is empty. As Max Saunders explains: 'The novel is structured around Christopher's central absence; and yet because the thoughts of all the other characters keep referring to him, he is as it were defined in silhouette by the way he impresses himself on the consciousness of others.'[32] While we gather quite a bit about Christopher's circumstances, which are both idyllic and troubled, we are shut out of the object of our readerly desire – his interiority. The narrative undermines our relationship with Christopher by denying us opportunities for cognitive empathy. We can no longer think with him, but only about him.

The very little we learn of Christopher's state of mind comes secondhand from Valentine: 'It was true that he was almost out of his mind about Groby and Groby Great Tree. He had begun to talk about that in his sleep, as for years, at times, he had talked, dreadfully, about the war' (p. 177). This bit of information is key. What it tells us is that we are still reading a story that is fundamentally about the effects of the war on the mind. Years later, the European conflict still haunts all the members of the Tietjens family. This haunting is manifestly clear in the thoughts of Marie Léonie (formerly known as Charlotte, now Lady Tietjens), who is barely mentioned in the first three books but becomes a central character in *Last Post*. She remains enraged that the Allies did not 'pursue the Germans in to their own country' (p. 26) to avenge France's sufferings. But what do we make of the fact that *Last Post* deprives us of Christopher's thoughts, giving us only the small clue that his psychological pain lingers in his dreams? This deprivation warns us about empathy's limits in a post-war, traumatic context. As Cathy Caruth's influential work on trauma has so persuasively shown, traumatic narratives make us ask: 'Is the trauma the encounter with death, or the ongoing experience of having survived it?'[33] Christopher's disappearance in *Last Post* suggests the latter. It tells us that he is living with a wound that is slow to heal. And while empathic narrative can help us 'feel into' the supposedly unrepresentable warfront experience, it is really the psychological pain of survival that complicates and prevents intersubjective understanding. The full story of Christopher's war experience, then, cannot be told without a final rebuff to readerly empathy. As Caruth explains, to establish history in the wake of traumatic events sometimes requires refusals of empathy or breaks in understanding.[34]

In its protection of Christopher, *Last Post* reflects some of the scepticism about empathy that Worringer expressed in *Abstraction and Empathy*. The novel puts the psychological distance back into fellow feeling, telling us that the knowledge that it provides, if we can call it knowledge, is very limited and perhaps limiting. Empathy, the final volume suggests, does not make us 'one' with another – that other is an autonomous subject who can jump into a plane and fly off to Yorkshire at any time. Or in the words of Marie Léonie: 'Naturally [Christopher] would be gone for a day and a half when he was most needed' (p. 122). From our readerly perspective, Christopher is most needed here, at the end of *Parade's End*. But what Christopher needs, perhaps, is to be separated from prying minds. Thus it seems that he is answering the urge to abstraction, the urge to take himself out of an 'entangled inter-relationship'.[35] But I want to suggest that he remains a viable object of fellow feeling by regaining some of the distance allowed by eighteenth-century sympathy.

In modernising Christopher's mind, the war has allowed him self-knowledge and effectively given him 'permission' to live with Valentine. But it has also given him a shattered past and an unclear future. His only words in *Last Post* describe to Mark the destruction wrought by the felling of Groby Great Tree: 'Half Groby wall is down. Your bedroom's wrecked. I found your case of sea-birds thrown on a rubble heap' (p. 202). Meanwhile, fearing for their unborn child's future, Valentine arrives to berate him for forgetting prints that they could have sold: 'Heavily, like a dejected bull-dog, Christopher made for the gate. As he went up the green path beyond the hedge, Valentine began to sob. "How are we to live? How are we ever to live?"' (p. 203). It is a depressing moment, to be sure. Without the old mutual belief that their minds 'march together', how are they to live in a post-war society where all that was once solid is now reduced to rubble? Yet there is hope in Christopher's silent dejection, hope that in maintaining the privacy of his mind he is not losing the ability to feel with others or know himself, but rather establishing borders around his much-altered interior land-scape. In this final moment, he is again the consummate eighteenth-century man. For, as Smith writes, 'we reverence that reserved, that silent and majestic sorrow, which discovers itself only in the swelling of the eyes, in the quivering of the lips and cheeks, and in the distant, but affecting, coldness of the whole behaviour'.[36] *Last Post*, for a brief moment, allows Christopher to be this kind of eighteenth-century man. We feel for him, but we cannot presume to feel with him. His disappearance from the last volume of *Parade's End*, then, might be read as a flight from the modernist era's new, specifically empathic, form of feeling with others.

The Present Object

Yet *Last Post* itself does not reject empathic thinking. True, Ford's novel allows Christopher to work through his trauma without exposing his interiority to readerly empathy, but it does not let that trauma fall away completely. Rather, it shows us how his warfront experience is connected to and continues on the home front. Here, too, Caruth's thoughts are helpful. Reading Freud, she writes: 'history is precisely the way we are implicated in each other's traumas'.[37] With the counterpoint of Mark Tietjens, who never saw battle, but is nevertheless left physically and mentally battered in the wake of the war, we begin to see a web of interpersonal traumatic implication develop in *Last Post*. Just when Christopher recedes from the action of *Parade's End*, Mark becomes a prominent object of our readerly empathy (although in many ways he remains deeply unsympathetic). As it turns out, the war has taken a great toll on Mark, whose 'indispensible' role in directing the nation's transport was not enough to secure the outcomes he hoped for. He apparently suffered a stroke while recovering from an illness just before the Armistice; Marie Léonie recalls: 'His face was dark purple and congested; he gazed straight before him' (p. 134). Nevertheless, his prodigious mind goes on thinking fluidly. Mark believes that he made a 'resolution never more to speak word. Nor yet stir a finger' (p. 13). Despite our access to his thoughts, the actual state of his body remains unclear – we do not know if he is indeed paralysed or if, as Marie Léonie believes, he 'could talk, walk, and perform the feats of strength of a Hercules' if he so chose (p. 25). What we do know is that, like his brother, Mark is exhausted after the war: 'once the idea of retiring, not only from the Office but the whole world, had come into his head it had grown and grown, on top of his mortification and his weariness' (p. 26).

Whatever the reason for his immobility, Mark becomes an incredibly vulnerable body. In this he is not alone. As he notes, the young children in the English countryside still suffer the effects of being born to a country at war: 'War-starvation in early years. . . . Well, that was not his fault. He had given the nation the transport it needed; they should have found the stuff. They hadn't, so the children had long, thin legs and protruding wrists on stem arms' (p. 13). Like these children, who remind us that the trauma of war does not end when hostilities cease, Mark is now upsettingly fragile. As *Last Post* opens, we find him in a singularly odd position, lying in a hut with no sides, where 'his view embraces four counties' (p. 9). According to his doctor, he is 'never to be left out of sight. [. . .] one day Mark might move – physically. And there might be great danger if ever he did move. The lesions, if lesions there were in his brain, might then be re-started with fatal effects' (p. 37). Marie Léonie, terrified at the thought that he might injure himself, has a bell running between his prone body and her bedroom in case he stirs in the night (p. 38). Her worries never stop: 'He was dying where he lay; he was beset by the spectral beings of the countryside; robbers, even, had crept upon him, though that was unreasonable' (p. 118). This physical vulnerability is, I believe, of deep importance to *Last Post*'s fellow feeling and circulation of trauma.

It is significant that Mark's suffering manifests in his body because it marks a split with earlier, eighteenth-century sympathetic values. Smith, for one, dismisses physical pain and suffering as an effective literary inducement to sympathetic imagination, writing:

> The loss of a leg may generally be regarded as a more real calamity than the loss of a mistress. It would be a ridiculous tragedy, however, of which the catastrophe was to turn upon a loss of that kind. A misfortune of the other kind, how frivolous soever it may appear to be, has given occasion to many a fine one.[38]

There is much in *Parade's End*, particularly in the first three volumes, to corroborate Smith's claim. For all its status as a great work of war literature, Ford's series does depend largely on affairs of the heart. And Christopher, of course, worries not about the integrity of his soldier's body, but rather of his prodigious mind. Yet *Last Post*, and in turn the resolution of *Parade's End*, absolutely depends on Mark's physical suffering. His vulnerable body is our way into the collective problem of fellow feeling that ends the series. Motionless atop his hill, Mark remains impenetrable for his family, but open to the reader's acts of in-feeling. Here, Ford troubles the 'inward turn' of modernism, for our access to Mark's mind seems to come only through the availability of his suffering body. Indeed, it is hard to separate interiority from the physicality of bodies when Christopher's mind has disappeared with his body and Mark's has suddenly opened up in conjunction with his immobility.

Lying out in the air, Mark is strangely open to the outside world – the family tries to cultivate a permeability that would break down the barrier that keeps him from answering Marie Léonie. They bring him material to read and turn him to show him new views of the countryside. But Mark shows a monumental resistance to their overtures, retaining an almost unbelievable sense of autonomy given his situation: 'Full of consideration for him, they were, all the lot of them. For ever thinking of developing his possible interests. He didn't need it. He had interests enough' (pp. 13–14). He displays not only a general lack of interest in the world beyond his mind and his memory, but also a desire that others should be thwarted from inflicting their interest on him. We read, for example: 'They kept the hedge low so that he should be amused by passers-by on the path, though he should have preferred to let it grow high so that the passers-by could not see into the orchard' (p. 14). His desire then, is to protect his land and his body, which in turn ought to protect his mind.

The family's experience with Mark seems to confirm what Margrit Shildrick describes as a longstanding, entrenched view of the mind's sovereignty within the body:

> Within conventional western discourse, to be a self is above all to be dis-tinguished from the other, to be ordered and discrete, secure *within* the well-defined boundaries of the body rather than actually being the body. We live, as sovereign selves, within our own skins, where to imagine inhabiting the body of another would be a special kind of madness, or to find our own bodies shared by another would constitute an invasion.[39]

Mark, in fact, will not even share the signs of his body that might betray his thoughts. Our first dip into his mind tells us: 'He would have grinned, but that might have been seen' (p. 9). From the beginning, then, we see him actively refusing to make his mind legible. He is also unconcerned about Marie Léonie's worries. She is sure, 'in her *for inté-rieur*', that Mark is mentally sound (pp. 26, 119), but she is baffled by what his thoughts might be. Feeding soup to his unmoving body with a syringe, she speaks to him: 'all this appears to be a madness. Why are we here? What is the meaning of all this? Why do you inhabit this singular erection?' (p. 22). Of one thing, however, she remains sure. Mark, she believes, vowed to stop speaking because of the Armistice terms that betrayed France: 'It was the first thing that had come into her mind, and no doubt it had been the first thing to come into Mark's' (pp. 26–7). Her belief, in fact, seems to line up with his own version of events. But he has no appetite to confirm that belief.

The long, comic scene in which Mrs de Bray Pape and Michael Mark find the intransigent Mark deals with the idea that the self is buried, hidden in the body. They repeatedly ask, with growing frustration, why he will not speak to them. Michael Mark exclaims 'it seems a little severe to refuse to speak to us!' while the silent Mark wonders 'at the breakdown in communications that there must have been' (p. 74). Mark's mind goes on and on while the two interlopers stand in front of him. The motionless body, it seems, is what separates them. This appears particularly true because of the misunderstanding his physical illness causes. Mrs de Bray Pape, following Sylvia's hints, believes Mark is suffering for 'the sins of [his] youth' (p. 62). What we know, however, is that his physical condition is intimately connected to a psychological one. The scene ends with Mark angrily thinking back to the time of the Armistice: 'he hated to be reminded of that day' (p. 82). To be reminded of that day is to remember his disappointments about the war's end and the inadvertent role he played in Christopher's ruin: first, by reporting false rumours about Christopher to their father, and second, by getting Christopher transferred home before the end of the war, thus depriving him of much-needed pay. Remembering against his will, he recalls the meal Marie Léonie was warming for him. It was, he thinks, 'Probably the last food to which he had ever helped himself' (p. 82). Mark's proneness and subsequent availability as an object of readerly empathy, then, are deeply connected to the trauma of the war and the most recent stage of his family's painful history.

A Final Connection

Mark Tietjens becomes, in the place of his missing brother, the primary object into which we project our readerly activity. This development, however, is not simply a matter of displaced libidinal investment. Rather, it makes space for fellow feeling in the future of the Tietjens family. Mark's final words, spoken to Valentine after Christopher walks away, are 'Hold my hand!' (p. 204). As Saunders has suggested, because Mark stays silent until the end and then speaks in his final moments, his death is 'strangely like a reanimation'.[40] But what is it that is reborn in this moment when Valentine reaches out and allows Mark's hand to close on hers? In this moment of physical touch, this moment of skin-to-skin connection, the possibility of psychological and emotional connection returns. It is significant that the pregnant Valentine, who is literally sharing her body with another, is the one to reach out to Mark at the moment of his death. It suggests that fellow feeling will be present in the future of this family, that despite lingering trauma, there is room for meaningful intersubjective connection.

Notes

1. On ways in which Christopher is connected to the eighteenth century, see Haslam, 'From Conversation to Humiliation'. In *Last Post*, Marie Léonie also associates him with the *dix-huitième*: Ford, *Last Post*, ed. Paul Skinner, p. 43. All further references are to this edition.
2. On the debates surrounding *Last Post*'s place in *Parade's End*, see Hawkes, *Ford Madox Ford and the Misfit Moderns*, pp. 141–3.

3. Ford, *A Man Could Stand Up –*, ed. Sara Haslam, p. 202. All further references are to this edition.

4. Ford, *Some Do Not . . .*, ed. Max Saunders, p. 34. All further references are to this edition.

5. For more on the relationship between empathic 'in-feeling' and typically modernist forms of narration, particularly in Ford's *A Man Could Stand Up –*, see Hammond, *Empathy and the Psychology of Literary Modernism*, Chapter 4.

6. Hawkes, *Ford Madox Ford and the Misfit Moderns*, p. 138.

7. Haslam, 'From Conversation to Humiliation', pp. 38–9.

8. Hume, *A Treatise of Human Nature*, p. 367.

9. Ibid. p. 390.

10. Ibid. pp. 626–7.

11. Ibid. p. 367.

12. Ibid. p. 367.

13. Smith, *The Theory of Moral Sentiments*, p. 2.

14. Ibid. p. 31.

15. Ibid. p. 32.

16. Hawkes, *Ford Madox Ford and the Misfit Moderns*, p. 159; Haslam, *Fragmenting Modernism*, p. 94.

17. Smith, *The Theory of Moral Sentiments*, p. 3.

18. Ibid. p. 2.

19. Ibid. p. 2.

20. Ibid. p. 392.

21. Stein, *On the Problem of Empathy*, p. 14.

22. Lee, *The Beautiful*, p. 63.

23. Ford, 'Joseph Conrad', *Critical Writings of Ford Madox Ford*, pp. 72–3.

24. Worringer, *Abstraction and Empathy*, p. 4.

25. Ibid. p. 23.

26. Ibid. p. 16.

27. Ibid. p. 7.

28. Lee, 'Anthropomorphic Aesthetics', p. 22.

29. Loeffler, 'The "Backbone of England"', p. 8.

30. Skinner, 'The Painful Process of Reconstruction', p. 66.

31. Haslam, *Fragmenting Modernism*, p. 108.

32. Saunders, *Ford Madox Ford*, II, p. 252.

33. Caruth, *Unclaimed Experience*, p. 7.

34. Ibid. p. 41.

35. Worringer, *Abstraction and Empathy*, p. 16.

36. Smith, *The Theory of Moral Sentiments*, p. 31.

37. Caruth, *Unclaimed Experience*, p. 24.

38. Smith, *The Theory of Moral Sentiments*, p. 42.

39. Shildrick, 'You are there, like my skin', p. 162.

40. Saunders, *Ford Madox Ford*, II, p. 251.

Chapter 5

The Self-Analysis of Christopher Tietjens

Barbara Farnworth

Throughout *Parade's End*, Christopher Tietjens continuously monitors and reflects on his thoughts and mental fitness. Tietjens enjoys his intellectual prowess in performing complex statistical calculations and in synthesising scattered bits of information. In *Some Do Not . . .*, he even refers to himself as 'more brain than body'.[1] In addition, Tietjens administers careful control over his affective responses, so he adopts a policy of not talking or thinking about unpleasant events, such as his wife's infidelity. In addition, he regulates how his neurological system deals with shock by waiting to confront the event until his mind can handle it calmly. Tietjens models his character on his ideal, an English gentleman, and carefully monitors his habits to shape his behaviour accordingly. His intense preoccupation with his mental processes reveals the tetralogy's engagement with William James's theories on selective consciousness and free will. In addition, the anxiety he expresses over his sanity as well as his experiences with trauma and repression suggest the text's negotiation with psychoanalytic theories of the unconscious mind. Through his continual introspective investigations, Tietjens performs an insightful self-analysis on his conscious and unconscious processes.

As T. J. Henighan argues, the 'dramatizing of Tietjens' inner consciousness is the great achievement' of *Parade's End*.[2] Throughout the majority of the first three books in the tetralogy, Ford places the reader in Tietjens' mind. This technique not only allows readers to view the action from Tietjens' perspective, but also gives an intimate portrait of his emotional reactions and potential psychological problems. Ford, however, extends this technique far beyond a simple representation of Tietjens' point of view to an examination of Tietjens' consciousness at work. Tietjens' thoughts reveal not only an acute self-awareness of his own consciousness, but also an almost obsessive need to monitor and control his thoughts and feelings. By controlling his thoughts and choosing which to attend to, Tietjens believes he has free will to structure his existence and his character. Similarly, Williams James based his psychological theories of consciousness on the importance of introspective analysis and selective attention.

After twelve years of study, James published his groundbreaking 1,200-page textbook, *The Principles of Psychology,* in 1890. His text synthesises his medical training, experimental results from his psychology laboratory at Harvard, his readings in philosophy, and his observations of his own thought processes, to produce a comprehensive psychology textbook. Although James was born and mainly educated in the United States, he was knowledgeable of the theories debated in the European intellectual community and, in fact, his textbook references some of these theories. During the 1870s, James travelled extensively in Europe 'visiting universities, attending laboratory sessions and lectures', meeting with dozens of leading psychologists and other scientists and establishing a long-term correspondence with many of them.[3] In his textbook, James identifies introspective analysis as a crucial method of investigation to develop a theory of mind. In examining our minds, we inevitably discover states of consciousness. Further, 'all people unhesitatingly believe that they feel themselves thinking and that they distinguish the mental state as an inward activity from all [outside] object'.[4] James characterises this belief in our consciousness as 'the most fundamental of all the postulates of Psychology'.[5] James's theories characterise consciousness as selective, intentional and self-aware, and a continuum or stream. In addition, the idea of a selective consciousness suggests humans have the freedom to 'organize and structure our existence' in a variety of ways.[6] By analysing Tietjens' thought processes, we can observe the tetralogy's engagement with James's theories, specifically those on introspection, the self-awareness of one's consciousness, stream of consciousness and selective attention. Most importantly, Tietjens negotiates with his ability to structure his behaviour, according to his principles, through a continuous, sometimes tremendously difficult, effort of will.

Tietjens' careful monitoring of his mental processes strongly resembles James's belief that the proper subject of psychology is the introspective analysis of the 'states of mind' that we are conscious of in daily life and of the 'functions they perform for the organism'.[7] In *The Principles of Psychology,* James stresses the importance of observing our conscious mental processes, thoughts and feelings, saying that introspection 'is what we have to rely on first and foremost and always' to investigate and understand our mental life.[8] Tietjens constantly performs this type of introspection in terms of his analysis of his intellectual prowess, his mental fitness, and his emotional control. Early in *Some Do Not . . . ,* for example, we learn about Tietjens' superior intelligence and his own awareness of it. His 'chief' in the Imperial Department of Statistics refers to Tietjens as 'a perfect encyclopaedia of exact material knowledge' (pp. 6–7). Tietjens not only acknowledges the compliment as his due, but also continually reflects on how his intellect operates. He spends a contented afternoon at the golf course, not playing golf, but picking up 'little pieces of workmanlike information' (p. 90). Although this information may have no current purpose, he feels that 'to know things was agreeable and gave him a feeling of strength' (p. 90). He derives satisfaction from the intellectual pursuit of knowledge rather than how that information may further his career. Macmaster recounts, for example, how Tietjens had no interest in earning a medal at school even though the honour was well within his grasp. Similarly, Tietjens does not regard his intellectual prowess in statistics as a means of advancement at work, but rather as a source of pleasure.

In a dramatic contrast with his earlier intellectual prowess, the second part of *Some Do Not . . .* represents Tietjens coping with memory loss after his first experiences in battle. Tietjens mourns that there were 'whole regions of fact upon which he could not call in support of his argument' (p. 221). His brain, he reports, feels two-thirds numb because 'half of it, an irregular piece of it, [is] dead. Or rather pale. Without a proper blood supply' (p. 168). In addition: 'A certain area has been wiped white' (p. 170). Although he previously expressed his disdain for encyclopaedias, Tietjens now employs one to rebuild his memory. His desperate struggle to remember specific words underlines the contrast between Tietjens' intellectual brilliance in Part I and his damaged memory in Part II. His despair also confirms how much he defines himself through his intelligence and how conscious he is of his loss of mental acuity. Earlier he enjoyed contemplating how his mind excelled at gathering and synthesising knowledge. Tietjens is painfully aware of how much he has lost. Despite his despair, however, Tietjens continues to examine his own consciousness and methodically 'retrains' his memory. He chooses to attend to his study of the encyclopaedia and ignores the rest of the world. Until, of course, his wife Sylvia demands his attention by throwing a plate of food at him.

Tietjens' focused attention on reconstructing his memory is a perfect example of his ongoing efforts to shape his experience by deliberately shifting his attention away from painful or unpleasant subjects. For example, in *Some Do Not . . .*, he refuses to think about or discuss Sylvia's elopement with Perowne. Instead, he employs himself in tabulating from memory the errors in the *Encyclopaedia Britannica*, describing this as a 'congenial occupation, like a long drowse' (p. 14).

According to William James, a person's experience is what he or she agrees to attend to, so that only those 'items which I notice shape my mind'.[9] James defines attention as the 'taking possession by the mind of one out of what seem several simultaneously possible objects or trains of thought'.[10] This voluntary selecting and attending determines our immediate actions and behaviour. In accordance with his policy of not talking about his wife's infidelity, Tietjens deliberately elects to attend to errors in the encyclopaedia and ignores his domestic problems. Tietjens speaks the minimal number of words necessary to deal with the practical issues surrounding Sylvia's elopement (moving in with Macmaster, informing his father of the facts, and arranging a new home for his son) and does not discuss the matter further. He is not even aware of how much his co-workers or social peers know about his domestic problems. Along with his policy of not talking, Tietjens refuses to attend to or acknowledge any emotional reaction to his wife's infidelity. He so successfully avoids thinking about how he feels that: 'his wife's flight had left him almost completely without emotions he could realise' (*Some Do Not . . .*, p. 8). Tietjens deliberately pursues this policy of verbal and emotional taciturnity as part of his ongoing project to shape his behaviour in accordance with the character of an English gentleman.[11]

Despite Tietjens' intellectual brilliance and his attention to his own consciousness, he often does not accurately interpret the thoughts and attitudes of others. For example, he describes his relationship with his father as one where they are so alike they understand one another without speaking. Unfortunately, when his father hears the rumours surrounding Christopher's 'dishonourable dealings', Mr Tietjens' reaction clearly indicates that he does not really know his son's basic character. Christopher's father neither rejects the rumours nor does he question his son directly. Instead, he asks his older son Mark to investigate and then chooses to believe Ruggles' libellous allegations against Christopher. Clearly, Christopher's interpretation of their mutual silence is false: it does not indicate an affinity between father and son. Similarly, William James warns against potential errors from introspection, what he calls the 'psychologist's fallacy'.[12] This error results from 'the confusion of his own standpoint with that of the mental fact about which he is making his report'.[13] An investigator, therefore, must be very careful of the tendency to 'attribute a particular content and awareness to the conscious state under consideration when that content and awareness is really present only in the experience of the investigator'.[14] In this example, Tietjens' rule of 'not talking' results in a disastrous lack of communication with his father. This scene should also serve as a warning to the reader of the pitfalls of experiencing a novel mainly through the consciousness of one character. It is all too easy for the reader to commit the fallacy of unconditionally accepting Tietjens' interpretation of reality, especially because the tetralogy emphasises Tietjens' superior intelligence. Although Ford's dramatisation of Tietjens' consciousness is compelling, we must also attend to the behaviour and thoughts of other characters in order to evaluate how accurately Tietjens' thought processes reflect the world of the novel.

In *No More Parades,* Tietjens continues his practice of ignoring his marital situation and burying his feelings about Sylvia until he receives an outside reminder of her. When General Campion unexpectedly mentions Sylvia in his note, Tietjens desperately engages in multiple activities at once in order to divert his attention from his estranged wife. Tietjens lives by a certain rule of conduct: '*Never think on the subject of a shock at a moment of shock*' because he prefers not to think about a difficult issue when his mind is 'too sensitized'.[15] In order to divert his attention, he simultaneously writes a sonnet, deals with the complex problems of his soldiers, speaks with a veterinarian about horses, and helps McKechnie solve a money issue. On this occasion, he has to exert a tremendous effort of will to avoid thinking of Sylvia. A soldier's record reminds him of Sylvia's cousin and he finds it difficult to shift his attention away from her. He encounters much greater difficulty in controlling his attention in *No More Parades*. His mind is already challenged to maintain his English imperturbability in the face of the extreme conditions of the war, especially O Nine Morgan's death, and his own ill health. Repressing his complex feelings surrounding his personal life becomes increasingly difficult.

During this scene, McKechnie describes Tietjens as 'doing eleven things at once' (p. 44). How is Tietjens able to handle all these tasks at the same time? According to William James, we cannot easily attend to more than one task at the same time unless 'the processes are very habitual'.[16] When the mental processes are less automatic, there must be a 'rapid oscillation of the mind' from one task to the next.[17] James bases this conclusion on attention experiments performed both in his lab at Harvard and by his peers in America and Europe. Similarly, Tietjens attends to all these tasks by rapidly shifting his mind from one thought to the next. James explains this phenomenon by theorising: 'There is no such thing as voluntary attention sustained for more than a few seconds at a time. What is called sustained voluntary attention is a repetition of successive efforts which bring back the topic to the mind.'[18] Tietjens' ability to attend to multiple talks is, according to James, a repetition of many efforts to redirect his attention. Tietjens' sustained effort in shifting his attention away from Sylvia demonstrates his tremendous investment in choosing to ignore her as well as the difficult situation she represents.

In Part II of *Some Do Not . . .*, Tietjens explains how he has used his own free will in order to adopt the best mode of behaviour:

> In electing to be peculiarly English in habits and in as much of his temperament as he could control – for although no man can choose the land of his birth or his ancestry, he can if he have industry and determination, so watch over himself as materially to modify his automatic habits – Tietjens had quite advisedly and of set purpose adopted a habit of behaviour that he considered to be the best in the world for the normal life. (p. 220)

According to this passage, Tietjens believes in the power of his will to control his automatic habits and his temperament in order to adopt his preferred behaviour patterns. To exert this control requires constant monitoring of his behaviour in order to modify them into 'peculiarly English habits'. Tietjens also states that his choice of behaviour derives not from his ancestry, but from his conscious decision that English habits are the best in the world. He clearly believes in and invests tremendous energy in his ability to control his habits in order to mould his character.

Similarly, William James stressed the importance of free will, both in terms of his own mental health and as the foundation for his theories about the interaction of attention and will. After suffering from an emotional crisis that left him incapacitated for many months, James's depression was finally alleviated when he read French philosopher Charles Renouvier's essay on free will. In his diary, James quotes Renouvier's definition of free will as the 'sustaining of a thought because I choose to when I might have other thoughts'.[19] In addition to relieving his depression, Renouvier's definition became an integral part of his theories. In Volume II of *The Principles of Psychology*, James states: 'the effort of attention is the essential phenomenon of will'.[20] The mind chooses our behaviour by the voluntary action of selecting and attending; the mind does not respond passively to outside influences. When Tietjens claims that he elected to adopt the behaviour of an English gentleman by attending to and selecting the correct habits, he exemplifies a conscious mind actively pursuing a preferred way of life. Similarly, when he chooses not to talk about Sylvia's elopement, this is also an act of free will, because 'not talking' is one of the peculiar habits of Englishmen. Tietjens' conduct follows from his decision to adopt the habits of an Englishman, even though Tietjens himself calls into question whether adopting this code of behaviour continues to be the most advantageous choice. He believes English behaviour is best for a 'normal life', but between his marital difficulties and his war experience, Tietjens does not live through 'normal' experiences.

Although James valued free will, he also understood the enormous effort involved in sustaining attention on one set of behaviours. In *Essays on Psychology*, he describes the experience of strong-willed people as those who:

> choose their attitude and know that the failing of its difficulties shall remain permanent portion of their task [. . .]. They find a zest in this difficult clinging to truth, or a lonely sort of joy in pressing on the thorn and going without it, which no passively warranted possession of it can ever confer. And thereby they become the masters and the lords of life.[21]

Tietjens' experiences certainly echo James's depiction of loneliness and difficulty. Tietjens speaks of the necessity for 'industry and determination' to 'watch over himself [. . .] to modify his automatic habits' in order to adopt the behaviour of an English gentlemen, 'the best in the world' (*Some Do Not . . .*, p. 220).

His behaviour certainly does not contribute to his domestic happiness or win sympathy from his peers. Although Sylvia is hardly an ideal spouse, his silences provoke her rage and, ironically, his moral integrity drives her to vengeance. According to Tietjens' code of ethics, he will not reveal Sylvia's infidelity even when his family and peers suspect him of being unfaithful. In addition, his intellectual interests set him apart from his peers, who find, for example, his interest in calculating trajectories at the golf course odd and incomprehensible. Although Tietjens refers to himself as an English public-school boy, his hatred of competitive pursuits is inconsistent with the overwhelming importance of games at public schools which Jonathon Gathorne-Hardy characterises as an 'obsession' that 'is universal [and] all embracing'.[22] Further, Leonard Woolf remembers public school as a place where the 'use of the mind, intellectual curiosity, mental originality [. . .] were violently condemned and persecuted'.[23] Certainly General Campion's 'rooted distrust of intelligence' in *Some Do Not . . .* (p. 91) confirms this public-school attitude. Although his moral integrity and intellectual pursuits isolate him from his peers, Tietjens perseveres in modelling his behaviour in accordance with his ideal – an English gentleman – and thus demonstrates his freedom to define his own identity.

In her analysis of Jamesian psychology, Francesca Bordogna identifies the implications for 'self-determination and individual agency' at the heart of the Jamesian self.[24] She examines James's theories of the self in the context of the changing social order of the late nineteenth and early twentieth century. According to Bordogna, the Jamesian self, with its techniques of self-cultivation and unification, emphasised 'self-mastery and moral autonomy' in order to assert independence from political and business organisations.[25] Similarly, in *Parade's End*, Tietjens pursues his ideal behaviour with the wish for autonomy from the current cultural and political order. In fact, Tietjens feels more affinity with eighteenth-century feudal England than with the political and moral climate of the early twentieth century. *Parade's End* contains numerous references to Tietjens' resemblance to an eighteenth-century man.[26] In his study of the tetralogy, Richard Cassell claims that Tietjens most resembles Edmund Burke's natural eighteenth-century aristocrat described in his 'Appeal from the Old to the New Whigs' (1791). Burke's natural aristocrat has a 'responsibility to the nation as well as to the convictions of his conscience' and has 'a guarded and regulated conduct'.[27] Undoubtedly, Tietjens strives for self-mastery and moral autonomy, the freedom to live according to his own principles.

Although James, like Tietjens, believed in free will, James saw it as a moral issue as well as an expression of freedom. According to James, the 'essential achievement of the will [. . .] is to attend to a difficult object and hold it fast before the mind'.[28] He also believed that when a man keeps that difficult object 'unwaveringly present to his mind [it] proves to be his saving moral act'.[29] In *Freedom and the Moral Life: The Ethics of William James*, John Roth examines the ethical implications of James's theories and finds 'a harmonious, unified life requires taking over experience in such a way that there is an honest facing of it and a projection of future goals that does not try to deny its existence'.[30] Further, the 'denial or repression' of difficult experiences 'may threaten [one's] identity'.[31] According to James, therefore, Tietjens cannot achieve a unified identity as long as he avoids confronting his marital difficulties. For Tietjens, however, emotional repression and taciturnity is not a moral issue, but the proper behaviour of an Englishman. Ironically, in *No More Parades*, Tietjens also expresses his ambition for Anglican sainthood, which he describes as the 'quality of being in harmony with your own soul' (p. 243). How can he reconcile his emotionally repressed English persona with his admiration for the principles of Anglican sainthood, which calls for facing difficult experiences? Ultimately, Tietjens realises he cannot repress his marital problems forever. Although he tries to ignore Sylvia, both by not talking about her and by not thinking about her, eventually his emotions break through.

In *Some Do Not . . .*, for example, Tietjens has successfully repressed the emotional impact of Sylvia's elopement for four months. Although he tries to maintain his detached and logical demeanour at the news of her return, he breaks down in the hotel while waiting for a wire from her. When Macmaster finds him in a state of near collapse, Tietjens blames his wife, saying: 'I shall be fit to talk about Sylvia after two more whiskies' (p. 60). Through a forty-page flashback of the day's events, we realise that Tietjens' breakdown is exacerbated by rumours about his relationship with Valentine Wannop. Despite his close relationship with Campion, Christopher does not convincingly defend himself, because he believes it is better for his son to have a 'rip of a father than a whore for mother' (p. 97). Between these allegations and the impending arrival of his unfaithful wife, Tietjens resorts uncharacteristically to great quantities of whisky. Similarly, in *No More Parades*, he works very hard at controlling his attention, but ultimately has to contemplate his marital situation before he is ready. The shock of hearing about Sylvia unexpectedly has, Tietjens fears, put him at a great disadvantage and rendered him unable to calm his mind.

In *No More Parades*, Tietjens continues his introspective habits but shifts his focus from his intellectual abilities to his psychological health. This quality is most striking during his long conversation with General Campion in Part II. At several points during their exchange, Tietjens pays far more attention to his own thoughts, feelings, and predictions than to his interaction with Campion. He anxiously monitors his mind's ability to handle Campion's probing questions. Tietjens feels his mind bordering on panic, especially when Campion inquires into Sylvia's infidelity. Up to this point, he has deliberately avoided thinking or talking about Sylvia, and now Campion forces him to openly discuss his failed marriage. Talking about infidelity, as Tietjens informs Macmaster early in *Some Do Not . . .*, is against his principles. When the conversation with Campion in *No More Parades* shifts from his domestic troubles to his next military assignment, Tietjens begins to express a new anxiety related to his mental health. As he anticipates his transfer to the Front, he occupies 'himself with his mind. What was it going to do?' (p. 223). A few pages later he states that 'there was now nothing left but to find out how his mind was going to take it' (p. 231). He continues to speculate on what will cause the greatest difficulty for his mind until he finally predicts that 'the fear of the mud was going to obsess him' (p. 231).[32] Tietjens anticipates and concentrates only on the threat to his sanity rather than on the obvious physical danger awaiting him at the Front. In addition, he has not yet fully recovered from his bout of pneumonia and, as a result, has received a C-3 rating, designating his unfitness for active duty. Despite his 'rotten chest' (p. 221) and the dangers of combat, Tietjens worries far more about his mental health. Although a return to the Front may well be akin to a death sentence for him, he has a far greater fear of insanity than of death. He consistently values a fit mind far more than a healthy body.

Tietjens' shift from monitoring his intellectual fitness to worrying about his mental health signals the tetralogy's engagement with psychoanalytic as well as Jamesian psychology. In *The Vanishing Subject*, Judith Ryan characterises the years from 1880 to 1940 as a 'period marked by [. . .] a most extraordinary symbiosis' between a multitude of new psychologies and the literature of the period.[33] According to Ryan, from 1880 to 1920 American and English authors focused their attention on the ideas of Williams James, who analysed the conscious mind. During the 1920s, authors began to assimilate psychoanalytic theories in their work, but Freudian psychoanalytic theory did not dominate the use of psychological theory in literature until the 1930s. Ryan theorises a 'gradual transition' during the 1920s from literary engagements with Jamesian psychology to psychoanalytic psychology, so that an author might participate in both Jamesian and psychoanalytic theories within the same novel.[34] *Parade's End*, written during the 1920s, invites an extremely fruitful psychological analysis because of its dialogue with both Jamesian theories of consciousness and psychoanalytic theories of the unconscious. Many scholars have speculated on Ford's knowledge of, and analysed the application of, Freudian theories in *Parade's End*.[35] Cassell, for example, points to Ford's use of terminology associated with psychoanalysis, such as 'subliminal consciousness [. . .] frustration, inhibition, mad doctors and complexes', as proof of his 'obvious familiarity with Freudian psychology'.[36] Although Cassell is correct in his identification of psychological terms, we cannot always apply a strict Freudian interpretation to these word-usages because of the diversity of British applications of Freud's work.

According to Suzanne Raitt's study of early British psychoanalysis, early practitioners of psychoanalysis did not agree with every facet of Freud's theories and used a watered-down version of Freudian theory, using 'military, rather than sexual, trauma' as the cause of hysterical neurosis, that eventually gained respectability within the medical establishment.[37] During the war years, an 'eclectic, diluted interpretation of Freudianism emerged that was quite popular with the lay public'.[38] So, although Freud's theories were not yet fully accepted by the medical establishment or even fully understood by the public, psychoanalytic terms became assimilated into popular British culture. Undoubtedly, *Parade's End* explores several psychoanalytic theories, including complexes, the repetitive nature of trauma, repression, and the use of writing as a form of talking cure. In each case, however, Tietjens remains conscious of his psychological experiences and he performs his own analysis of the cause(s). Although he does not deny the existence of unconsciousness, Tietjens continues to monitor the effect on his consciousness as well as theorise about the processes of his unconscious.

Tietjens employs the psychoanalytic term 'complex' several times, including in reference to his guilt over O Nine Morgan's death and his feelings for Valentine. W. H. R. Rivers explores the diverse meanings of this term in his book *Instinct and the Unconscious* (1920). The original definition of the term emphasised its pathological nature and its inaccessibility to consciousness. By 1920, the term 'has so caught the general fancy that it is becoming part of popular language' and has come to be used for the 'worries and anxieties arising out of recent and fully conscious experience'.[39] When Tietjens tells Campion in *No More Parades* about his reaction to O Nine Morgan's death, he calls it 'a sort of . . . Complex' (p. 217). Tietjens refers to an event he clearly remembers, a recent and conscious experience. When he experiences flashbacks of traumatic images, he is fully aware of their connection to his shock and guilt over Morgan's death. His awareness suggests that Tietjens uses 'complex', at least in this context, according to its colloquial meaning. More significantly, Tietjens continues the same introspective habits he applies to his intellectual fitness in order to study the mental processes behind these flashbacks.

Tietjens' flashbacks echo Freud's theory of the compulsion to repeat traumatic events. In his 1914 paper 'Remembering, Repeating and Working-Through', Freud theorises that patients may repeat patterns of thinking, feeling and behaving from their earlier lives in an attempt to master a past trauma.[40] On numerous occasions after O Nine Morgan's death in *No More Parades*, Tietjens experiences a hallucination of 'the glowing image of O Nine Morgan's blood', which are repetitions of the traumatic experience of witnessing O Nine Morgan's death (p. 85). Tietjens reveals his awareness of the source of these visions by referring to his 'accursed obsession with O Nine' (p. 228). These involuntary hallucinations are especially striking in a man like Tietjens, who invests a great deal of energy in controlling his thoughts and emotions. Although he cannot control these flashbacks, however, he performs his own analysis to interpret their meaning.

Tietjens' fear of the mud represents another traumatic experience repeated throughout *Parade's End*. The trauma originates in *No More Parades* when he witnesses German deserters crawling across a field covered in mud 'with only their eyes visible' and hears their references to the mud, 'it is unbearable; it is that that has ruined us' (pp. 231–2). Tietjens describes this scene in terms of death, eternity, and the last day of the world. He interprets the 'obscene whisper' of one of the Germans as 'the voice obviously of the damned; hell could hold nothing curious for those poor beasts' (p. 232). Although he has never fought in the mud, his memory of the Germans clearly makes a deep impression on his mind. When he first hears of his return to the Front, he reacts with a sensory image, feeling himself 'clambering over slopes of mud with his heavy legs and labouring chest' (p. 102). When Campion orders him back to the Front, Tietjens ponders what his mind will fear most. He finally settles on the mud, 'the fear of mud that was going to obsess him' (p. 231). Crucially, however, Tietjens is not overcome by fear while he is in the trenches. In *A Man Could Stand Up –,* he is buried up to the waist in mud, but his sanity survives and he is able to save one of his men and direct the rescue of the other. Significantly, just as with his traumatic hallucinations of Morgan's blood, Tietjens predicts and analyses his own fears and obsessions. His traumas do not arise from events hidden in his unconscious, but from recent memories.

As noted earlier, in *No More Parades* Tietjens expresses his rule for dealing with a stressful event as: '*Never to think on the subject of a shock at the moment of a shock*. The mind was then too sensitized. [. . .] If your mind thinks when it is too sensitized its then conclusions will be too strong' (p. 38). His method exemplifies James's theory on the ability of the brain to choose when it will attend to a subject, but it also resembles Freud's principle of constancy. In *Beyond the Pleasure Principle,* Freud states: 'the work of the mental apparatus is directed towards keeping the quantity of excitation low' and anything that 'increases that quantity is bound to be felt as adverse to the functioning of the apparatus'.[41] Similarly, Tietjens theorises that his mind, at the moment of shock, is sensitised, which will adversely affect its functioning, so his conclusions will be too strong. Just as Freud theorised that the mind functioned best with a lower amount of excitation, Tietjens speaks of the need for equilibrium in his brain before he can think logically and calmly.

From the beginning of *Parade's End,* Tietjens has habitually repressed unpleasant experiences, such as Sylvia's elopement, as well as his feelings about these experiences. In both situations, he deliberately casts these painful experiences out of his mind, although they do remain accessible to his conscious mind. In contrast, in 'The Psychotherapy of Hysteria', Freud describes repression as a defence mechanism used when the 'patient's ego had been approached by an idea which proved to be incompatible' and, as a result, the ego repels this idea out of consciousness and out of memory.[42] These ideas will be inaccessible (without analysis) to the conscious mind. In contrast, in 'The Repression of War Experience', Rivers describes repression as an active process, which attempts to 'remove some part of the mental content out of the field of attention'.[43] Rivers theorises an active repression process with the disturbing memory still accessible in the conscious mind. Both men agree, however, that repression 'under conditions in which it fails to adapt the individual to his environment' can be harmful.[44] In *Some Do Not . . .*, Tietjens echoes this theory when he worries that his habit of suppressing his emotions will put him at 'a great disadvantage in moments of unusual stress' (p. 220). As he predicts, Tietjens' ability to control his emotions and shift his attention becomes compromised under stress. Tietjens represses his feelings about Sylvia's elopement for four months, but he finally breaks down, despite his attempts to distract himself with cards and calculations, when he encounters Valentine Wannop. In *No More Parades*, he strives to control his thoughts and emotions until he can contemplate the situation calmly. This proves enormously difficult because of the stress of war, O Nine Morgan's death, and Sylvia's unexpected appearance. Because of these pressures, along with Perowne's presence, Tietjens becomes increasingly unable to repress his feelings for Valentine. Indeed, Tietjens can't avoid thoughts of Valentine and cannot explain why thoughts of Valentine keep 'wriggling in at all hours of the day and night' (p. 65). Previously, he expressed confidence in his freedom to decide what thoughts and feelings to attend to and what mode of conduct to adopt. Tietjens continues to monitor his mental processes, but without his earlier confidence in his control over his mind and his identity.

In her article on therapeutic treatment at Craiglockhart War Hospital, Meredith Martin analyses poetry composition as a therapeutic practice for traumatised soldiers. W. H. R. Rivers, for example, practised a 'Freudian psychotherapy' by asking his patients to narrate 'traumatic experiences in order to move through them'.[45] Tietjens attempts his own version of narrative therapy in *No More Parades* when he writes an account of his marriage, in order to 'set about a calm analysis of his relations with his wife' (p. 73). As he writes his story, he contemplates the possibility of a future with Valentine Wannop. Eventually, he declares that writing 'gave him no sort of psychological pointers' and claims 'he wasn't himself ever much the man for psychology' (p. 77). Despite his criticism of psychology, this exercise gives him an important insight. He realises that he has a passion for Valentine, 'deep and boundless like the sea' (p. 78). Tietjens states that he wasn't the 'sort of fellow who goes into his emotions' so he hadn't been aware of 'passionately loving her' until that morning (p. 78). Clearly, Tietjens has gained insight into his own repressed emotions from this form of talking therapy. By the end of the war, Tietjens conflates a happy marriage with the ability to talk to Valentine, a striking contrast with his earlier motto of 'not talking'.

Parade's End creatively explores both Jamesian theories of consciousness as well as psychoanalytic theories of the unconscious mind. Tietjens' introspective monitoring of his mental acuity as well as his self-awareness of his own thought processes echo James's theories of consciousness. In addition, Tietjens displays a Jamesian belief in his freedom to shape his identity through selective attention. On the other hand, while under stress from the war and his disastrous marriage, Tietjens relies on early twentieth-century psychoanalytic theory to examine the effects of trauma and repression on his mind. Tietjens approaches the exploration of his unconscious mind with the same introspective techniques he brings to his examination of his consciousness. Rather than identifying himself as a victim or a patient in need of psychiatric therapy, Tietjens examines his psychological experiences – his trauma, repressions, obsessions and complexes – and performs his own self-analysis. Ultimately, the tetralogy does not deny the validity of psychoanalytical theory, but it does privilege James's model of self-awareness through the introspective examination of mental processes and self-mastery through practices of selective attention.

Notes

1. Ford, *Some Do Not . . .*, ed. Max Saunders, p. 288. All further references are to this edition.
2. Henighan, 'Tietjens Transformed', p. 145.
3. Hunt, *The Story of Psychology*, p. 151.
4. James, *The Principles of Psychology*, I, p. 185.
5. Ibid. p. 185.
6. Roth, *Freedom and the Moral Life*, p. 16.
7. Hunt, *The Story of Psychology*, p. 151.
8. James, *The Principles of Psychology*, I, p. 185.
9. James, *The Principles of Psychology*, I, p. 402.
10. Ibid. p. 403.
11. On Tietjens' taciturnity, see Attridge, '"A Taboo on the Mention of Taboo"', pp. 23–35.
12. James, *The Principles of Psychology*, I, p. 196.
13. Ibid. p. 196.
14. Roth, *Freedom and the Moral Life*, p. 24.
15. Ford, *No More Parades*, ed. Joseph Wiesenfarth, p. 38. All further references are to this edition.
16. James, *The Principles of Psychology*, I, p. 409.
17. Ibid. p. 409.
18. Ibid. p. 420.

19. Boring, *A History of Experimental Psychology*, p. 149.
20. James, *The Principles of Psychology*, II, p. 561.
21. James, *Essays in Psychology*, pp. 233–4.
22. Gathorne-Hardy, *The Old School Tie*, p. 145.
23. Ibid. p. 153.
24. Bordogna, 'Inner Division and Uncertain Contours', p. 536.
25. Ibid. pp. 508–9.
26. On Tietjens and the eighteenth century, see Chapter 4 in this volume and Haslam, 'From Conversation to Humiliation', pp. 37–51.
27. Cassell, *Ford Madox Ford*, p. 215.
28. James, *The Principles of Psychology*, II, p. 561.
29. Ibid. p. 563.
30. Roth, *Freedom and the Moral Life*, p. 33.
31. Ibid. p. 34.
32. On mud in *Parade's End*, see O'Malley, 'How Much Mud Does A Man Need?', pp. 119–28.
33. Ryan, *The Vanishing Subject*, p. 5.
34. Ibid. p. 5.
35. See, for example, Brown, 'Remains of the Day'; and Haslam, *Fragmenting Modernism*.
36. Cassell, *Ford Madox Ford*, p. 223.
37. Raitt, 'Early British Psychoanalysis and the Medico-Psychological Clinic', p. 70.
38. Ibid. p. 77.
39. Rivers, *Instinct and the Unconscious*, p. 85.
40. Sandler et al., *Freud's Models of the Mind*, p. 33.
41. Freud, *Beyond the Pleasure Principle*, p. 3.
42. Freud, 'The Psychotherapy of Hysteria', p. 239.
43. Rivers, 'The Repression of War Experience', p. 2.
44. Ibid. p. 2.
45. Martin, 'Therapeutic Measures', p. 37.

Chapter 6

Composing the War and the Mind; Composing *Parade's End*

Alexandra Becquet

Testifying to the First World War seems to have gone hand in hand with the war itself: the vast amount of literature, both fiction and non-fiction, alongside works of art in various other media produced by those involved in the hostilities, attests to a profound need to bear witness to the experience of 'Armageddon'. However, the time which elapsed between the experience of war itself and the act of relating it points to the extreme complexity of testifying. When Ford set out to write *Parade's End*, in 1923, he was acutely aware of the difficulties artists desiring to testify were faced with. Since he considered that overstating the horrors and the heroisms of the war would create indifference,[1] he endeavoured above all to depict the conflict in such a way that would not blunt the sensitivity of his readers, so shunned exaggeration:

> I have not exaggerated either the physical horrors or the mental distresses of that period. On the contrary I have selected for treatment less horrible episodes than I might well have rendered and I have rendered them with more equanimity than might well have been displayed.[2]

Yet, as the first fully mechanised war, World War One was unprecedented in many respects, especially in terms of destruction – which it brought to a whole new scale and, as a result, generated entirely new visual and aural experiences – and in terms of its impact on the psyche, as the attrition rates and psychical losses during the conflict show.[3]

Ford was attuned to looking at and listening to the world with an artist's eyes and ears from an early age, not least because of his childhood amongst the second-generation Pre-Raphaelites and his musical training. Highly sensitised to the world, Ford was naturally very much interested in the visual as well as in the aural and acoustic aspects of the Great War, as his letters from the Front to Joseph Conrad prove.[4] Moreover, while he was 'a writer, a complete writer – nothing but a writer'[5] who considered that the arts mirror life and saw the latter through the prism of the former, he strove to transpose his sensory experience into his writing by resorting to all the arts he knew, understood and even mastered as he wished to 'present [. . .] only what [he] observed and heard' at the Front (*No More Parades*, p. 4). Ford was also acutely interested in the workings of the human mind and psychology and, perceiving that the war's impact on the psyche was one of the respects in which the conflict was most unprecedented, he proved to be primarily concerned with the effects of the war on the mind. Indeed, all of his war writing actually focuses less on combat than on its perception and its psychological consequences, which more often than not either involve, or result in, shattered minds. As he states in the dedicatory letter to *A Man Could Stand Up –*, he aimed to expose chiefly 'how modern fighting of the organised, scientific type affects the mind' (p. 3). Ford's war writing is therefore saturated with images and sounds, which reveal as many subjective perceptions and so correspond to states of mind, disclosing the impact of the war on the soldier's psyche.

In *Parade's End* (as in all his writings), Ford employs not only the visual arts, with which his Impressionist aesthetics is most readily associated, but the performing arts as well as music, and he embeds them in his text, thus turning it into an art composition, that is, a composition rallying a vast array of art forms to create a unified, composite, single, and singular, artwork. For in *Parade's End*, arts are not only present through references and quotations: they are assimilated into the text's own fabric. As a result of this assimilation, the text stands at the juncture of two or more media, mixing and using them in the writing itself, and so is genuinely intermedial. It is on that intermedial dimension of Ford's aesthetics and prose, its use and its effects, that this chapter focuses, in order to consider in particular the structure of *Parade's End* – or its lack thereof – and bring out the 'whole design'[6] of the tetralogy. For the arts appear to enable Ford to structure and aestheticise what was for him, as for countless others, a traumatic experience, and thus to properly render it while simultaneously anaesthetising his response to it.

This chapter, therefore, addresses the act of composition which intermediality entails and which engages a double process: on the one hand, a process of decomposition, thanks to which the arts are translated into the text, and can be studied in it; on the other, a process of recomposition which calls upon the reader's cooperation to fully realise the narrative. This intermedial composition forges a new aesthetic code encompassing all the arts involved at the same time and fitting to perfection the medium in which the final artwork is produced. This newly created, original code, partaking of the syntax of all the arts imported into the intermedial work, makes the latter artistically composite: in other words, an art composition through which Ford can truly present 'what [he] observed and heard' at the Front and show 'how modern fighting of the organised, scientific type affects the mind'. Indeed, it is through such composition, and thanks to it, that *Parade's End* does, as Ford wanted, 'constitute an attempt simply to reflect [. . .] our own times'.[7]

Impressionism, the War, and the Mind

According to Freud, the cure for all neuroses, including the two kinds of war neuroses, derives from catharsis, a process fundamental to the development of the psychoanalytical method based on anamnesis. When war neurosis stems from the repression of a traumatic experience, a talking cure encourages recollection of that experience to give rise to abreaction, which in turn leads to catharsis. In the case of a neurosis due to a conflicted ego, the recovery of a unified one, as Guillaume Piketty explains, is operated through a process akin to mourning, which prompts the individual to go back to his (pre-war) intimate sphere and undivided self:

> coming out of the war thus goes hand in hand with the reconstruction of an identity and the recovery of an image of self, with learning anew a kind of body economy, or again discovering anew hygiene and decency. Returning to oneself at the end of the war [. . .]. For many, that return to their intimate sphere at the end of the war is synonymous with mourning [. . .].[8]

Consequently, for both types of neurosis, healing is carried out through the return of the repressed, which is a reflection of the more or less distant past, in other words, a recovery of the past through its repetition in the duplication that 'reflection' entails. The duplication on which that healing process relies matches the one found in representation; while both words, 'reflection' and 'representation', share the prefix 're', which indicates a return to the past thanks to its repetition (or duplication) in the present. Duplicating the past thus allows traumatised soldiers to contemplate and (re)integrate the past into their present and so to recover a unified self – or a sense of one.

As with many forms of representation, Ford's Impressionism functions along these lines, as he shows when he details how 'momentary' his aesthetics is and describes the workings of an Impressionist mind in a moment caught in a time paradox since the time frame of that moment is at once present and past:

> Impressionism is a thing altogether momentary.
>   I do not wish to be misunderstood. It is perfectly possible that the remembrance of a former observation may colour your impression of the moment.

> [. . .] It is [. . .] perfectly possible that a piece of Impressionism should give a
> sense of two, of three, of as many as you will, places, persons, emotions, all
> going on simultaneously in the emotions of the writer.[9]

Perception in the Impressionist moment is anchored in the present,
which is fleeting and mingled with another moment proceeding from
the past, and thus ultimately coincides with genuine perception, as
defined by Henri Bergson, that is, 'an occasion upon which to remember'.[10] The momentariness of Impressionism, stamped by a heightened
consciousness and approaching the 'moments of being' Virginia Woolf
held dear,[11] readily compares with the involuntary memory engaged in
Marcel Proust's *À la recherche du temps perdu* (1913–27) and epito-
mised by the episode of the madeleine. Furthermore, the Impressionist
moment is a present perception captured in a time complex which associates not only past and present but also the future, as the image of the
window, Ford's leading metaphor for Impressionist writing, displays:

> And there is nothing in the canons of Impressionism, as I know it, to stop
> the attempt to render those superimposed emotions. Indeed, I suppose that
> Impressionism exists to render those queer effects of real life that are like so
> many views seen through bright glass – through glass so bright that whilst
> you perceive through it a landscape or a backyard, you are aware that, on its
> surface, it reflects a face of a person behind you. For the whole of life is really
> like that: we are almost always in one place with our minds somewhere quite
> other.[12]

Several spaces are joined in this window: the image beyond it and the
reflection of the space behind the spectator, respectively corresponding
to the outside and the inside. However, if 'a face of a person behind you'
is reflected in the glass, the spectator's face must be reflected in it too and
there are no longer two but three spaces coexisting in the glass. Besides,
while Ford here refers only to space, we can also regard it, with Max
Saunders, in terms of time and see 'the temporal superimposition' on
which Ford insisted in describing the Impressionist moment, to conclude
that the Impressionist writer, and so his text, 'is almost always in one
time with his mind some*when* quite other'.[13]

   Furthermore, all the images presented in the glass are the perceptions
of the spectator and are therefore reflections of his own mind, while the
inside, to which the glass belongs, appears to denote the interiority of
the individual. The window thus reveals the time construct in which the
individual's mind is consigned, that is, in what Henri Bergson termed
'duration', as opposed to 'time' measured by clocks in fixed, discrete
units (seconds, minutes, hours). Duration is the present of perception
and of the individual, a time frame which is perpetually present and

perpetually re-formed as, in it, the present proves itself to be 'the unseiz-able progress of the past nibbling at the future'.[14] It is thus stamped by fluctuation, not only in its content but also its form, and both the per-ception and the identity of the individual are constantly changing, never definite.

Fordian Impressionism therefore emerges as an aesthetics of percep-tion which triggers memory as Proust's madeleine does, and which at the same time encapsulates the complexity of memory and its ties to the present. Thus Impressionism unveils the individual's mind through his or her perceptions to expose the essential fragmentation of the psyche and that of the self. Being 'founded so entirely on the observation of the psychology of the patron',[15] Impressionism scrupulously adheres to the realities of the individual's psychical activity and so is thoroughly appropriate to the rendering of the psychological experience engen-dered by the war as well as its impact on the mind, while the inherent fragmentation of Impressionism enables it to mirror that of the soldier's psyche. Although, as Max Saunders notes, 'Ford finds the war has left his Impressionism in an impasse',[16] as is apparent in the 1916–17 essays 'Arms and the Mind' and 'War and the Mind', Impressionism turns out to be a fitting writing method for the mediation of war experience. It appears so in *No Enemy*, Ford's autobiographical novel completed in 1919 though only published in 1929, in which the Compiler is endlessly frustrated by Gringoire's tales of the war because battles are almost absent from them, while his impressions of and intimate feelings at the Front dominate his stories. In *Parade's End*, of which *No Enemy* can be considered as a 'raw', more personal version, scenes of combat are quite scarce but individual perceptions of them abound.

Furthermore, Impressionism enables Ford to present the war itself through the soldier's perception of it, since the perceptions he presents stand at the juncture of the individual's interiority and the outside world being perceived. Impressionism thus appears to be structured by a dual perspective which Ford first enunciated in what may be regarded as his first Impressionist treatise, that is, the dedicatory letter to *Ancient Lights* (1911).[17] Here he declares: 'The earliest thing that I can remember is this, and the odd thing is that, as I remember it, I seem to be looking at myself from outside.'[18] It is that same dual perspective which governed the writing of *Parade's End* for which Ford '[fell] back on the old device of a world seen through the eyes of a central observer'.[19] Thanks to that dual perspective – of which *No Enemy*, with its two narrators, can be seen as a first draft – Ford acquires the necessary distance from his experience of the war to present it and is enabled not only to associate the charac-ter's point of view and interiority with an external viewpoint standing at a remove, but also to engage and combine 'sympathetic imagination' and 'critical attitude' in the reader as his Impressionism allows him to 'mediate between impressionist subjectivity and omniscience'.[20]

While perceptions clearly emanate from an individual and are therefore determined by a point of view, they are framed in the space afforded by the window, which coincides with the rectangle elected by the painter to inscribe his representation before proceeding to producing it, as Alberti explains in *Della Pittura* (1435):

> First I trace as large a quadrangle as I wish, with right angles, on the surface to be painted; in this place, it [the rectangular quadrangle] certainly functions for me as an open window through which the *historia* is to be observed, and there I determine how big I want the men to be [. . .].[21]

That chosen space corresponds to the canvas and thus delineated stands as a frame for the image projected, whether there is an actual frame around it or not. As it appears, the frame duplicates the limits of the field of vision and 'determines the space to be painted',[22] in the strongest sense of the word, that is to say, the frame regulates the construction of perspective. While representation is a duplicate of a perception meant to present it to another, perspective representation is genuinely mimetic as it involves distortions which are 'the visual expression that this world is being sighted'.[23] Besides the network of lines on which perspective rests and whose organisation is dictated by the frame, converges at the vanishing point (usually there is one but there can be more), a point which, within the image, indicates where the original onlooker was standing and so assigns a spot to the spectator from which he should contemplate the representation, thus fundamentally including him in the representation as a double of the original onlooker. Furthermore the frame acts as 'an iconic [. . .] deictic',[24] a pictorial device which draws the spectator's attention to the representation. It is especially true when there is an actual frame present but it is also the case when considering the mere limits of the representational space, as with the window, depending on whether we include its contours or not. As a consequence, Ford's window is not merely a space onto which an image is projected, whether we look at it or through it: it is a structuring and deictic device which reveals Impressionism as a true aesthetics of representation. For the Impressionist text actually frames its content to really be 'monstrous', as Ford would have it, his narrative being meant to be 'a frame absolutely monstrous' 'for the purpose of proper bringing out of a very slight Impressionist sketch', and Impressionist writing therefore effectively 'produce[s] an illusion of reality in the mind of [the] reader' as it actually makes it present in and projects it into the reader's mind.[25]

Moreover, Impressionism is a realism and even a heightened one with regards to perception in the sense that it is what I elsewhere term an 'objective subjectivity'[26] as it exhibits the world through its perception in the individual's mind, rendering that perception without altering it. Malcolm Bradbury first described Ford's Impressionism as 'a heightened realism' and celebrated it in *Parade's End* as:

> a technique for dematerialising the solid world, partly in order to extend its historical significance, relating one part of life to another, partly in order to move the action inward into consciousness and allow for its anguish and disordered movement, the movement that itself mirrors a decomposing world.[27]

As Bradbury notices, the subject qualifies the form and vice versa and so, as Impressionist writing dematerialises 'the solid world' by its projection into the characters' consciousness, the text focuses on the psyche and thus reveals the impact that world has on the mind. The text therefore renders the character's perceptions and, to do so, resorts to intermediality which dematerialises the media translated into the Impressionist text and the text itself. Conversely, intermediality leads to the reinforcement of the text's materiality, that is, as textual medium. Indeed, as the Impressionist intermedial text incorporates other media into its own fabric, both the media utilised and the text itself come to exist together, as one, in their immaterial realisation in the reader's mind, thus moving beyond their respective materiality – that of a picture in the case of painting, for example, and that of the writing as text on a page. However, such a dematerialised projection of the intermedial text into the reader's mind is achieved by the reinforcement of the materiality of all the media involved, especially the textual medium, that is, their technique, for understanding and mastering the technique of all the media involved in the work produced by the artist – here, the novel – is central to medial translation and so to intermediality.

That Ford paid considerable attention to technique may be demonstrated by the title of his essay, 'Techniques', as well as his higher regard for those he called 'conscious artists', 'craftsmen', or 'masters' because they mastered the technique of their medium, whether they be writers, painters or musicians. As his essays show, Ford understood and mastered the techniques of those arts even though he did not himself practise them all, while he came to master narrative technique thanks to his collaboration with Conrad through which they evolved 'the New Form' for the novel[28] with the aim 'to make you *see*'. As a result, and as 'On Impressionism' proves, much goes through sight and vision set in a solid formal structure throughout Ford's writing, and *Parade's End* is no exception.

Sights and Sounds in the War and the Mind

The visual arts used in the tetralogy map the evolution of society in the decade depicted in the four volumes. This comes strikingly to the fore at the beginning of each novel. The opening paragraph of each acts as a formal threshold and offers an arresting example of the Fordian composition. These are moments of descriptive prose which suspend the progression of the story; yet they still carry the narrative forward as they introduce it and help the reader to find his or her bearings in new circumstances. That is particularly true of the tetralogy's opening in *Some Do Not ...* which launches the narrative *in medias res*, but it applies to every beginning throughout *Parade's End* since time-shifts between novels, also between parts and between chapters, disrupt time and space continuity, so readers have to each time familiarise themselves with the new circumstances and environment of the story. Indeed, moving from the end of *Some Do Not ...* to the beginning of *No More Parades* takes the reader from Whitehall in the dead of night to a dark shelter near the French trenches; then from the kitchens at the base camp in the last paragraphs of *No More Parades* to a London school playground with the first words of *A Man Could Stand Up* –; and we finally turn from the riotous dance in Tietjens' living room at Grays Inn in the last words of *A Man Could Stand Up* – to the panorama of quiet green country at the beginning of *Last Post*.

Each opening sets the scene and tone of the text it introduces, as well as the point of view that will dominate that part of the novel, following the same precise organisation: space is first delineated, then surveyed in detail, before the surroundings are taken in and the first, or the sole, point of view of the chapter is introduced. Whether it is the compartment of the railway carriage in *Some Do Not ...*, the shelter near the Front in *No More Parades*, the school playground in *A Man Could Stand Up* – or the hut in *Last Post*, each novel opens onto a framed space which calls for contemplation, and the prose unfolds following the three moments which distinguish the progress of a spectator's eye on a visual surface: the image is first taken in as a whole, then explored closely, before the spectator proceeds to a retroreading of the picture, looking at it again as a unit, the apprehension of which is modified by the import of the details. Moreover, these opening paragraphs call upon other senses than sight: namely, smell and hearing, thus projecting the reader into the environment as if to make it his own and realise Ford's ambition of making him 'entirely oblivious [. . .] of the fact that he is reading a book'.[29]

Those opening descriptions strike the note of the text to follow and outline the thematic and aesthetic course of the tetralogy which, as a whole, traces the history of art from the nineteenth to the early twentieth century as *Parade's End* illustrates it, the aesthetics used in each volume matching its theme so that the one comes to reinforce the other. The academic aesthetics of the first paragraph of *Some Do Not . . .* establishes a Victorian setting infused with order, social and visual, the perfection of 'virgin newness' and comfort, and a sense of security in the permanence of an order so absolute that even 'eccentricities are expected'.[30]

> The two young men – they were of the English public official class – sat in the perfectly appointed railway carriage. The leather straps to the windows were of virgin newness; the mirrors beneath the new luggage racks immaculate as if they had reflected very little; the bulging upholstery in its luxuriant, regulated curves was scarlet and yellow in an intricate, minute dragon pattern, the design of a geometrician in Cologne. The compartment smelt faintly, hygienically of admirable varnish; the train ran as smoothly – Tietjens remembered thinking – as British gilt-edged securities. (p. 3)

This secure environment is, however, threatened by the progress which marks it, and its order and perfection have been clearly wiped out in *No More Parades*, where they are replaced by disorder and hysteria bursting with each bomb drop:

> When you came in the space was desultory, rectangular, warm after the drip of the winter night, and transfused with a brown-orange dust that was light. It was shaped like the house a child draws. Three groups of brown limbs spotted with brass took dim high-lights from shafts that came from a bucket pierced with holes, filled with incandescent coke and covered in with a sheet of iron in the shape of a tunnel. Two men, as if hierarchically smaller, crouched on the floor beside the brazier; four, two at each end of the hut, drooped over tables in attitudes of extreme indifference. From the eaves above the parallelogram of black that was the doorway fell intermittent drippings of collected moisture, persistent, with glass-like intervals of musical sound. The two men squatting on their heels over the brazier – they had been miners – began to talk in a low sing-song of dialect, hardly audible. It went on and on, monotonously, without animation. It was as if one told the other long, long stories to which his companion manifested his comprehension or sympathy with animal grunts. . . .
>   An immense tea-tray, august, its voice filling the black circle of the horizon, thundered to the ground. Numerous pieces of sheet-iron said 'Pack. Pack. Pack.' In a minute the clay floor of the hut shook, the drums of ears were pressed inwards, solid noise showered about the universe, enormous echoes pushes these men – to the right, to the left, or down towards the tables, and crackling like that of flames among vast underwood became the settled condition of the night. (pp. 9–10)

The prose here presents motley, fragmented, rudimentary forms, words that no longer have meaning but are mere animal-like sounds, men as anonymous fragments, dejected-looking silhouettes. Moving from one group of men to another in a regular and circular fashion, the text suggests a vortex and thus stamps the composition with Vorticist aesthetics.[31]

The first lines of *A Man Could Stand Up –*, visually more rudimentary still as they attend to the solid noise surrounding Valentine, are redolent of Futurist or even abstract painting which endeavoured to represent sound on canvas – here, we will think of Gino Severini's ideographic pictures such as *Cannon in Action* (1915), which aspires to make the sounds of war heard by resorting to dynamic shapes, bright colours, words and onomatopoeias, and of Wassily Kandinsky's abstract canvases such as *Impression III, Concert* (1911) which relies on synesthesia for the visual material to be equated with sounds.

> Slowly, amidst intolerable noises from, on the one hand the street and, on the other, from the large and voluminously echoing playground, the depths of the telephone began, for Valentine, to assume an aspect that, years ago it had used to have [. . .]. (p. 7)

With quietness and beauty regained, the infinite view and the grass whose colour harks back to the brightness of Ford Madox Brown's pictures such as *The Pretty Baa-Lambs* (1851–9) or *Carrying Corn* (1854–5), the opening of *Last Post* testifies to the post-war 'retour à l'ordre' in the arts and dramatises the nostalgia and trauma left by the events of the last decade.

> He lay staring at the withy binders of his thatch; the grass was infinitely green; his view embraced four counties; the roof was supported by six small oak sapling-trunks, roughly trimmed and brushed from above by apple boughs. French crab-apple! The hut had no sides.[32]

This opening paragraph contrasts with and seems to answer the one of *Some Do Not . . .*, while, in *No More Parades* and *A Man Could Stand Up –*, the visual aesthetics of the early twentieth-century avant-gardes along with the noise trace the mutation of society and the arts as the fragmentation of the old order gives way to an abstracted, virtually shapeless, world.

Although the visual is very much insisted on when it comes to literary Impressionism, the openings of *No More Parades* and *A Man Could Stand Up –*, in particular, are dominated by sound, thus indicating, on the one hand, that images and sight were displaced by noise and hearing during the war, and showing, on the other, that Impressionism is not solely about pictorial representation but can also take on that of sound, which is indispensable for the treatment of the war. For, with the use of camouflage, artillery and aviation as well as trench warfare (in which the first three were all resorted to), the enemy was at a distance from its target and thus remained invisible, while many attacks, as most of those described in *Parade's End*, were carried out at night. Consequently, rather than sight, sound prevailed, as Fernand Léger, a French painter who fought in the war, highlights: 'No one saw the war, hidden, concealed, on all fours, mud colour the useless eye could see nothing. Everyone "heard" the war. It was an enormous symphony which no musician or composer has yet equalled: "Four years without colour"'.[33] The invisibility of the war and the subsequent difficulty for painters to represent it through their medium motivated the title of Philippe Dagen's book *The Painters' Silence* (1996). For painting is fundamentally silent and therefore cannot render what is essentially characterised by sound, just as it struggled to represent the movement that distinguished the war.

In that respect, writers benefitted from a superior medium compared to painters as words may translate sound and can also actually be sound, something that Ford was very much aware of. The two central volumes of *Parade's End* are saturated with the sounds heard at the Front, as the steady repetition of the word 'noise' confirms.[34] Sound also occupies a prominent place in the memories left by the attacks, even though during them, as Tietjens ponders in *A Man Could Stand Up –*, the 'din [was] so overwhelming that you could not any longer bother to notice it' (p. 69). Besides, while the voices of the men no longer carry meaning and are drowned by the noise of the artillery to the point of becoming inaudible, objects seem to have something to say, such as the shell falling close to the hut at the onset of *No More Parades* with 'its voice' (p. 9), the soldiers' steps chanting 'Cannon fodder. . . . Cannon fodder. . . .' (p. 92), or the cornet singing Herrick in *A Man Could Stand Up –* (pp. 86–8). Tietjens listens attentively to the surrounding noises, even though he is bad at identifying sounds, whether it is telling the difference between a key-bugle and a cornet, identifying artillery or distinguishing between a regular strafe and 'a little extra Morning Hate' (*A Man Could Stand Up –*, pp. 88, 132, 144).

More frequently still, sounds are rendered through onomatopoeias, the only form of language which is genuinely akin to music as there exists a 'necessary link between the signifying and the signified facets of the linguistic sign'.[35] For not only does Ford insist a lot on sound in his narrations, he also uses all the resources the written text provides him with and even extends them by making use of those afforded by an intermedial text so as to fully expose the 'drab fabric of sound' the war was (*No More Parades*, p. 180). If in the second paragraph of *No More Parades* quoted above, the shrapnel goes 'Pack. Pack. Pack' (p. 10) and further 'pop-op-ops' (p. 23), sounds as onomatopoeias pervade *A*

Man Could Stand Up – where accounts of attacks are most numerous: for instance, bullets go 'Snap! Snap! Snap!' (p. 177); shells fall with a 'F.R.R.R.r.r.r.!' (p. 62) or a 'Wee ... ee ... ry.... Whack!' (p. 70); cannons blurt out 'Phoh.h.h.h.h.h.h.' (p. 100) then 'Pho.o.o.o.h.' (p. 101); unidentified artillery emits a 'Crumb!' (p. 130) or 'Crump' (p. 142), while the German guns roll on 'Pam ... Pamperi ... Pam! Pam! .... Pa ... Pamperi ... Pam! Pam! ... Pampamperipampampam ... Pam ....' (p. 131). As these examples show, Ford also uses the visual when he manipulates onomatopoeias, exploiting typography and punctuation with capital letters, strings of the same letter, suspension dots, and so on, thus practising a kind of writing which coincides with Filippo T. Marinetti's 'words in freedom'[36] that are manipulated by the Futurist to render the sounds of modernity, and of war in particular. All in all, the few artillery attacks which occupy the pages of *Parade's End* are either 'a conversation [...] of mastodons' (*A Man Could Stand Up* –, p. 174) or the productions of orchestras, the one at the Hotel de la Poste in Rouen described by Sylvia being comparable to Luigi Russolo's noise-makers as she remarks that the tumult generated by the bombardment involves 'all the instruments for making noise' (*No More Parades*, p. 177), while the other in the trenches detailed by Tietjens is equated by him to 'an opera orchestra' (*A Man Could Stand Up* –, p. 131).

Yet, however powerful the word may be as a vehicle to convey sound, the text or page, like painting, remains essentially silent and, as is the case with visual description, for sound to be realised, the efficacy of Ford's intermedial composition fundamentally depends on the transfer of the narrative onto the reader, all the more so as it is produced with that aim for, if Ford paid a great deal of attention to technique, to him, having 'your eyes forever on your Reader [...] alone constitutes ... Technique!'[37]

Time-Shifting the War and the Mind: The Music of *Parade's End*

Ford thus immerses his readers into his text by appealing to their senses, thanks mainly to the intermediality of his writing, while he calls upon them to work, that is, exhorts them to get wholly involved in the text through their memory by the technical mainspring of his Impressionism: the time-shift. The time-shift appears at first to fragment the text rather than help combine its elements as it disrupts the classical, chronological standard which dominated novel writing up to the nineteenth century.[38] While text time in *Parade's End* is multiple and destabilised by the descriptions the numerous time and space dislocations call for, story time is complex for it is disrupted by the time-shift which makes the narrative go forward and backward. The story even becomes unstable as the chronology of some time-shifted episodes doesn't work, and time may be 'join[ed] up' as events may be 'cut out' (*Some Do Not . . .*, p. 346).

Nevertheless, as Max Saunders insists: 'the cutting and joining of time that is Fordian impressionism cuts not in order to efface, but to face'.[39] Indeed, the time-shift makes an event recur within different time frames where it often appears from the perspectives of various characters. Readers can then contemplate the scene from a diversity of points of view to see how the pattern may be rearranged according to perspective, which calls for a different interpretation as the composition is each time created anew while it is necessarily mingled with the previous occasions. Readers then find themselves in the same position as Christopher and Valentine in front of a soap advertisement, 'standing at different angles and though [they] both look at the same thing [they] read different messages'. However, contrary to the characters, the readers come to occupy both positions in turn and then a third one combining the first two which shall yield 'yet a third [message]' (*Some Do Not . . .*, p. 285).

So, if fragmentation resulting from local division suggests the Impressionist painters' visual style and substantiates the parallel between Fordian Impressionism and the nineteenth-century French painters' style, the multiplicity of perspective embedded in Fordian texts creates holographs which intimate Cubist aesthetics as the various holographic images are eventually superimposed to compose one embracing those multiple perspectives on the same object. *Parade's End* thus offers a complex reflection of the times of the war, not only because Impressionist writing, being intermedial, is composite, but also because the characters, scenes, and situations the novel presents are. The reader is then called upon to memorise all the appearances or occurrences of the character or scene to combine their different renderings into a single, unified one which, in line with Gestalt theory, exceeds the impressions composing it as does the third message of the soap advertisement.

The time-shift therefore relies on the reader's memory while it exposes the workings of memory. Indeed, the time-shift and the impression it produces illustrate the subjective perception and treatment of time ('duration') as they engage the association of different moments or ideas. The time-shift thus reveals duration as the paradigmatic time construct it is, and which depends on the subjectivity of the person – or character – who remembers and the moment of remembrance. Highly subjective, duration is then detached from the time continuum and the outside world to always be set in the present, thus making the remembered past part of the present, as a work of art is always part of the present of perception while it *re*presents what is (perforce) past.

Because of the recurrence of images or scenes in *Parade's End* and because of the multiplicity of elements which constitute those images or scenes, the novel comes across as de-articulated. However, the same principles make the patterns of the tetralogy come out strikingly and powerfully as the narrative calls upon the reader's memory and effort to synthesise the numerous elements they have been provided with. For recurrence does not mean sheer repetition: each appearance of a motif sheds new light on its previous occurrences, and vice versa. While such a process compares with the retroreading at work in the contemplation of a painting, that process also corresponds to one of the major principles operating in music, which relies on the memory of the listener to discover the themes and their variations in the pieces performed.

Music has a special ring when linked with Ford due to his musical education and training, the musical compositions he produced, or his qualities as a stylist – and as a lyrical poet – and all appear to motivate his insistence on 'cadence' and 'rhythm'. Although Ford tends to use those words rather loosely, they acquire a most definite musical meaning when considered in the light of 'The Making of Modern Verse' (1902), in which Ford details the process of poetic composition with his own poem 'Lavender' and so exhibits how the poem develops along the lines of the tonal and thematic layout of the classical sonata. As it provides language with a structural model, music invests it with a 'rhythm' that conveys the writer's personality and which points directly to the etymology of *'rhuthmos*, rhythm, the impress on matter of the body's internal energy, in the mobility and vibrancy of its somatic rhythms'.[40] The structure thus provided is not rigid, as the 'experiments' Ford operates in 'Lavender' testify, and, as Norman Bryson points out, 'rhythm' enables us to apprehend form 'in dynamic terms, as matter in process'.[41] Despite Ford's minute detailing of the musical principles governing the composition of his poetry, most of his criticism insists on the overall structure music provides to his works in prose. The operating model, nevertheless, is still the sonata form, which Ford praises in H. G. Wells's novels[42] and returns to in *Provence* (1935) to show how he adopts the operatic form whose layout is directly derived from the sonata's.[43]

The occurrence of 'composition' in *Parade's End* supports that perspective on music. 'Composition' appears more often as 'composed' or 'composedly' and therefore points to a mode of bringing and holding separate elements together in a comprehensible form. One of the leading motifs in *Parade's End* is indeed to counteract fragmentation and each character in his or her own way endeavours to emulate Christopher whose mind 'picks up useless facts' and 'arranges [them] in obsolescent patterns' (*Some Do Not . . .*, p. 169), for, as Mark underlines, 'you must have a pattern to interpret things by. You can't really get your mind to work without it' (*Last Post*, p. 200). If Mark's pattern has always been provided by 'Transport' (p. 200), Ford's writing appears to be governed by the same principle: on the one hand, it strives to carry the story forward and to transfer the text onto the reader to move him or her as a picture should, since to Ford: 'A picture should come out of its frame and seize the spectator.'[44] On the other hand, Ford follows in the footsteps of his Master, Henry James, as his prose endeavours to pattern the text so as to create 'a picture of the life we live',[45] and to 'make out the pattern of the bewildering carpet that modern life is'.[46] In this regard, Ford puts to use the lessons he learnt while working with Conrad, who passed on to him the belief in the supremacy of the architectonics of the novel which Ford had so far dismissed with almost contempt.[47]

Time-shifted as *Parade's End* may be, it thus progresses implacably to its end and could be described as a linear three-part work, a form which, as Joseph Wiesenfarth underlines in the introduction to *No More Parades*, Ford imported into his writing from his collaboration with Conrad (pp. xvii–viii). That structure also matches the layout of the sonata, a three-movement form from which was derived a four-part structure used by composers for the symphony. Following the format of a three-part sonata, the pre-war period presented in *Some Do Not . . .* exposes the theme in the main tone, then *No More Parades* and *A Man Could Stand Up* – dealing with the war develop the theme in modulations set in the dominant tone, and, with post-war reconstruction, *Last Post* finally gets back to the theme in the main tone to round up the piece. Or, to draw parallels with the four-part symphony, *Some Do Not . . .* introduces the two themes in the main tone, which are modulated in *No More Parades* then re-exposed in the main tone in *A Man Could Stand Up* –, while *Last Post* constitutes the coda – which is how Arthur Mizener qualifies the fourth novel to defend it: 'the sonata form allows for a coda, so that *Last Post* does not really break the pattern'.[48] Analyses relying on finer distinctions between themes and tones can be presented but, however detailed the study of the structure may be, and despite the fact that the numerous aspects of sound have been here left aside, dissecting *Parade's End* in such a way discloses one aspect of the musical quality of Ford's writing. The time-shift, both in itself and in its effects, relies on principles operating in music composition and listening; it thus reveals the structural role played by music in the formal and intermedial composition of Ford's work, as it brings out the process of de-composition and re-composition through which the text goes at the moment of both writing and reading.

While the visual fragments have to be collected and collated to create a complex 'impression' of a character, a picture or a scene, the musical principle forces those fragments together. It thus forges the design of *Parade's End* which indeed appears when we look at the tetralogy as a whole, and from there so do parallels and comparisons with operatic works. *Parade's End* compares with Erik Satie's *Parade*, a ballet performed at the Théâtre du Châtelet in 1917 by Serge Diaghilev's Russian ballets, with music by Satie, libretto by Jean Cocteau and decor, curtain and costumes by Pablo Picasso. Besides the Cubist visual element the works share, both stage parades and (mockingly) reveal the antics of society as their spirit is stamped by what we now call the absurd. 'Absurd' also constitutes one of the lexical motifs in *Parade's End* and, through its etymological and first, though now rare, meaning as 'inharmonious, jarring, out of tune' (*OED*), is directly linked with music and composition as well as with the crisis of the beginning of the century which culminated in the First World War. It is highly likely that Ford knew Satie and his ballet as Satie appeared twice in the *transatlantic review* (May and August 1924), when Ford was writing *Parade's End*. Satie's *Parade* seems even to be referred to in *Some Do Not . . .* when Sylvia, Claudine Sandbach and General Wade go to see 'Russian dancers' the night of Macmaster's wedding announcement and knighthood party, before Christopher's return to France in 1917 (p. 245).

Parade's End also compares with Richard Wagner's four-part *Der Ring Des Nibelungen* (composed 1848–74): it shares the immense scale of Wagner's cycle in which, as in *Parade's End*, more than thirty characters appear along with over eighty leitmotifs, and the unit of both works is constituted retrospectively thanks to the effect of their leitmotifs. Ford's adoption of the operatic form, however, reverses Wagner's logic of composition, the structure of *Parade's End* being constituted of three movements with a coda whereas the structure of the *Ring* is composed of a prologue – *The Rhine Gold* – and three parts: *The Valkyrie*, *Siegfried*, and *Twilight of the Gods*. *Parade's End*, and Ford's intermedial writing generally, appear to owe a great deal to Wagner's artistic practice and theories: although music regulates the structure of the text in Ford when the text governs the music in Wagner, the German composer's theory of the total artwork, exemplified by the *Ring*, fits Ford's work as its intermediality extends to include the theatre, music, poetry and painting which Wagner aspired to bring together in the lyrical drama.[49]

Yet *Parade's End* is not so much a total artwork as a work of total art. If not all the arts, then a plurality of arts are integrated in the artistically composite syntax of the novel to embrace and represent the world, above which the writer stands as the 'creating deity'.[50] It is also the spot which Ford reserved for the readers to take once the writer's work is done so that they could see the characters living, see with them and see them seeing too. It is from this elevated place that the readers can distinguish the design of the work, just as an Impressionist painting, or one of the Gobelin tapestries in *Parade's End*, need the spectator to stand at a remove from the picture so that it comes to make sense. For, as Ford insists: 'if you hold your nose too close to a carpet, it is useless to hope to see its pattern'.[51]

With *Parade's End*, Ford reveals the 'novelist in his really proud position as historian of his own time'[52] for he presents time as duration to expose an intimate experience. He thus exposes the trauma engendered by the war, rendering it through its subjective perception by the characters, and transfers it onto his readers. Indeed, on the one hand, the readers are deeply involved in the book, through sympathetic identification with the characters and story, seized by the representation the text offers which is thus set in the readers' present to become their own experience. On the other hand, they need to take a step back from it all and call upon their memory to see the design of the work, which depends on that process to appear. The effectiveness of the tetralogy's moral design, Ford's hope of obviating all wars, relies on that process which also turns the readers' sympathy to the author. For it is so that the Impressionist transfer takes place and is complete.

Although *Parade's End* may be hailed as 'the greatest war novel ever written by an Englishman'[53] and 'the finest novel about the First World War',[54] it also traces the history of society and of the arts in the early twentieth century, demonstrating how an artwork is produced (as the study of the intermediality of Ford's *oeuvre* reveals), and reflecting on the nature and function of Art itself. Moreover, *Parade's End* unveils the (predominantly psychological) horrors of the war as it discloses the individual's perceptions thanks to its intermediality and the arts it rallies, and so mirrors the subject's psyche, its fragmentation as well as that of the world in the trenches and the experience that environment and situation provided. Simultaneously the arts, and ultimately intermediality, function as patterning forces for they offer a structure in which to assemble the fragments of the experience and make sense of them as it totalises them. Besides, the arts grant a distance from the trauma the conflict induced through artistic construction and organisation and through aesthetisation which functions as anaesthetisation of the trauma. Meant not 'to efface but to face',[55] the intermedial representation of traumatic experience thus enables Ford to 'reflect' and to 'reflect on'[56] the effect of the war on the mind, while the Fordian text also encourages such critical reflection in his readers.

In reconstructing the conflict, *Parade's End* then stands as a return to the trauma, a return of the repressed, thanks to which not only the psychoanalytical process but also the reconstruction of the individual and his unified psyche is carried out. At the same time, while shying away from overstating the horrors of the war to secure his readers' sensitivity, Ford's artwork succeeds in transferring these horrors onto the reader's psyche thanks to its intermediality, thus fulfilling the Impressionist aim of offering a vicarious experience, and in the hope here of 'obviating all future wars'.[57] *Parade's End* is, in this very last respect, a failure; in all the others, no superlative will suffice.

Notes

1. See Ford, 'To William Bird' (dedicatory letter), *No More Parades*, ed. Joseph Wiesenfarth, p. 4. All further references are to this edition.
2. Ford, 'To Gerald Duckworth' (dedicatory letter), *A Man Could Stand Up –*, ed. Sara Haslam, p. 4. All further references are to this edition.
3. See Piketty, preface, Freud et al., *Sur les névroses de guerre*, pp. 14–15; my translation. All further translations from French texts are mine unless otherwise stated.
4. Ford to Joseph Conrad (September 1916, 6 September 1916, 7 September 1916), *Letters of Ford Madox Ford*, pp. 71–3, 73–4, 75–6.
5. Bowen, *Drawn from Life*, p. 80.
6. Ford to Percival Hinton (27 November 1931), *Letters of Ford Madox Ford*, p. 204.
7. Ford, 'To Gerald Duckworth', *A Man Could Stand Up –*, p. 3.
8. Piketty, preface, Freud et al., *Sur les névroses de guerre*, p. 10.
9. Ford, 'On Impressionism', *Critical Writings of Ford Madox Ford*, p. 40.
10. Bergson, *Matière et mémoire*, p. 68.
11. See Woolf, *Moments of Being*, in particular 'A Sketch of the Past', pp. 61–159.
12. Ford, 'On Impressionism', p. 41.
13. Saunders, *Ford Madox Ford*, I, p. 69.
14. Bergson, *Matière et mémoire*, p. 167.
15. Ford, 'On Impressionism', p. 40.
16. Saunders, introductory note, 'True Love & a GCM', *War Prose*, p. 78.
17. As Max Saunders underlines, 'the "Dedication" [. . .] reads as a manifesto for literary impressionism in all but name': Saunders, 'From Pre-Raphaelism to Impressionism', p. 59.
18. Ford, *Ancient Lights*, p. viii.
19. Ford, *It Was the Nightingale*, p. 195.

20. Saunders, *Ford Madox Ford*, II, p. 275.
21. Alberti, *On Painting*, p. 39.
22. Arasse, *Histoires de peinture*, p. 84.
23. Arnheim, *Art and Visual Perception*, p. 294.
24. Marin, *De la représentation*, p. 348.
25. Ford, 'On Impressionism', p. 44.
26. Becquet, 'Impressionist Confusion, Dissolving Landscape', p. 120. Here I oppose Peter Stowell's conception of literary Impressionism as 'a mode of "subjective objectivism"': Stowell, *Literary Impressionism*, pp. 16–17: quoted in Matz, *Literary Impressionism and Modernist Aesthetics*, p. 26.
27. Bradbury, 'The Denuded Place', pp. 199, 200–1.
28. Ford, *Joseph Conrad*, p. 35.
29. Ibid. p. 186.
30. Ford, *Some Do Not . . .*, ed. Max Saunders, p. 3. All further references are to this edition.
31. For more on the 'Vorticist opening' of *No More Parades*, see Piette, 'War and Division in *Parade's End*', pp. 141–52.
32. Ford, *Last Post*, ed. Paul Skinner, p. 9. All further references are to this edition.
33. Léger, 'Couleur dans le monde', p. 206.
34. For a detailed discussion of *Parade's End*'s soundscape, see Vandevelde, 'Are You Going to Mind the Noise?', pp. 53–66.
35. Backès, *Musique et littérature*, p. 123.
36. Marinetti, 'Imagination sans fils et les mots en liberté: manifeste futuriste', pp. 142–7, in particular p. 146.
37. Ford, 'Techniques', *Critical Writings of Ford Madox Ford*, p. 71.
38. As Dowell underlines in *The Good Soldier*, a person telling a story delivers it in 'a very rambling way': Ford, *The Good Soldier*, p. 119. Ford and Conrad 'agreed that the general effect of a novel must be the general effect that life makes on mankind. A novel must therefore not be a narration, a report': Ford, *Joseph Conrad*, p. 180.
39. Saunders, *Ford Madox Ford*, II, p. 277.
40. Bryson, *Vision and Painting*, p. 131.
41. Ibid. p. 131.
42. Ford, 'English Literature of To-Day II', *The Critical Attitude*, p. 103.
43. Ford, *Provence*, p. 67.
44. Ford, 'On Impressionism', p. 48.
45. Ford, 'On the Functions of the Arts in the Republic', *The Critical Attitude*, p. 33.
46. Ford, 'English Literature of To-Day I', *The Critical Attitude*, p. 66.
47. Ford, *Joseph Conrad*, p. 24.
48. Mizener, *The Saddest Story*, pp. 508–9.
49. On Wagner's influence on *Parade's End*, see Wrenn, 'Wagner's *Ring* Cycle and *Parade's End*', pp. 67–80.
50. Ford, 'Techniques', p. 60.
51. Ford, 'The Woman of the Novelists', *The Critical Attitude*, p. 164.
52. Ford, *It Was the Nightingale*, p. 180.
53. Hynes, 'The Genre of *No Enemy*', p. 140.
54. Burgess, 'Literature', p. 97.

55. Saunders, *Ford Madox Ford*, II, p. 277.
56. 'these books, like all my others, constitute an attempt simply to reflect – not in the least to reflect on – our own times': Ford, 'To Gerald Duckworth', *A Man Could Stand Up –*, p. 3.
57. Ford, *It Was the Nightingale*, p. 225.

Chapter 7

The Work of Sleep: Insomnia and Discipline in Ford and Sassoon

Sarah Kingston

While contemplating the various hierarchical powers within the military, Christopher Tietjens comes to the conclusion that for an army to run effectively, the bodies of its members, no matter their rank, must be completely submissive to military authority. In *A Man Could Stand Up –*, Tietjens argues that this submission to discipline is especially significant in the case of any physical or mental illness: 'the moment [the Colonel] becomes sick the fact that his body is property of His Majesty the King, comes forcibly into operation'. He concludes: 'Sick bodies are not only of no use to the King, but are enormously detrimental to the army that has to cart them about.'[1] Though uncomfortable with the necessity of submitting one's body to the discipline of the military, Tietjens accepts this condition as 'very reasonable and proper' (p. 107) and regards the care for one's well being as 'a duty to your children. And the King' (p. 150). George Sherston, the central character of *Memoirs of an Infantry Officer* (1930) by Siegfried Sassoon, expresses a similar belief, that as a soldier he 'could no longer call [his] life [his] own'.[2] Both characters share a fundamental and problematised sense of accountability, not to themselves, but to their society, their comrades and superiors, and their king. They display, and often resist, this accountability by sometimes offering and sometimes withholding their bodies for use in the war. Their habits and failures of sleep are one of the means through which they express their ambivalence towards subjection and discipline. For instance, Tietjens, at times of stress, chooses not to sleep despite both exhaustion and the opportunity for rest, and Sherston describes numerous occasions when he cannot sleep given his physical and emotional circumstances. As this chapter will demonstrate, sleep signifies more than just a biological function in these novels: the failure or refusal to sleep acts as a point of resistance against becoming a disciplined subject.

As Michel Foucault argues: 'The body becomes a useful force only if it is both a productive body and a subjected body.'[3] Sleep is central to this utility, as lack of sleep reduces an individual's capacity to be productive. Consequently, those in control of the military during World War I were extremely concerned with the sleep habits of soldiers, and studies in fatigue were important to military efforts.[4] Anson Rabinbach refers to the First World War as 'a war of exhaustion': 'Even the term *attrition* suggests a fatigue, and in many ways the problem of fatigue was central to both military and nonmilitary aspects of the war.'[5] According to Rabinbach, the health of troops was a significant concern because success in combat was largely dependent upon the troops' medical and psychological fitness, both of which are reliant upon getting the necessary amount of rest.[6] Thus, in wartime especially, sleep is not a matter of individual comfort, but of national import. As such, sleep becomes not only a behaviour essential to productivity, but also one that is subject to discipline, therefore within the realm of disciplinary mechanisms. In essence, control over sleep becomes a point of threshold between public and private behaviour, and, as these novels show, a point of resistance to the subjection of the body for public interest.

In addition to the disciplining of sleep as a mechanism of subjection, the failure to sleep under discursively appropriate spatial and temporal conditions, whether by accident or choice, presents a particularly salient point of analysis of the soldiers' relationship to war through an exploration of its phenomenology. The wakefulness associated with the failure to sleep (in other words, insomnia) must be distinguished from the ordinary wakefulness associated with everyday activity. Peter Schwenger, a researcher interested in the role of sleep in literature, provides a concise and useful definition of insomnia: 'being awake when one ought to be asleep'.[7] Schwenger's 'ought', I will argue, is both discursively determined and contingent upon social circumstance. Traditionally, the civilian should sleep at night in a bedroom and the soldier should sleep where and when he can, as opportunity provides. One who fails to do so, whether by disposition or choice, has insomnia. For Schwenger, sleep entails a loss of the ability to determine and define the self.[8] Coincidentally, both Tietjens and Sherston are men who display a resistance to the loss of self involved with being a soldier, and both show similar resistance to the loss of self that sleep requires. This instance displays one of the ways in which the experience of insomnia mirrors the experiences of these characters in the war, as well as providing evidence of their ambivalent attitudes towards their own participation.

Gender-based scholarship presents a means of examining the subjected body's physical behaviours and responses as a direct reaction to and rebellion against social practices and discourses. Scholars such as Susan Bordo and Elaine Showalter argue that in many instances pathological conditions such as hysteria, shell shock, and anorexia are produced by and reflect the social conditions of the afflicted individual. Bordo sees 'the psychopathologies that develop within a culture, far from being anomalies or aberrations, to be characteristic expressions of that culture; to be, indeed, the crystallization of much that is wrong with it'.[9] Showalter makes a similar observation with regard to soldiers' shell shock, which she asserts 'was related to social expectations of the masculine role in war. [...] In a sense, the long-term repression of signs of fear that led to shell shock in war was only an exaggeration of the male sex-role expectations, the self-control and emotional disguise of civilian life'.[10] Virginia Woolf's character Septimus Smith, in *Mrs Dalloway* (1925), provides a relevant and informative literary example of Showalter's argument. Of Septimus, a notably brave and heroic soldier, Woolf writes: 'When [his comrade] Evans was killed, [...] Septimus, far from showing any emotion or recognising that here was the end of a friendship, congratulated himself upon feeling very little and very reasonably. The War had taught him', yet, the consequence is that 'something failed him; he could not feel'.[11] His symptoms are an exaggeration of the expectations of masculine stoicism placed upon him as a soldier; he is taught to act without feeling, and this lack of emotion becomes the permanent condition of his life after the war, displaying the danger of extending wartime values to peacetime existence, but also exposing the detrimental effects of being required to accept such values in the first place.

Similarly, in *Parade's End* and *Memoirs* insomnia presents an exaggeration of and response to the conditions of World War I, and Tietjens' and Sherston's insomnia serves much the same function as Septimus' lack of feeling. The relationship between insomnia as behaviour or symptom and insomnia as reflective ontological state rests in its liminality. By liminality, I refer to a point of threshold, a state between two or more other states, sharing characteristics of each, yet existing independently of both. The most obvious threshold involved in insomnia is as a state between sleeping and waking or consciousness and unconsciousness. The moment between sleeping and waking, argues Schwenger, is 'a threshold between two states that are literally as different as night and day – and yet can change into each other and perhaps even interpenetrate'.[12] Insomnia, which Schwenger refers to as 'almost always more liminal than simple wide-awakeness',[13] is an extension of this threshold between sleeping and waking. During insomniac time, one is typically not performing one's daily activities, nor is one getting the rest(oration) necessary for productivity. For a soldier, time spent actively awake is not the same as time spent not sleeping: time awake would be devoted to the performance of one's duties, whether in battle or in preparation for or recovery from battle, and time spent asleep is time necessary to maintain health and well-being necessary for duty, yet insomniac time is not active in the sense of contributing to waking productivity. Insomniac time is time often considered wasted, especially given the importance placed on the maximisation of efficiency and time related to recent advances in industrialisation, such as those made by American industrial consultant Frederick Taylor. Eluned Summers-Bremner argues: 'Actual insomnia both mimics Taylorist paranoia about untrackable uniqueness with its clock-watching and twists it by playing back to worker measurement its greatest fear: time-wasting.'[14] Insomnia is both product of anxiety over wasted time and an expression of time being wasted. It simultaneously brings to light and resists the societal importance placed upon efficient use of time. Insomnia is the threshold between activity and passivity.

However, insomnia is a threshold in other senses as well. It represents a threshold between public and private behaviour. Sleep is private in the sense that it isolates the sleeping individual completely, both from the self and others, reinforced by the typical relative isolation of the sleep space (the bedroom). Yet, by virtue of sleep's failures being subject to intervention and correction, it becomes a public behaviour as well, one through which an individual can contribute to or detract from the greater social good, and, as a result, it is observed by others accordingly. And, notably, during wartime, the sleep space for the typical soldier is rarely private. In fact, in *A Man Could Stand Up –*, Tietjens observes that as an officer, his men 'watched [him] eternally and knew the minutest gestures of [his] sleep' (p. 94). Thus, insomnia can result from an exaggerated sense of the lack of privacy felt by the soldier during war, something with which Tietjens struggles. In *No More Parades*, Ford relates Tietjens' thoughts on privacy:

> No scenes. Obviously for the sake of the servants – who are the same thing as the public. No scenes then, for the sake of the public. And indeed, with him, the instinct for privacy – as to his relationships, his passions, or even as to his most unimportant motives – was as strong as the instinct of life itself. He would, literally, rather be dead than an open book.[15]

Interestingly, Tietjens has these thoughts just prior to his decision to forego sleep in order to write the history of his relationship with his wife, Sylvia, and her infidelities so as to formulate an approach to the situation of his failed marriage. Because his marital situation is discussed publicly in the camp, he realises that his privacy has been violated, and his response is to refuse to enter into the private state of sleep in the presence of others (who are awake around him). Indeed, when Tietjens sleeps, his privacy is violated, much to his mortification. The next morning, Tietjens' friend Levin reveals having learned about Tietjens' relationship with Valentine specifically because Tietjens talks in his sleep (p. 194). In this situation, insomnia becomes an expression of anxiety over the lack of privacy consequent to living in close quarters with other soldiers, and is a physical response to social circumstance.

Like Tietjens, Sherston also has difficulty sleeping in close quarters. One instance of insomnia he recounts comes as he tries to sleep in a crowded room: 'The night was cold and sleep was impossible, since there was no space to lie down in' (p. 426). In this case, insomnia is the result of lack of physical comfort, yet still revelatory of the crowded, cramped, and claustrophobic conditions of life in the trenches, a physical response to social circumstance. In another example of insomnia, Sherston is in an army hospital, unable to sleep because the soldier in the next bed will not stop screaming. Sassoon writes that the wounded soldier's:

> voice went on, in the low, rapid, even tone of delirium. [. . .] Someone called Dicky was on his mind, and he kept on crying out to Dicky. [. . .] All the horror of the Somme attacks was in that raving; all the darkness and the dreadful daylight. [. . .] I watched the Sister come back with a white coated doctor; the screen glowed comfortingly; soon the disquieting voice became inaudible and I fell asleep. (p. 366)

The second case, more distressing than the first, uses Sherston's inability to sleep due to shared space to reveal the horror of the soldier's experience, but also presents the close sleeping quarters as the means of exposing the innermost thoughts of Sherston's room-mate. Sherston's failure to sleep is in direct response to another soldier's shell shock brought on by an intense sense of anxiety and loss. Proximity forces Sherston's exposure to this other soldier's experience, and Sherston can only rest once the other soldier is quieted.

An additional example of insomnia as threshold entails an intersection between the autonomic and the willed. Many late nineteenth-century and First World War-era medical texts posit that conscious control over habit, environment, and the mind can lead to regularised, healthy behaviours. According to William James, habit is necessary to function without exhausting ourselves with the need to constantly make conscious decisions regarding our behaviours.[16] Discipline is a means of establishing habit or, in other words, action without the necessity of thought or consideration. General Campion illustrates this idea when he asks: 'What was discipline for if subordinates were to act on their consciences?' (*No More Parades*, p. 226). In this case, habit eliminates the need for the conscience, an unfortunate necessity of war. Sleep is a type of habit, so resistance to sleep is arguably a resistance to giving oneself over to unconsciously established habit.

Medical texts from the period reflect both the idea of sleep as habit and insomnia as resistance to habit. For example, in an article entitled 'Broken Sleep', published in a 1918 issue of the *British Medical Journal*, physician Guthrie Rankin writes: 'In order to effect this desirable end [good sleep] an attempt ought to be made by every middle-aged person who suffers from insomnia in whatever degree to mend matters by some attention to the details of routine habits.'[17] Earlier texts that discuss insomnia include A. W. MacFarlane's *Insomnia and Its Therapeutics* (1891) and Silas Weir Mitchell's *Fat and Blood: An Essay on the Treatment of Certain Forms of Neurasthenia and Hysteria* (1885), and both present treatment for insomnia in terms of establishing control over both habit and one's mind. MacFarlane argues that: 'A brain which is properly used is adequately nourished and, consequently, vigorous. Its functions (such as sleep) are healthily performed.'[18] And Mitchell describes his widely famous 'rest cure' (used to treat Virginia Woolf, among others), which emphasises the importance of discipline and routine in the treatment of insomnia and other mental disorders.[19] Texts like Rankin's, MacFarlane's, and Mitchell's suggest that insomnia is treatable through routine, which strengthens self-control. Yet self-control does not always result in a desired physical response, and the insomniac can often only wait for sleep to come. The treatment of insomnia is presented as a procedure of discipline, yet many insomniacs can only wish getting sleep was this simple.

Discipline is a means of corralling the will or the body in order to have it meet (typically) external demands. For Foucault, the function of discipline is to 'increase the docility and utility of all the elements of [people within] the system'.[20] Tietjens, however, feels uncomfortable having his body disciplined and disciplining the bodies of other soldiers: 'It was detestable to him to be in control of the person of another human being – as detestable as it would have been to be himself a prisoner . . . that thing he dreaded most in the world' (*A Man Could Stand Up –*, p. 153). His attitude in this passage suggests that discipline is something against which he would rebel, and, ultimately, he does, if not intentionally. Tietjens is a master of controlling his mental faculties. In order to avoid thinking about the death of O Nine Morgan, for example, he forces himself to write a sonnet while holding conversations and fulfilling his military duties (*No More Parades*, p. 44). Yet even he cannot always control his thoughts and his mental habits overtake him. When confronting the imminent move to the Front, he can no longer control his mind: 'He wished his mind would not go on and on figuring. It did it whilst you weren't looking. As a well-trained dog will do when you tell it to stay in one part of a room and it prefers another. It prefers to do figuring' (*A Man Could Stand Up –*, p. 73). Tietjens is in a paradoxical situation. He has trained his mind so well to do calculations that his own training has surpassed his control. He inadvertently reveals the potential failure of habit as a means of asserting self-control. Just as sometimes the desire to sleep is exactly what prevents sleep from coming, an over-reliance on habit as a means of self-control can cause the forfeiture of control over the self.

A further correlation exists between the liminality of insomnia and the liminality of war experience, as is shown in Ford's and Sassoon's novels. Many affected by the war were often in some version of a liminal state, on a constant and excruciating threshold between life and death or hope and fear. In the trenches, this liminality occurred in the time spent awaiting impending attack or action, yet not engaging in outright battle, as well as the state between the relative safety of time off duty and the imminent danger of combat. As the insomniac waits for sleep, not knowing when it will come, the soldier waits for an impending, yet often surprising, onslaught. In *A Man Could Stand Up –*, Ford describes 'the process of eternal waiting that is War':

> You hung about and you hung about, and you kicked your heels and you kicked your heels: waiting for Mills bombs to come, or for jam, or for generals, or for the tanks, or transport, or the clearance of the road ahead. You waited in offices under the eyes of somnolent orderlies, under fire on the banks of canals, you waited in hotels, dug-outs, tin sheds, ruined houses. There will be no man who survives His Majesty's Armed Forces that shall not remember those eternal hours when Time itself stayed still as the true image of bloody War! (pp. 92–3)

The sense of frozen time spent waiting for the action of war is similar to the sense of infinite yet frozen time the insomniac spends waiting for sleep. Civilians experienced the tensions of waiting as well: they existed in a state between hope for their loved ones' safe return and fear that their loved ones were dead or injured. This state, extended over time, created a great deal of anxiety, which, as Trudi Tate argues, for some civilians became neurosis, similar to the shell shock experienced by soldiers, a condition, which, though first refuted by doctors as impossible, finally came to be accepted by the public and medical establishments.[21]

Additional to liminality of the external circumstance of war, in *Parade's End* and *Memoirs*, the characters lived in liminality of personal circumstance. Tietjens' marriage to Sylvia is liminal: they are in a state of legal marriage, but emotional and physical separation. This liminality extends to Tietjens' relationship with Valentine Wannop: in *Some Do Not . . .* he hesitates to pursue her while he is married, but feels bound to her nonetheless. Notably, he first becomes interested in her after they have been up all night together, helping her friend escape.[22] The scene of their carriage ride superimposes the liminality of their relationship on the liminality of their shared experience of insomnia. They are both physically lost in fog, often unsure of their proximity to each other, and psychologically placed in uncertain social and personal relations.

Similarly, Sherston has a liminal social position too, as he hovers in a state between desire to do his patriotic duty and an eventual refusal to accept the validity of the war. As a result, he is between sanity/delinquency and insanity/unaccountability. He escapes punishment for his resistance to the war only through renouncing his ability to understand the nature of his own resistance and allowing himself to be hospitalised. Remaining between two states reveals the tension of Sherston's opposition, as well as resistance, to categorisation. Consequently, both characters, as well as others connected to them, experience a great deal of stress, which manifests as the insomnia they and many other characters suffer. They experience this insomnia in moments when they must confront their liminality; Tietjens with regard to his marriage and Sherston with regard to his duties. Insomnia, then, is both liminal and reflects the liminal. It is created by the liminality of their circumstances, yet expresses itself through its liminality.

Tietjens also exists in a state of liminality between two eras. He is often referred to as being of an earlier time, yet is devoted to the preservation of his society and family line for years to come. Ford identified Tietjens as a man 'whose body is tied in one place, but whose mind and personality brood eternally over another distant locality'.[23] This brooding is often a product of anxiety, from which Tietjens certainly suffers, but his anxiety is more related to, as Jeffrey McCarthy argues, 'instrumentalizing relations', or his innate opposition to 'the shaping of human will to the designs of technical administration'.[24] In moments of physical or emotional exhaustion, when experiencing visual illusions, Tietjens often sees 'a woman in eighteenth-century dress' (*No More Parades*, p. 155). When he senses a lack of control, his mind's reaction is to focus itself on a scene from which he takes comfort, a scene from an earlier era. When Tietjens is unable to sleep, it is primarily because he is concerned with interpersonal, not instrumental, relationships, such as those between himself and his wife or Valentine (*Some Do Not . . .*, pp. 101, 70). Modernity reduced the need for interpersonal relations, through factors such as increased bureaucracy, rationalisation of industry, mass production, and mechanised warfare. Tietjens, however, focuses his mental energy not on solving problems of productivity but on working out conflicts related to human relationships, illustrating his valorisation of antiquated values and resistance to present conditions of depersonalisation.

Insomnia caused by this anxiety of interpersonal relations occurs in *No More Parades* when Tietjens learns that he will see Sylvia again after he believes they have parted permanently. Significantly, her supposed parting takes place in the early morning hours when Tietjens cannot sleep, and he overhears her telling her driver to take her to Paddington Station (p. 39). Rather than sleeping after an exhausting day, Tietjens has 'appointed this moment of physical ease that usually followed on his splurging heavily down on to his creaking camp-bed in the doctor's tent hut, for the cool consideration of his relations with his wife' (p. 70). In this instance, Tietjens chooses insomnia, deciding to use his insomniac time as time to confront the liminal state of his marriage. However, his marital difficulties are not all that keep him awake. This scene takes place shortly after the death of O Nine Morgan, and visions of Morgan's end continue to occupy his mind, despite his efforts to think about something else.

As thoughts of Morgan overtake him, he begins to equate his exhaustion with mortality, illustrating the liminality of the soldier's experience of life with the perpetual threat of death:

> And at the thought of [Morgan] as he was alive and of him now, dead, an immense blackness descended all over Tietjens. He said to himself: *I am very tired*. Yet he was not ashamed. . . . It was the blackness that descends on you when you think of your dead. . . . It comes, at any time, over the brightness of sunlight, in the grey of evening, in the grey of the dawn, at mess, on parade [. . .]. Or at the thought of the dead that you have never seen dead at all. . . . Suddenly, the light goes out. . . . (p. 86)

Here, Tietjens is overtly contemplating death, the description of which parallels the onset of sleep with its descending blackness, but he is also thinking about the idiosyncrasy of his experience as a soldier, trying to live when death could arrive at any time, and the isolation lack of consciousness creates, whether through sleep or through death. Sherston draws the same parallel when he sees soldiers and 'was doubtful whether they were asleep or dead, for the attitudes of many were like death, grotesque and distorted' (p. 431). It is their isolation, their 'attitude' of being cut off from the rest of humanity that Sherston finds grotesque. He asks: 'The soldiers who slept around us in their hundreds – were they not like the dead, among whom in some dim region where time survived in ghostly remembrances [. . .]?' (p. 358). Insomnia mimics the condition of human mortality, with its revelation of the idiosyncrasy of the arrival of lack of consciousness and the isolating effects of this lack, thus phenomenologically reflects lived circumstance.

Sherston also suffers from anxiety of anticipation of death, making sleep difficult. After he returns from Army School, he learns of an impending raid on the enemy trenches and this news keeps him awake. He 'could think of nothing else. [His] month [of rest] at Flixécourt was already obliterated' and he 'wouldn't mind going up there and doing [the raid] now' (pp. 296–7). The liminality of his situation, being neither in imminent danger nor safe from it, prevents sleep. He would rather take action, though that action entails significant risk, than spend time waiting. He would prefer combat to the anxiety preceding it, resulting in insomnia.

Of course, just as soldiers were not the only ones to experience war trauma, they were not the only ones to have insomnia, illustrating Tate's argument about civilian shell shock. Civilian insomnia also expresses liminality in terms of the state between hope and fear engendered by loved ones' participation in the war. It reflects the sense of helplessness felt by the non-combatant population. Sylvia and Valentine both acknowledge being unable to sleep at night due to their concerns regarding Tietjens and the war itself. Valentine, for instance, exclaims: 'I can't sleep . . . Never . . . I haven't slept a whole night since . . . Think of the immense spaces, stretching out under the night . . .' (*Some Do Not . . .*, p. 285). And Sylvia says: 'I'm dog-tired. . . . I haven't slept for six nights. . . . In spite of drugs. . . .' (*No More Parades*, p. 184). Sylvia's insomnia relates to her lack of control over Tietjens, and she seeks to mute her thoughts through the use of sedatives. However, Valentine's insomnia is similar to Tietjens' in that one of its causes is the horror of war itself; she displays no concern for herself, and, while she is concerned for Tietjens' safety, she is more focused on the general suffering of all involved. She mentions 'immense spaces', echoing Tietjens' anxiety over the 'hugenesses of landscapes' he envisions as part of the war (*No More Parades*, p. 17). Valentine, like Tietjens, is willing to stay awake with her thoughts, using her insomnia as time for contemplation. Valentine's insomnia, in particular, further exposes the horror of the soldiers' position and her sense of helplessness, as well as her sense of Tietjens' similar helplessness.

If insomnia is, at least in part, a product of a sense of helplessness, then eliminating helplessness can arguably be its cure. Because of insomnia's liminality, I have argued thus far that insomnia echoes the anxiety created through the often liminal circumstances of the soldiers' experience. However, during the era of the First World War, this view was certainly not the prevalent one, and insomnia was often viewed as a failure on the part of the individual. Soldiers in particular were expected to be masters of both their bodies and their minds, exemplified by the medical community's general belief that, as Paul Lerner argues, 'traumatic events do not make healthy people sick, but rather sick people react pathologically to traumatic events'.[25] The soldier who has control over body and mind can handle any event, no matter how horrific, without adverse effects. As mentioned before, in the medical literature of the time, the ability to control oneself, regardless of circumstance, came through the cultivation of proper habits. For example, in the 1905 child-rearing book *The Care and Feeding of Children*, A. B. Barnard, much like James, asserts that once a behaviour or task is repeated regularly, the habit becomes second nature, allowing a form of automatism (ingrained discipline) to control the behaviour and will, which is especially important in the training of children.[26]

More significantly, however, Barnard equates good habits with 'morality and intellectual efficiency' and notes that 'the bad habit usually arises from the defect of some quality', a defect which must be 'cured'.[27] In his 1918 essay, Rankin refers to insomnia as 'the evil habit of broken sleep'.[28] Since sleep is a habitual behaviour, one who cannot control the habit can be perceived as having a moral or character flaw, thus becoming subject to normative measures. With regard to the process of normalisation, an informative parallel may be drawn here between the insomniac and the criminally delinquent. Foucault argues that in the case of the criminal, delinquency is seen as an attribute of the person rather than merely a consequence of the crime; thus, the individual, rather than the offence, becomes the subject of scrutiny.[29] Extended to insomnia, the case can be made that one is not an insomniac simply because one cannot sleep, but because some other attribute of one's personality causes one to become an insomniac, making the insomniac one, who, as Foucault says of the delinquent, 'is not only author of his own acts (the author responsible in terms of certain criteria of free, conscious will), but is linked to his offence by a whole bundle of complex threads (instincts, drives, tendencies, character)'.[30]

Interestingly, the term 'insomniac' did not appear in written medical discourse until 1908, an early instance of its emergence occurring in the medical journal *The Lancet*: '[An increase in urinary secretion] is, like the phenomenon of sleeplessness, most evident in the neurotic insomniac' (*OED*). The coining of a new diagnostic label for an individual has significant implications: the focal point of insomnia itself has shifted from an event or state happening to a person to a specific identity category. The inability to sleep is now regarded not as an external condition but as an internal trait; the label itself allows for a person to be defined in terms of his or her insomnia. Thus, through the act of labelling the 'insomniac', the individual is now implicated as cause of the insomnia. This semantic shift, in part, indicates a larger shift in medical discourse rooted in attributing 'unhealthiness' to some flaw of personality, character, or constitution, evident in both of the novels and medical literature of the time. This value given to disciplined behaviour, including sleep, fosters not only biographical inquiry into the allegedly undisciplined individual, but also into the family, a sentiment Tietjens expresses in *Last Post*: 'Mind doctors of to-day said that all cases of nervous breakdown occurred in persons whose parents had not led harmonious lives.'[31]

With regard the regulation of behaviour, Foucault argues that there are three primary means of control: 'establish rhythms, impose particular occupations, regulate the cycles of repetition'.[32] He points to the presence of such tactics in modern establishments such as armies, hospitals, and schools, all of which mirror the practices of religious institutions through emphasis on ritualised behaviour.[33] The goal of this regularity is to establish discipline, which, in essence, eliminates waste; time spent liminally (waiting for sleep, waiting for battle) is time wasted. To eliminate waste, or lack of productivity, the cause of the waste must first be defined and then it must be corrected. Thus, a function of discipline is to dispense with liminality, which can be detrimental to the maintenance of discipline. For instance, Sherston never questions the war until he is physically removed from and has the mental freedom to consider it, after which he exclaims to his friend: 'But I can't drop [this anti-war business]. [. . .] Don't you realize that I'm a man with a message?' (p. 510). While he is involved in the rigours of active duty, he performs his job admirably. When he is given time to rest (and think) while on leave, he questions the war. He may consider this time for thought extremely productive, as does Tietjens when he is able to pause to think about his marriage; however, neither character is being outwardly productive. The time spent on personal thought detracts from social productivity: Tietjens' ability to perform his duties and Sherston's determination to fight in the war; therefore, the time used is subject to corrective measures from outside authorities, which we see in the novels as Tietjens' friends attempting to help wake him up mentally after a sleepless night (*No More Parades*, p. 95) and Sherston's hospitalisation to avoid punishment as a detractor (pp. 513–14).

The emphasis in Foucault's passage on discipline is on training the body through repetition and regularity, of which physical exercise is an example. Foucault's argument parallels a passage in which Valentine considers her job as an athletic instructor. In *A Man Could Stand Up –*, Ford writes:

> The military physical developments of the last four years had been responsible for a real exaggeration of physical values. [Valentine] was aware that in that Institution [the girls' school], for the last four years, she had been regarded as supplementing, if not as actually replacing both the doctor and the priest. (p. 50)

In this case, Valentine acts as the disciplinarian. She is responsible for replicating the discipline associated with Foucault's previously cited authoritative establishments. Additionally, Valentine understands physical discipline in relation to its ability to disrupt or prevent thought, but also to guard against socially inappropriate behaviour. For example, when thinking of the possibility of an affair with Tietjens, she considers the notion that her 'hard condition' had not 'moved' him to get her 'into trouble before going to be killed' (*Some Do Not . . .*, p. 330).

The essential argument being made by the medical establishment and disciplinary entities is that lack of discipline, at least partially manifested in the insomniac, points to immorality and weakness of character. Daniel Pick illustrates this sentiment, as he notes that 'the wider presumption that mental illness was an index to the moral state of the nation – as though the sum of individual physical and psychological conditions formed a collective mind and body'.[34] In theory, discipline leads to a stronger and more moral citizen and country. However, the novels reveal the problematic nature of this argument. For instance, in *A Man Could Stand Up –*, Ford discusses the function of discipline in war:

> It was a very great achievement to have got men to fire at moments of such stress with such complete tranquility. For discipline works in two ways: in the first place it enables the soldier in action to get through his movements in the shortest possible time; and then the engrossment in the exact performance begets a great indifference to danger. (p. 108)

Here, discipline is not only presented as control over one's thoughts, but controlling them through the ceding of one's thoughts to training. Discipline eliminates liminality and waste: the disciplined soldier will not stop to consider his actions – or his safety. However, while it can make one a better soldier, it does not necessarily make one a stronger individual. Despite its discursive presentation as a marker of individual strength and morality, discipline is not only self-control taken to an excess; it is the willing relinquishment of that control to a series of prescribed motions and behaviours and the relinquishment of the body to the consequence of those actions.

Sherston gives another example of the ramifications of the internalisation of discipline:

> a tentative patch of brightness revealed somebody half hidden under a blanket. Not a very clever spot to be taking a nap, I thought as I stooped to shake him by the shoulder. He refused to wake up, so I gave him a kick. [. . .] My nerves were on edge; and what right had he to be having a good sleep, when I never seemed to get five minutes' rest? [. . .] Then my beam settled on the livid face of a dead German whose fingers still clutched the blackened gash on his neck [. . .]. Stumbling on, I could only mutter to myself that this was really a bit too thick. (That, however, was an exaggeration; there is nothing remarkable about a dead body in a European war, or a squashed beetle in a cellar.) (p. 437)

Later, commenting on his exhaustion, Sherston describes viewing the world with 'the haggard clarity of insomnia' (p. 508). This clarity enables him to see the effects of war as the creation of a state of mind allowing one to equate a dead human with a 'squashed beetle' (one whose sleep he is jealous of). He attempts to humanise the dead soldier, noting the obvious fear with which the German died, but his discipline prevents him from dwelling on the horror for too long. The dark irony of the tone of this passage foreshadows his later refusal to return to fighting – he knows what he should think, but he cannot quite accept it as right. Consequently, this passage reveals an inadvertent effect of a level of discipline that desensitised people to each other's humanity, a victory for discipline, but not necessarily one for human interaction.

Ultimately, the insomniac is one whose mind and body, while they remain in the liminal state of insomnia, resist discipline, whether by choice, circumstance or countless other factors. Insomnia becomes a point of both exposure and resistance to social intervention into personal autonomy. Discursively, discipline is presented as self-control, but the novels reveal discipline as the relinquishment of control over the self. Discipline only constitutes self-control inasmuch as it entails one's ability to give up that control for what one perceives to be the greater good, whether that consists of doing one's duty as a soldier or being a productive member of the workforce. Further, while discipline is equated with morality, that same discipline creates dehumanisation, as in the case of a soldier who can look at a dead human being as no more significant than a squashed beetle. That the condition of insomnia exists proves that the mind cannot be fully in control of the body all of the time, nor can the individual be fully in control of the mind. Insomnia allows time for thought, yet ultimately points to our inability to harness those thoughts, mirroring the regulations and hierarchy of the military imperfectly imposed on the chaos of battle. In attempting to instil discipline, thereby both controlling thought and maximising productivity, disciplinary mechanisms reveal their frustration with liminal space, a space not readily categorised or colonised.

Notes

1. Ford, *A Man Could Stand Up –*, ed. Sara Haslam, p. 107. All further references are to this edition.
2. Sassoon, *Memoirs of an Infantry Officer*, p. 359. All further references are to this edition.
3. Foucault, *Discipline and Punish*, p. 26.
4. Rabinbach, *The Human Motor*, p. 260.
5. Ibid. p. 259.
6. Ibid. p. 260.
7. Schwenger, *At the Borders of Sleep*, p. 51.
8. Ibid. p. 48.
9. Bordo, *Unbearable Weight*, p. 141.
10. Showalter, *The Female Malady*, p. 171.
11. Woolf, *Mrs Dalloway*, pp. 94–5.
12. Schwenger, *At the Borders of Sleep*, p. ix.
13. Ibid. p. ix.
14. Summers-Bremner, *Insomnia: A Cultural History*, p. 121.
15. Ford, *No More Parades*, ed. Joseph Wiesenfarth, p. 69. All further references are to this edition.
16. James, *Habit*, p. 40.
17. Rankin, 'Broken Sleep', pp. 77–8.
18. MacFarlane, *Insomnia and Its Therapeutics*, p. 40.
19. Mitchell, *Fat and Blood*, p. 59.
20. Foucault, *Discipline and Punish*, p. 218.
21. Tate, *Modernism, History, and the First World War*, p. 11.
22. Ford, *Some Do Not ...*, ed. Max Saunders, pp. 164–75. All further references are to this edition.
23. Ford, *It Was the Nightingale*, p. 197.
24. McCarthy, '"The Foul System"', pp. 178–9.
25. Lerner, 'Psychiatry and Casualties of War in Germany, 1914–18', p. 15.
26. Barnard, 'Habit', p. 99.
27. Ibid. pp. 99–100.
28. Rankin, 'Broken Sleep', p. 78.
29. Foucault, *Discipline and Punish*, p. 252.
30. Ibid. pp. 252–3.
31. Ford, *Last Post*, ed. Paul Skinner, p. 156.
32. Foucault, *Discipline and Punish*, p. 149.
33. Ibid. p. 149.
34. Pick, *War Machine*, p. 243.

Representing Shell Shock:
A Return to Ford and Rebecca West

Charlotte Jones

In 1922, as the spectacularly equivocal report by the War Office Committee of Enquiry into 'Shell-Shock' was published, 65,000 ex-soldiers were either hospitalised or drawing disability pensions for war neurosis.[1] Estimates for the total number of First World War soldiers who suffered from shell shock severely enough to require a discharge from the army range from 80,000 to 200,000.[2] Of course these are just the official statistics; as Richard Aldington later said: '[w]e talk of shell-shock, but who wasn't shell-shocked, more or less?'[3] Most soldiers, and many non-combatants, were affected by the sights and sounds of total war, and shell shock was only one manifestation of the harrowing impact of mechanical warfare on the mind.

One of those 'more or less' shell-shocked by the war was Ford Madox Ford. He was sent to France in July 1916, after joining the army the previous year, and was 'blown into the air' by a shell near Bécourt Wood which resulted in a concussion and amnesia so severe he temporarily forgot even his own name.[4] Although he was released from the Casualty Clearing Station at Corbie just thirty-six hours later, Ford would later claim that: 'I had completely lost my memory so that [. . .] three weeks of my life are completely dead to me.'[5] He suffered from what he called his 'nerve tangle'[6] or 'Corbie-phobia'[7] until 1923, the year he began writing *Parade's End*. Its influence on the tetralogy is clear: Tietjens' shell shock, manifesting itself like Ford's as amnesia, is a crucial structural aspect of the book's panoramic survey of war and Edwardian society, as well as its literary modernism.

Yet just as *Parade's End* is in many ways born of its author's direct experience, it seems also to be in dialogue with another earlier exploration of shell shock, Rebecca West's *The Return of the Soldier*. In a letter to Sylvia Lynd in 1918, soon after her novella was published, West recounts how:

> I had a weekend with Violet [Hunt] and Ford during which Ford explained to me elaborately the imperfection of *The Return of the Soldier* compared to any of his works – a statement with which I profoundly agree but which oughtn't to be made, because it rouses emulation.[8]

What this 'imperfection' was – and whether it was of a literary or factual nature – isn't known, but 'emulation' is an interesting concept here. West, of course, is referring to her own admiration of Ford, who, at this early stage of her career, despite her runaway success on Fleet Street, she still saw as something of a mentor. But the notion of 'emulation' undergoes a curious inversion when the obvious similarities between her novella and the later *Parade's End* are examined. Both feature soldiers returning from the war suffering from amnesia. Both dwell on the latent aggression underlying sexual relationships (indeed one suspects these points may not be unrelated; as Celia Malone Kingsbury observes: 'both memory losses are appropriate to the characters' circumstances', namely unhappy, repressive marriages).[9] Both are set in an upper-class conservative milieu whose traditional values are encapsulated by ancestral estates: Baldry Court and Groby. And, perhaps most tellingly of all, both protagonists share the same name: Christopher. Seamus O'Malley has posited reading *Parade's End* as in many ways an emulation of *The Return of the Soldier*, arguing 'not only was Ford directly influenced by *The Return of the Soldier*, but that we can read *Parade's End* as a more complex and ultimately more optimistic rewriting of West's novel'.[10]

To read *The Return of the Soldier* and *Parade's End* alongside one another in this way is to trace, amongst other things, the literary aetiology of shell shock over the immediate post-war period. Published between 1918 and 1928, although West maintains that her novel was 'complete in my mind in the middle of 1915',[11] their representation of shell shock both reflects and in many ways contributes to society's nascent understanding of the condition. It is important to note, therefore, that as well as referencing one another, both West and Ford engage with other paradigms increasingly shaping society's response to shell shock at the same time: medical definitions, military classifications and emergent psychoanalytic models of memory, trauma, and repression. I want to argue that in working through the returns of their respective soldiers, Ford and West are 'rewriting' these contemporary narratives of shell shock in their attempts to imagine and represent the reintegration of the mind after war.

Representing 'Shell Shock'

A previously unprecedented phenomenon, shell shock quickly captured the public's attention as the First World War raged on; as Ted Bogacz notes, by 'mid-1916, the shell-shocked soldier had become a virtual cliché in the English press'.[12] Yet at the same time there was no coherent or unanimous understanding of what the condition actually was; no two experiences were the same and symptoms could range from fatigue, depression, paralysis, deaf-mutism, temporary blindness, recurring nightmares, convulsions or trembling of the limbs, amnesia, dissociation and many more, in any combination. Shell shock was in fact only recognised as a single condition, as Peter Leese has argued, through a 'narrative of diagnosis, treatment and representation'.[13]

It is impossible to survey comprehensively the myriad contemporary medical, military, and popular responses in this chapter, but one crucial thing to note for my purposes is the role played by the phrase 'shell shock' ('shell-shock' in some publications) in these problems of definition. Introduced by Charles Myers in 1915 in *The Lancet*, and immediately seizing the public imagination, 'shell shock' implied, as fellow practitioner John MacCurdy criticised, 'a single etiology' [*sic*] – 'the physical effects of high explosive shells'.[14] In 1940, Myers recalled that '[l]ater familiarity with the disorder, however, showed that the emotional disturbance alone was a sufficient cause', and 'shell shock' quickly came to seem both inaccurate and misleading.[15] A multitude of alternative terms were subsequently deployed – 'traumatic neurosis', 'war neuroses', 'battle fatigue', 'war shock' – but none were used consistently by medical practitioners and 'shell shock' persisted in popular publications.

In 1915 the British Army attempted to clarify the taxonomical situation by imposing a traditional military distinction between casualty and coward. A soldier whose breakdown was directly triggered by a shell explosion was labelled 'Shell-shock, W' (for wound), while those whose breakdown was deemed not 'due to the enemy' were 'Shell-shock, S' (for sickness) and did not receive either a wound stripe or pension.[16] The battle for official definition between 'wounded' and 'sick' encapsulates the struggle to categorise shell shock, where linguistic instability reflects the condition's indeterminate somatic status, and as Ben Shephard notes: 'The effect of this policy was to exacerbate an already confused situation.'[17] Aside from the heavily freighted value-judgements underlying 'wounded' and 'sick', the qualifier 'due to the enemy' was almost impossible to interpret. There are records of scenarios in which men who broke down during or just after an attack or bombardment were labelled 'W', while those who attempted to continue before succumbing were labelled 'S', on the assumption that they had survived unscathed and then 'funked'.[18]

By 1917 a British soldier 'who without visible wound become[s] non-effective' was given the blanket label 'Not Yet Diagnosed, Nervous', a phrase whose hesitancy condenses into four words the inadequacy of available medical terminology.[19] The diagnosis became simultaneously a deferral of diagnosis: the soldier has been diagnosed as 'nervous', but at the same time has 'not yet' been diagnosed at all. Shell shock's elusiveness, coupled with its public persistence, clearly reflects the profoundly disturbing questions it was posing to the medical and military communities. Are the mental effects of war the same as the physical? Can they be described using the same language? Can they be cured in the same way?

It is in this context of epistemological uncertainty that *The Return of the Soldier* was published. Chris Baldry's return home is dominated by ambiguity as to what exactly he is suffering from, yet the other characters' ability to welcome him back hinges upon their attempts at definition. The narrator, Chris's cousin Jenny, insistently physicalises his condition, describing him as 'disabled', 'slightly bent, as though he had been maimed', and sitting 'like a blind man'.[20] Chris's wife, Kitty, similarly deploys standard military terminology in an attempt to absorb his illness to a pre-existing medical category: to her, he is 'wounded' (p. 11), simply suffering from 'concussion' (p. 12). His trauma is only valid if it produces physical effects or can be rendered in physical terms.

Chris's childhood sweetheart Margaret – the woman who delivers news of Chris's condition to Baldry Court and with whom he believes, in his amnesiac state, that he is in love – offers a different interpretation. As the text's 'intuitive therapist', in the words of Steve Pinkerton, Margaret's narrative is juxtaposed to medical establishment discourse.[21] Her repetition of Kitty's phrase, 'Yes [. . .] he's wounded' (p. 11), pointedly changes the significance of the word: she redefines what it is to be wounded by incorporating an emotional nuance – 'he's hurt' (p. 11) – creating an alternative diagnostic category which combines the concussion of the 'shell burst' (p. 12) blamed for Chris's amnesia with a sense of the less tangible strain of combat. The war of words eventually culminates in 'shell-shock' (p. 12), though Margaret's immediate qualification, 'Anyway, he's not well' (p. 12), refuses to submit completely to the phrase. Chris never speaks about the condition for himself, and throughout the story West implies that something intrinsic to shell shock resists articulation and representation: it defeats existing linguistic frameworks. Just as the war overwhelms Chris's mind, his shell shock exceeds the interpretative abilities of the other characters.

Debates about the nature of shell shock reached their most heated in publications such as *The Lancet* between 1917 and 1923. After the war ended, and as the War Office Committee of Enquiry failed to establish an absolute method of diagnosis or treatment, the emphasis shifted to reintegration and recovery. Concomitantly, Ford's concern in *Parade's End* is to place shell shock in the context of the wider mental effects of war, rather than define it, and extrapolate its significance for the post-war era. In *Parade's End*, medical attitudes to shell shock are framed as a subset of an official Army establishment discourse which prioritises 'national efficiency' over individual well-being. Men are referred to in *Some Do Not . . .* as 'figures of millions of pairs of boots', ideological counters whose existence in reality ceases to matter except as figures to be manipulated at the Imperial Department of Statistics.[22] Individual experience is lost in the reductive language of sheer quantity. The military classification of traumatised men as 'S', 'W' or 'NYDN' is then simply another aspect of this language of objectification and dehumanisation, the culmination of a discourse espoused by men such as Sir William Bradshaw in Virginia Woolf's *Mrs Dalloway* (1925) with his reverence for 'Proportion, divine proportion'.[23]

The tension Ford identifies underlying Bradshaw's notion of 'proportion' is whether efficiency prioritises the mass or the individual: 'men. Not just populations. Men you worried over there', as Tietjens says in *No More Parades*.[24] The trauma of the individual, the microcosmic, is what Sylvia cannot understand when she condemns male 'hypocrisy', accepting 'the deaths of men in inconceivable holocausts of pain and terror. Then they had crises of agony over the death of one single man' (p. 178). Yet to Tietjens, the individual is not 'one single' entity; as he observes in *A Man Could Stand Up –*: 'To a sensitive officer [. . .] the psychology of the men makes itself felt in innumerable ways.'[25] For Ford, whose own role in the army was more bureaucratic than frontline, witnessing the 'innumerable' dimensions of individual suffering is as much a part of war's impact on the mind as the shock of combat. As Tietjens explains to Valentine when justifying his decision to leave the Imperial Department of Statistics for the infantry in *Some Do Not . . .*: 'these things are official [. . .]. You see it means such infinite deaths of men, such an infinite prolongation . . . [. . .] helping them means unnumbered deaths' (p. 288). 'Innumerable', 'infinite' and 'unnumbered' are all numbers beyond proportion, the ultimate failure of proportion; they are numbers that literally undo numbering. The suffering of the First World War is not quantifiable and cannot fit into this linguistic framework.

Ford addressed the topic more explicitly still in 'Epilogue', an unpublished essay written at the end of the war:

We *don't know how many men have been killed* . . . . . . [. . .] one saw, on the one hand, such an infinite number of our own male dead, or, on the other, such an infinite number of dead – and frequently mouldering – Huns [. . .] the operations of counted millions of men moving million against million – you think again of Armageddon. And the War seems of infinite importance.[26]

In its repetition, 'million' becomes meaningless, revealing the paradox of 'counted millions': the millions of dead cannot be 'counted' because they 'don't know' how many have been killed since 1914. The 'infinite number' of dead is seemingly justified by the 'infinite importance' of the war, but Ford's repetition is cruelly ironic. Looking back on such infinite agony, it is not just the shell-shocked soldier that evidences the mind's inability to process the war; the whole situation appears utterly unintelligible. Max Saunders has demonstrated the crucial role of writing in Ford's own recovery, explaining that the panoramic dimensions of *Parade's End* could help him to '[reconstruct] a sense of perspective and proportion'.[27] But the alignment is perhaps not as stable as it first appears; here, one term excludes the other: *Parade's End*'s sense of historical perspective exposes the senseless lack of proportion the war entailed. If madness is, as Sir William Bradshaw asserts, losing a 'sense of proportion' (p. 109), then, Ford asks, who is really mad?

The 'Barrier in the Brain': Visualising Trauma

The problem Ford encountered with the notion of 'infinite' is that, just like 'shell-shock' for West, it falls beyond normal modes of thought and as such becomes almost impossible to represent. The war affects therefore not only the mind of the soldier, but also that of the writer. In an unpublished essay, 'Arms and the Mind', written in September 1916 soon after his own memory loss and signed ironically 'Miles Ignotus' (the unknown soldier), Ford states that his aim as a writer is to 'visualize things'.[28] 'Visualize' here stands both for Ford's own ability to imagine, but also the ability to convey a scene, emotion or experience to a reader. Since the war, he explains, he is conscious of 'an invisible barrier in my brain [which] seems to lie between the profession of Arms and the mind that puts things into words'.[29]

To a certain extent, this 'barrier in the brain' can be seen as a defensive mechanism: being unable to put things into words avoids the visualisation, if not the recollection, of traumatic memories. For Tietjens, this becomes a conscious strategy. Confronted by a wounded soldier in *No More Parades*, Tietjens describes him as having: 'draped half his face and the right side of his breast with crape' (p. 28). This substitution of material for blood evades the horror of the scene, abstracting and displacing it as the metaphor inserts a layer of distance between Tietjens and the wound. The scene is further abstracted several sentences later when Tietjens describes how: 'In the bright light it was as if a whole pint of scarlet paint had been dashed across the man's face on the left and his chest. It glistened in the firelight – just like fresh paint, moving!' (p. 28). The incident culminates with a description of another soldier 'pinned down' by this body 'resembling one girl that should be combing the hair of another recumbent before her' (p. 28), which Sara Haslam convincingly argues recalls Degas's painting 'A Maid Combing a Woman's Hair' (1883).[30]

Haslam characterises Tietjens' response as a division between the abstract and the concrete, where mental detachment is the result of his inability to confront the physical reality of the scene (which may explain why at this stage the soldier remains anonymous; he is not O Nine Morgan in the particular, just a generic wounded man). If Ford's difficulty visualising things is not the product of a failure of words or imagination, but an inability to conjoin the two – to 'put things into words' – the solution here, as Haslam observes, is not to put them into words at all but to endlessly displace them. The incident operates through allusion, rather than direct description, which falls short of visualisation even as it facilitates it. Tietjens represents the scene to himself, rather than experiencing it. This reliance on reference and citation, however, moves the scene beyond abstraction and towards aestheticisation. Ford constantly shifts the terms of representation, moving from clothing to paint to a painting; the final allusion to Degas avoids naming (and visually conjuring) Morgan's blood, not only distancing the scene but simultaneously transforming it into art. Tietjens elevates it to a plane of contemplation above the trenches, not just passively avoiding the experience but actively reconfiguring it. Representation turns defence into creation.

Representation becomes a crucial mediatory function not only for coping with immediate trauma, such as the death of O Nine Morgan, but also as a way of protecting the self from the constant fear and anxiety of the trenches. In *A Man Could Stand Up –*, Tietjens becomes obsessed with a 'particular splash of purposeless whitewash':

> Tietjens had stood extremely wishing that his head were level with a particular splash of purposeless whitewash. Something behind his mind forced him to the conviction that, if his head – and of course the rest of his trunk and lower limbs – were suspended by a process of levitation to that distance above the duckboard on which, now, his feet were, he would be in an inviolable sphere. (p. 59)

The whitewash is transformed from a banal 'splash' into an 'inviolable sphere'; by an overdetermination of significance it becomes a symbol of safety, an attempt to imagine a space where a man can stand up above the sanctuary of the trenches and yet be invulnerable. The 'inviolable' is a recurring idea in Ford's work: *No Enemy* (1929), for example, is preoccupied with Gringoire's 'vision of the inviolable corner of the earth'.[31] He is obsessed with finding a 'nook' or 'sanctuary' (p. 33) to provide a refuge from the horrors of war. In its particularly spatial sense of impregnability, however, Ford's 'inviolable sphere' bears a striking resemblance to Freud's 'stimulus shield', formulated in his own war text *Beyond the Pleasure Principle*, which was translated into English the year before Ford began *Parade's End*. To Freud, consciousness is a:

> fragment of living substance [...] suspended in the middle of an external world charged with the most powerful energies; and it would be killed by the stimulation emanating from these if it were not provided with a protective shield against stimuli. It acquires the shield in this way: its outermost surface ceases to have the structure proper to living matter, becomes to some degree inorganic and thenceforward functions as a special envelope or membrane resistant to stimuli.[32]

The stimulus shield encases the 'suspended' consciousness, protecting lower layers by filtering and resisting stimuli, just as Tietjens is 'suspended by a process of levitation' and enclosed within his sphere. The crucial difference between the two, however, is that whereas in Freud's physiological metaphor the shield is internal, a mutation of the outermost layer of consciousness, Ford's sphere is projected outwards: it is a figure of the mind which is imagined to encompass the body. It is of course a specious kind of mental security, irrationally emanating from 'behind [Tietjens'] mind' and representing a hiatus – a 'suspension' – of fear, but at the same time it does radically redefine the self's relation to the outside world. When Tietjens is blown up he associates it with being 'suspended in space. As if he were suspended as he had wanted to be in front of that cockscomb in whitewash. Coincidence!' (*A Man Could Stand Up –*, p. 174). The association is less a coincidence than a retrospective use of the whitewash by Tietjens as a way to interpret and assimilate the experience of being blown up; it provides an alternative framework in which he can confront reality. The whitewash functions as a self-reflexive way for Tietjens to represent the self as inviolable, which creatively re-interprets his bodily vulnerability and makes it bearable. The barrier in the brain becomes a barrier around the brain.

The Return of the Soldiers

Tietjens' shell-shocked representational strategy is a practical and intuitive response of the mind to war when at war. Yet what is of equal concern to both West and Ford is what happens when the mind must adjust to a context other than war: how does the mind react when the soldier returns home? As a manifestation of trauma, amnesia epitomises the difficulties inherent in writing about the First World War. Paul Fussell has stated that 'the Great War was perhaps the last to be conceived as taking place within a seamless, purposeful "history" involving a coherent stream of time running from past through present to future', and amnesia literalises this disjointed relation between pre- and post-war.[33] The temporal dislocation of these texts – *The Return of the Soldier* indistinguishably overlays Chris's adolescent past onto his present and *Parade's End* proceeds according to a disorienting achronological timeline – is a corollary to the protagonists' shell shock; memory as a linear narrative is literally disrupted by the gaps of the traumatised subject.

In *Shell Shock and the Modernist Imagination*, Wyatt Bonikowski reads both texts against Freud's concept of the death drive to consider the traumatic dimension of the relationship between the returning soldier and the women who receive him. 'Bringing war home', however, does not for Bonikowski constitute a space of healing, and amnesia instead represents a 'fantasy of a return to wholeness' which hides the irreconcilable divisions between self and home.[34] The fragmentation of both history and the self signalled by amnesia also has implications for narrative form. Rob Hawkes argues for reading this structural relation between amnesia and narrative in *Parade's End* and *The Return of the Soldier* as 'only the most overt of the innumerable ways in which war destabilises and undermines the prospect of recovering a coherent narrative sequence that might reconnect pre-war, war, and post-war'.[35] Time is 'suspended' during war, and the return of the soldier inherently challenges the very notion of narrative. The multiple meanings of 'return', therefore, are crucial to understanding the different visions of shell shock and recovery that Ford and West offer.

In *The Return of the Soldier*, Monkey Island is Chris's version of a 'nook', a state of temporal suspension resulting from his amnesia which enables him to reject Baldry Court and the social values it signifies, and create instead an alternative utopian world embodied by the allegorical figure of his childhood, Margaret. Monkey Island is extra-temporal and extra-spatial, 'a magic state' (p. 49) primarily existing in the realm of the mind rather than external reality. His return to the past is a retreat into the mind as a sanctuary from the traumas of the present; Monkey Island represents a mode of existence rather than a setting, and within its 'magic circle' (p. 70) Chris and Margaret appear to Jenny 'englobed in peace as in a crystal sphere' (p. 70), almost as though they have withdrawn to their own 'inviolable sphere'. Like Tietjens, Chris abstracts experience, representing a version of reality to himself in a way which reinvents not only the world around him, but also himself. He wakes up believing he is fifteen years younger, unmarried and in love with Margaret.

Chris's repressive response to trauma in *The Return of the Soldier* is clearly in dialogue with psychoanalysis. Despite West's claim that 'my novel has fundamentally nothing to do with psychoanalysis', citing it as 'an unimportant device', the discipline has long been recognised as an important frame of reference for the novella.[36] Yet while Steve Pinkerton claims that it 'stands as a remarkably prescient testament [. . .] to ongoing Freudian theorisations of trauma', it is perhaps more accurate to read West's story as contemporaneous to, rather than prescient of, psychoanalytic theories of trauma.[37] Freud's 1914 essay 'Remembering, Repeating and Working-Through' is a crucial early draft of ideas which would be explicated more fully in *Beyond the Pleasure Principle* and is the first Freudian text to fully define the relation of repetition to memory and trauma by introducing the concept of 'working-through'.[38] Here Freud proposes three paradigms of memory: remembering, which constitutes a linear chronology of experience with a distant and separate past; 'the compulsion to repeat, which now replaces the impulsion to remember'[39] and in its insistent return to the trauma signals repression; and 'working-through', which is the movement from repetition to memory which enables recovery. These ideas very quickly became common currency in contemporary discussions of shell shock: a psychoanalytic register was regularly employed even by those opposed to Freud's ideas and West could hardly have been unaware of the concepts.[40] Chris's return to an idyllic adolescent relationship with Margaret is clearly to be read as a function of his resistance to reality; their affair becomes, in Freud's words, 'a transference of the forgotten past'.[41] Chris creates a narrative of temporal conflation, living in a pre-war, prelapsarian state that cannot be remembered as past and gone, but must instead be repeated insistently. Margaret and Monkey Island are thus re-figured as an unhealthy impulse to deny experience – both the war and his restrictive bourgeois family life – which must be confronted in order for the trauma to be 'worked through'.

In another act of transference, albeit an authorial one, the gaps in Chris's narrative are filled by Jenny, the archetypal intrusive and unreliable narrator. As a result of his amnesia, Chris never describes his feelings or experiences, yet perhaps even more disturbingly Jenny denies Chris the right to his own imaginative or recollective visualisations of war. She not only usurps the narrative voice and Chris's ability to relate his experiences, she also usurps the experiences themselves. All visions of war in *The Return of the Soldier* emanate from Jenny: her mind is the only one through which the 'dreary place of death and dirt' (p. 7) is visualised, like set pieces seen 'on the war-films' (p. 5). The talking cure becomes an act of ventriloquism. Unlike Tietjens, Chris does not represent events *to* himself. Tietjens' abstraction is predicated on reimagining himself in relation to the things he is experiencing so that both are transformed simultaneously. Chris, however, erases both his experiences and the reality of Baldry Court so that his fantasy of the self as whole is abstracted from context; he cannot conceive his existence in relation to war, and as a result he cannot re-conceive himself after it.

This decontextualisation reflects upon both dimensions of Chris's return: his return to the past, and his return as a soldier. As has often been remarked, the origin of Chris's trauma remains elusive and unarticulated throughout the novella,[42] but less remarked upon is the elusiveness of the ending. The obvious and oft-noted ironies of Chris's 'cure' aside, his return to the Front apparently signals, if not his return to sanity, at least his return to reality. Yet as much else in the text, this is only gestured at; the final apocalyptic imagery of Baldry Court covered by a 'sky more full of flying death than clouds' from which 'bullets fall like rain' (p. 90) seems unambiguous, but Jenny's focalisation (these images are hers) renders this far from objectively stable. In destabilising the ending of her novella, West emphasises that the 'cure' is not just about identifying the origin of trauma; how can you be cured if you can't visualise a future? Her disclaimer about psychoanalysis does not reject the discipline per se, but rather the 'psycho-analytical novel – that is a novel cut to a pattern and not spontaneously created'.[43] Her concern was to avoid the psychoanalytic 'pattern', a simplistic linear trajectory which projected that a return to the cause will necessarily produce a cure. Chris's return to the Front applies pressure to this paradigm. It is simply the repetition of an act undertaken four years ago; in going to war Chris is reproducing the trauma, as Freud explains: 'not as a memory but as an action' (p. 150). It is impossible in *The Return of the Soldier* to imagine a future. Where could a soldier go in early 1918 except back to the Front? The link between past, present, and future cannot be forged because at this historical juncture one part of the triptych is absent.

If *Parade's End* is to be read, as Seamus O'Malley suggests, as an 'optimistic' rewriting of *The Return of the Soldier*, the change in context is crucial, and Tietjens' burial by a shell blast in *A Man Could Stand Up –* becomes the fundamental pivot of the tetralogy. In *The Return of the Soldier*, as Chris returns to Baldry Court, and by extension the Front, he is transformed into an automaton; he walks 'with the soldier's hard tread upon the heel' and 'wore a dreadful decent smile' (p. 90), an image which brings to mind Wilfred Owen's 'Mental Cases' whose 'heads wear this hilarious, hideous, / Awful falseness of set-smiling corpses'.[44] In 1918 the returning soldier is a walking corpse. Tietjens' return, by way of contrast, is symbolically a moment of rebirth, a suspension between life and death succeeding the funeral alluded to at the end of *No More Parades* and preceding the Armistice Day 'wedding' which will end *A Man Could Stand Up –*. The language of the scene mimics that of birth in its emphasis on an organic imagery of fluids: 'The earth sucked slowly and composedly at his feet. It assimilated his calves, his thighs. [. . .] Tietjens tried to kick with his feet. Then he realised it was better not to kick with his feet. He was pulled out' (*A Man Could Stand Up –*, p. 175). As Santanu Das notes: 'This is one of the few moments in First World War writings when the mud is figured in its regenerative, womb-like function.'[45] Representation becomes reinvention; the metaphor of rebirth represents a creative reconception of the self. The returning soldier cannot connect the pre-war to the post-war self; there is no 'coherent stream of time' uniting the two. Yet while Chris regresses, Ford imagines Tietjens as reborn, literally, out of the experiences of the trenches, ready to live with Valentine and abandon Groby.

The idea of rebirth can be found not just in *Parade's End* but across Ford's post-war texts. In *No Enemy*, Gringoire describes the death of a Lieutenant Morgan, whose initials he can't remember:

> He was buried so that, in the morning when they found him, only his feet and legs were showing. He was probably not buried alive, because the officer who found him said that he was smiling. I like to think of that. (p. 98)

The image returns later in the book when Gringoire contemplates the idea of death as a 'sanctuary': 'For I like very much to remember the smile that was on the face of Lt. Morgan when they dug him out from under the dirt of the communication-trench' (p. 140). Between the two instances, however, there is a crucial shift. The first episode is reported, Morgan's smile relayed to Gringoire by the 'officer who found him'. In the second, Gringoire 'remember[s]' it himself. Moreover, this is not the O Nine Morgan of *Parade's End*, the 'bloomin' casualty' whose chest is blown away in *No More Parades* (p. 28) or Lance Corporal Duckett who dies after being buried in *A Man Could Stand Up –* (pp. 176–80).

Are these discrepancies purely authorial inconsistency, or is there a more deliberate strategy behind them? It seems as though Gringoire has appropriated, perhaps even generated, this memory. It is fictionalised, the representation of an experience which may or may not have actually taken place. Like Tietjens, Gringoire has invented himself. Reconstruction becomes a vision of doubleness, a dialectic of remembering and forgetting: of rewriting and inventing. This of course is the ultimate solution to amnesia. Freud's paradigm of the unconscious in 'Remembering, Repeating and Working-Through' is predicated on the assertion that the ability to construct a completely coherent narrative is a sign of repression; gaps and inconsistencies become, ironically, crucial indicators of accuracy. Ford extends this one step further, making inconsistency part of recovery. In 'The Repression of War Experiences' (1918), W. H. R. Rivers proposed that instead of repressing their traumatic memories, shell-shocked soldiers must find a way to turn them into 'tolerable, if not even pleasant, companions instead of evil influences'.[46] The smile on Morgan's face in *No Enemy* has a different tenor to that of Chris Baldry and Wilfred Owen; despite, or perhaps because of, its quasi-fantastical quality, the memory has become a 'pleasant companion', and by representing it thus to himself Gringoire has turned this pseudo-memory into a source of potential consolation and possible recovery. Recovery is a function of representation; experience will follow the imagination.

Max Saunders has argued that: 'All [Ford's] post-war work is in some sense a fantasy of reconstruction.'[47] Fantasy is the key word here. Many soldiers and writers alike felt that it was not possible to seamlessly reconnect the pre-war and post-war self: the division was simply too violent and abrupt. There is, accordingly, no cure in *Parade's End*: Tietjens' symbolic rebirth is not the single moment of regenerative catharsis it appears, and he still suffers from nightmares and amnesia in *Last Post*. But over the course of the tetralogy Ford does imagine a narrative arc, pivoted on the rebirth in *A Man Could Stand Up –*, which can begin to represent how recovery in the post-war era might be possible. What West couldn't visualise in 1918, Ford can begin to gesture at by 1923.

Notes

1. Babington, *Shell-Shock*, p. 121.
2. Babington gives 80,000: *Shell-Shock*, p. 168; while Laurinda Stryker posits that it may be closer to 200,000: 'Mental Cases', p. 160.
3. Aldington, *Death of a Hero*, p. 376.
4. Ford, *It Was the Nightingale*, p. 175.

5. Ibid. p. 175.
6. Ford to H. G. Wells (14 November 1923), *Letters of Ford Madox Ford*, p. 154.
7. Ford, 'Shell Shock', *War Prose*, p. 222.
8. West, *Selected Letters of Rebecca West*, p. 40.
9. Kingsbury, *The Peculiar Sanity of War*, p. 122.
10. O'Malley, '*The Return of the Soldier* and *Parade's End*', pp. 156, 161.
11. West and Hutchinson, 'On *The Return of the Soldier*', p. 67.
12. Bogacz, 'War Neurosis and Cultural Change in England 1914–22', p. 234.
13. Leese, *Shell Shock*, p. 10.
14. Shephard, *A War of Nerves*, p. 1; MacCurdy, *War Neuroses*, p. 1.
15. Myers, *Shell Shock in France 1914–1918*, p. 13.
16. Ibid. pp. 93–101.
17. Shephard, *A War of Nerves*, p. 29.
18. See Shephard, *A War of Nerves*, especially pp. 21–32.
19. British Army Order of 7 June 1917, quoted in Binnevald, *From Shell Shock to Combat Stress*, p. 138.
20. West, *The Return of the Soldier*, pp. 19, 24, 61. All further references are to this edition.
21. Pinkerton, 'Trauma and Cure in Rebecca West's *The Return of the Soldier*', p. 6.
22. Ford, *Some Do Not . . .*, ed. Max Saunders, p. 288. All further references are to this edition.
23. Woolf, *Mrs Dalloway*, p. 109. All further references are to this edition.
24. Ford, *No More Parades*, ed. Joseph Wiesenfarth, p. 16. All further references are to this edition.
25. Ford, *A Man Could Stand Up –*, ed. Sara Haslam, p. 111. All further references are to this edition.
26. Ford, 'Epilogue', *War Prose,* pp. 59–60.
27. Saunders, *Ford Madox Ford*, II, p. 90.
28. Ford, 'Arms and the Mind', *War Prose,* pp. 36–42.
29. Ibid. p. 37.
30. Haslam, *Fragmenting Modernism*, pp. 91–2.
31. Ford, *No Enemy*, p. 34. All further references are to this edition.
32. Freud, 'Beyond the Pleasure Principle', p. 236.
33. Fussell, *The Great War and Modern Memory*, p. 21.
34. Bonikowski, *Shell Shock and the Modernist Imagination*, pp. 125, 96.
35. Hawkes, *Ford Madox Ford and the Misfit Moderns*, p. 139.
36. West and Hutchinson, 'On *The Return of the Soldier*', p. 68. Most recently, both Cristina Pividori and Steve Pinkerton have reassessed the links between the two, focusing on the role of Margaret as an alternative source of healing to Gilbert Anderson, the 'Freudian' doctor. See Pinkerton, 'Trauma and Cure'; and Pividori, 'Eros and Thanatos Revisited'.
37. Pinkerton, 'Trauma and Cure', p. 3
38. Freud, 'Remembering, Repeating and Working-Through', pp. 147–56.
39. Ibid. p. 151.
40. Bogacz explains that a 'number of war-time articles on shell-shock employed a terminology indebted to Freud (even if their authors rarely acknowledged him). In the last years of the war, some of the once arcane

vocabulary of psychoanalysis was being casually employed by journalists':
'War Neurosis', p. 9.
41. Freud, 'Remembering, Repeating and Working-Through', p. 151.
42. Steve Pinkerton has charted the 'unreachable origins' of Chris's trauma,
    which could include not just the war and the death of his son, but also his
    restrictive marriage, the traumatic break-up with Margaret and potentially
    his relationship with his parents: 'Trauma and Cure', p. 3.
43. West, 'On *The Return of the Soldier*', p. 69.
44. Owen, 'Mental Cases', p. 30.
45. Das, *Touch and Intimacy in First World War Literature*, p. 47.
46. Rivers, 'The Repression of War Experience', p. 174.
47. Saunders, *Ford Madox Ford*, II, p. 69.

Chapter 9

'I hate soldiering': Ford, May Sinclair, and War Heroism

Leslie de Bont

A friend of Ford and Violet Hunt, May Sinclair (1863–1946) enlisted in 1915 as the 'Secretary and Reporter' of an ambulance unit from the Medico-Psychological Clinic, which she had helped found two years earlier.[1] Like Ford, she wrote extensively about the war and tried to depict the complexity of the soldier's experience. Her fictional and non-fictional works lay a similar emphasis on the psychological issues faced by soldiers involving shell shock, the influence of war on the relationships between genders, the return to civilian life, fear of and fascination with death, the anxiety of loss, and the difficulty of articulating pre-war, war and post-war times. Such perspectives seem at odds with traditional definitions of war heroism in literature. Several studies have shown how heroic discourses, ranging from Greek mythology to Arthurian romances or adventure stories, were embedded in Victorian life and literature, as they relied on empirical or historicised figures that were all associated with successful adventures and 'a moral paradigm'.[2] World War I heroism seems to challenge this diverse and complex heritage: the soldier is no longer 'a man of superhuman strength, courage, or ability, favoured by the gods' (*OED*). With Ford and Sinclair, war heroism becomes an adventure of the mind, of the self, its neuroses and its unconscious mechanisms. Tietjens, just like Sinclair's hero Tasker Jevons, seems driven, at least temporarily, by military duty, yet their heroic narratives are given minor importance. Ford 'carefully avoid[s] the word "hero"',[3] and in *Some Do Not . . .* Tietjens describes war as the context for 'the incidental degeneration of the heroic impulse'.[4] This chapter argues that Ford's and Sinclair's depictions of war heroism are paradoxically constructed on their heroes' fear and war neuroses, as well as on their relation to the civilian world. War heroism has thus become a complex matter that relies on the soldiers' antecedents, on their thoughts, impressions and unconscious, rather than on their 'heroic' impulses. Ford and Sinclair also integrate the soldiers' relations and interactions with other characters to their representations of heroism, thereby underlining particular behaviours and reactions or chaotic self-representations, in the manner of the case studies conducted by Freud at the turn of the century. Heroism is then transferred from the expected war records to the many battles fought by the soldiers' minds.

Fragmenting the Soldier's Mind: Heroic Ambiguity

Fordian and Sinclairian war imagery is particularly dense. Shells are represented as a bigger, impersonal force singularly bearing human resemblance. For instance, the 'mortal vomiting'[5] of shells in *Parade's End* can remind the reader of several metaphors from Sinclair's war prose:

> We saw the first shell [. . .]. There was a deadly attraction about the thing that made you feel that it and you were the only objects in God's universe, and that you were about to be merged in each other. It looked as if it were rushing out of heaven straight for us.[6]

An unknown and worrying enemy, both similar to and different from the soldiers themselves, the shell explosion also evokes Freud's literary *Unheimliche*, which he first developed in his 1919 essay 'The Uncanny'. Referring to traditional tales of war heroism – be they Arthurian romances or Victorian adventure stories – makes little sense: Ford's and Sinclair's soldiers face problems – and machineries – of a new kind as the novels develop a psychoanalytical interpretation of modern military deeds. The intensity of explosions enables Ford and Sinclair to represent their characters' perplexing attraction for death – 'a deadly attraction' (*Tasker Jevons*, p. 321) – which can be read, in Sinclair's texts, as a reference to the death drive, first studied by Sabina Spielrein[7] and adapted by Freud in *Beyond the Pleasure Principle* (1920).

Making sense of this complex war is the soldier's first battle. In 'Arms and the Mind', Ford depicts war as a puzzling, intense, and alienating religious experience:

> There must have been [. . .] a million men [. . .] impelled by an invisible moral force into a Hell of fear [. . .]. As for explanation I hadn't any: as for significant or valuable pronouncement of a psychological kind I could not make any [. . .]. I just had to fall back upon the formula: it is the Will of God.[8]

Just as in *Parade's End*, Armageddon looms large in Ford's reminiscence. A religious dimension is equally at stake for Sinclair: the bombardments give Tasker Jevons the impression that he has been chosen, as shells rain down onto him, 'rushing out of heaven straight for us' (p. 321); and in *The Tree of Heaven* (1917), Michael Harrison:

> saw how the War might take hold of you like a religion. It was the Great War of Redemption. And redemption meant simply thousands and millions of men in troop-ships and troop-trains coming from the ends of the world to buy the freedom of the world with their bodies. (p. 370)

In her 1917 essay *A Defence of Idealism*, Sinclair theorised something close to Ford's 'invisible moral force' as the expression of a pantheistic will, prompting soldiers, but also artists, mystics and lovers, to sublimate their libido:

> Lovers and poets [. . .] and mystics and heroes know them: [. . .] moments when things [. . .] change to us in an instant of time [. . .]; moments of danger that are sure and perfect happiness, because then [. . .] Reality gives itself to our very sight and touch.[9]

For Sinclair, 'moments when things change', like 'moments of danger', are so intense that they enable a form of revelation of what she refers to as 'Ultimate Reality'.[10] Yet such visionary experiences are often problematically close to dissociation – first described in 1893 by Pierre Janet in his seminal *État mental des hystériques* – and which Sinclair divides into two categories: mystical dissociation and hysterical dissociation. The former amounts to the sublimation of the libido, which is what the soldiers and poets experience; the latter reveals a psychological disorder as the individual loses all rational contact with empirical reality. The soldiers' mystical dissociation is best described in *The Tree of Heaven* as Michael Harrison observes that, on the Front: 'your body and its nerves aren't in it at all. Your body may be moving violently, with other bodies moving violently round it, but you're still' (p. 395). The violence of the war experience dissociates body and mind, which is, according to Sinclair, both a sign of heroism and a mental strategy for self-preservation.

But the ambiguity of Ford's and Sinclair's fiction actually questions Sinclair's distinction, as it shows the difficulty of fully grasping the soldier's experience. Indeed, mystical dissociation does not prevent episodes of psychological confusion, nervous breakdowns and disturbed sanity. Fordian and Sinclairian fiction thus creates complex situations endowed with parameters that shed doubt on their likely theoretical framework. However, in their descriptions of anxiety, fear and ecstasy, Ford's and Sinclair's war novels use Freudian terminology and give their readers a clinical account of the soldier's experience. *Parade's End* gives us examples of complex hallucinations, which might echo the 'sort of madness'

(p. 334) that is described in *Tasker Jevons* or what Ford relates as his own experience in 'Arms and the Mind'.[11] Compared to Sinclair, Ford's use of psychological terms is at times loosely adapted – 'self-suppression' (p. 15), for example, in *No More Parades*, instead of 'repression' or 'suppression' – and sometimes purposefully echoes popular conceptions: 'the repressions of the passionate drive them mad' (*No More Parades*, p. 15). Significantly, despite a recurring use of Freudian terminology emphasising the complexity of the soldiers' disorders, *The Tree of Heaven* also conveys a sense of distrust of popular psychology:

> That poem he sent me that somebody wrote, making out that this gorgeous fight-feeling [. . .] is nothing but a form of sex-madness. He thinks that's all there is in it, he doesn't know much about war, or love either. [. . .] They're all wrong about it, because they make it turn on killing and not on your chance of being killed. (pp. 368–9)

Michael's comment disavows the popular interpretation of Freud's sexual theory, while echoing, perhaps more precisely, Sabina Spielrein's 1912 study on self-sacrifice and destruction.[12] A similar distrust of traditional psychoanalysis is voiced by Tietjens in *No More Parades*: 'what those fools called a complex' (p. 65). Such distance – and phrasing – is frequent in Sinclair's and Ford's fiction.[13] It takes part of a broader questioning of Freud's emphasis on sexuality, which Sinclair, a follower of Jung, rejected in her essays, but it also reveals a form of reasoning in progress, including confusions and contradictions, on the multifold interpretations of war-time behaviour – thereby imitating the contemporary evolution and diversity of psychoanalysis itself.

War ecstasy, another heroic quality for Sinclair,[14] is also subjected to irony, perversity and hallucination. In *The Tree of Heaven*:

> It is absolutely real. I mean it has to do with absolute reality. With God. It hasn't anything to do with having courage, or not having courage: it's another state of mind altogether. [. . .] Your body and nerves aren't in it at all. Your body may be moving violently, with other bodies moving violently around it; but you're still. [. . .] Why should the moment of extreme danger be always the 'exquisite' moment? Why not the moment of safety? [. . .] Actually you lay hold on eternal life, and you know it. [. . .] You keep on wanting to get near it. Wanting it to happen again. (p. 347)

In *No More Parades*: 'It was sheer exhilaration to freeze here' (p. 92). Both extracts hint at the fighter's pleasure, but Ford's sentence also bears ironic undertones. War duties are not solely sublime or pleasurable, they are also simultaneously absurd, hard to bear, exhilarating and nerve-wracking. Such concentration is also present when Michael Harrison, in the above quotation, like Tietjens, describes the soldier's experience mostly through hesitations, negations, questions and approximations ('another state of mind altogether'). The war experience actually becomes so intense and complex that it requires distance and analysis. John Mackenzie argues that Victorian heroic literature relied on 'a mediator figure, in effect a priest who constructed, developed and interpreted the [heroic] myth'.[15] In Ford and Sinclair, the soldiers are left alone and making sense of the war situation becomes a heroic challenge in itself. Tietjens' accounts often convey deep confusion, betraying his difficulty to build a coherent discourse on his situation:

> They mopped and mowed, fantastically; grey, with black shadows; dropping like the dishevelled veils of murdered bodies. [. . .] This was fear. This was the intimate fear of black quiet nights, in dugouts where you heard the obscene suggestions of the miners' picks below you; tranquil, engrossed. Infinitely threatening. . . . But not FEAR.[16]

Here, is it actually *fear* that Tietjens experiences? A few pages later, he still seems unable to answer the question. Heroism and war ecstasy are no longer the focal points. For Ford's and Sinclair's soldiers, the complexity of the war experience raises many perplexing contradictions and puzzling questions. Even a brilliant mind like Nicholas Harrison in *The Tree of Heaven* seems to contradict himself and be forced into silence:

> In Nicholas's brain images gathered fast, one after another; they thickened; clear, vivid images with hard outlines. They came slowly but with order and precision. While the other talked [about war], he had been silent and grave. (p. 280)

This short passage depicts a two-step cognitive process. We read that, in Nicholas's mind, 'images gathered fast' and then that 'they came slowly'. Yet there is no contradiction per se. War functions as a strongly evocative subject that quickly compels images into Nicholas's mind, but the text tells us that the images are processed slowly and orderly because Nicholas is aware of the complex density of war. War heroism is thus also intellectual and psychological. It is anchored into the psychological capacities of the soldiers, which are the core elements of Tietjens' and of the Sinclairian protagonists' portrait. Rather than rejecting the idea of heroism outright (as we often tend to think World War I writers did), Ford and Sinclair introduce new versions of heroism. Their soldiers are indeed depicted as heroes, because of the many and unrelated battles fought by and against their unprepared consciousnesses.

Literature, Culture, and Heroism

Writing is also central to the lives of Fordian and Sinclairian soldiers. Two of Sinclair's heroes, Jevons and Michael Harrison, are writers and produce war fiction and Tietjens also displays writing skills when he sets out to write a sonnet in limited time in *No More Parades* (p. 37). By granting the soldiers sound general culture, artistic skills or techniques, the novels give them a sense of chivalric nobility and thus single them out as potential heroic figures. Yet a 1922 report of the War Office mentions that having an 'artistic temperament' is a predisposition for shell shock.[17] Both authors are thus taking a stand against the official psychology of their time while anticipating the later development of art-therapy: in Ford's and Sinclair's fiction, art and culture help, not hinder, the mind to make sense of the world – and of the war. Tietjens, for instance, resorts to bibliotherapy as he tries to recover memory on reading the *Encyclopaedia Britannica*.[18] However, literary attempts are often incomplete and both authors create a condensed and dislocated network of fragmented elements: in the trenches, texts (such as Tietjens' sonnets), bodies, minds, and time cannot avoid fragmentation.[19]

Interestingly, culture and literature also provide the protagonists with a sense of continuity. Not only are they part of the soldiers' identities, they are also seen as a private objective or as a personal goal to achieve. In *No More Parades*, 'misplaced erudition' (p. 224), devising rhymes and doing Latin translations are thus also seen as ways to cope: soldiers seem to resort to texts and culture as a way back to the known, reassuring, chartered territory of their consciousness. Such a perspective was thoroughly studied by Ella Sharpe, a psychoanalyst and colleague of Sinclair at the Medico-Psychological Clinic.[20] Repetitions, even with significant alterations, of words and rhythms also seem to unite the soldier's mind to his situation. For instance, the play on the multiple abbreviations of military titles and lexis (*No More Parades*, p. 35) contrasts with the rhyme scheme of Tietjens' sonnet (abba) highlighted soon after (p. 37). The literary code seems to temporarily take over from the military signs, enacting a complex rhetoric of fragmentation, enabling the erudite soldier's mind to try and make sense of his predicament.

Ford's and Sinclair's texts also entail multiple fragmentations of diegetic time and space. For example, a certain sense of nostalgia for the land can be found in their novels. It bears on both space and time when Tietjens exclaims in *A Man Could Stand Up –*: 'The land remains. . . . It remains!' (p. 89). In Sinclair's *Anne Severn and the Fieldings* (1922), the land also functions as a stable landmark for all the main characters as well as a way to rekindle memories. A harmonious, peaceful space, the land embodies an idealised, peaceful past. Significantly, the only character who seems to endow the fields with a sense of violence is John Conway, who is characterised by his unhealthy aggressiveness and perverse behaviour and who fails as a traditional hero. By contrast, fieldwork, for the aptly named Colin Fielding, also works as a means to partially cure shell shock. During and after the war, the introspection processes of the soldiers hardly ever imply a sense of longing, and when it does, the result is a rather grim prospect, rendered by the 'no more parades' repetition in *Parade's End*, or in Sinclair's *Far End* (1926): 'it's going to be damnable, every minute of it. There won't be any glory, there'll be filth [. . .], there'll be fleas and there'll be lice, and I shall be frightened, trembling with funk half the time.'[21] For World War I soldiers, traditional war heroism has been defeated by war itself.

In Ford's and Sinclair's novels, the soldiers' disturbed and complex look backwards also provides them with the ability to escape the present. Evoking memories, just like their literary escapes, appears as a way for the soldiers to reach balance and mental homeostasis. For example, memories enable Tietjens to find peace in the trenches: 'You felt at peace [. . .]. Like being in [. . .] Groby' (*A Man Could Stand Up* –, p. 72). The past thus functions both as a coping technique enabling the soldier to (re)construct his own narrative through the renewed processing of memories, and as a means of repression of the horrors of combats. Memories, or streams of memories, also play a central role in the construction of the soldier figures and even participate in the characters' psychological anamnesis. Tietjens experiences the tranquilising memory of Valentine Wannop (*A Man Could Stand Up* –, p. 133) because he has seen Duckett, a lance corporal, who makes him think of Valentine. Yet as Tietjens himself admits, in a stream-of-consciousness passage, Duckett does not look like Valentine at all. The entire passage thus places emphasis on the memory of Valentine and what it signifies for Tietjens: love, of course, but also pre- and post-war times. Surviving thus also implies re-appropriating one's past, while repressing the present situation.

Interestingly, thoughts and memories, rather than feelings and perceptions that the soldiers' minds try to fight, are often the starting points of Sinclair's and Ford's streams of consciousness. Thus, stream-of-consciousness passages never fail to hint at the temporal dissociation structuring the soldier's mind. This discrepancy can be attributed to Ford's theories of Impressionism and to both authors' practice of what Freud terms *Nachträglichkeit* (afterwardness) in *Studies on Hysteria* (1895), according to which, events can be experienced without being fully grasped and thus tend to reappear afterwards under various forms

– hence the soldier's jumbled sense of temporality and fragmentary understanding.

Soldiers' thoughts are also turned towards a future that is made of technical reworkings of medieval war props instead of human endeavours. As Nicholas Harrison dreams of building 'a Moving Fortress', a tank, in *The Tree of Heaven* (pp. 159–62), Tietjens fantasises about a cannon attacking the moon:

> It was quiet; the wet cool air was agreeable. They had autumn mornings that felt like in Yorkshire. [. . .] He was more free in the chest than he had been for months.
>   A single immense cannon, at a tremendous distance said something. Something sulky [. . .]. It would be a tremendous piece of frightfulness to hit the moon. Great gain in prestige. (*A Man Could Stand Up –*, pp. 60–1)

What first stands out in this extract is the dialogue between body and mind. Peaceful perceptions ('it was quiet') and physical sensations ('free in the chest') enable perspectives and flights of fancy, showing how Tietjens (like Nicholas Harrison) temporarily escape the hardships of the trenches. Such scenes also further deconstruct traditional war heroism as they show the positive influence of a peaceful environment on the working of the soldier's mind. Building up projects and gaining perspective or keeping his mind active and focusing on other subjects appear as coping techniques: 'They wanted their minds taken off [. . .]. Thus, you talk to men, just before the event, about [. . .] the hind-legs of the elephant at the old Lane' (*A Man Could Stand Up –*, p. 133). Reminding soldiers of pre-war times is a strategy to keep the thought of danger at bay. Yet being unable to think might also become a sign, and possibly a symptom, of a greater perplexity: 'of course, you might lose control of your mind in a reeling cellar where you cannot hear your thoughts. If you cannot hear your thoughts how the hell are you going to tell what your thoughts are doing?' (*A Man Could Stand Up –*, p. 76). This perplexity reverberates on the soldier's own military engagement. A striking common point between Tietjens and Sinclair's Tasker Jevons and Eliot Fielding, Colin's elder brother, is their uncanny capability to utter accurate predictions about the upcoming war – and they are thus endowed, antebellum, with potential heroic skills. But such powers seem to keep them away from any form of traditional heroism as all join the army for non-traditional reasons. Tietjens enlists to be 'kept out of England' (*No More Parades*, p. 59), Colin Fielding also tries to be recruited in order to escape from his wife, while Jevons engages in the military forces as a showcase for his virility.

'I hate soldiering': Portrait of the Soldier as a Misfit

In Ford's and Sinclair's war fiction, a new relationship to soldiering seems to arise. War is first seen as pointless for both Tietjens and Michael Harrison: military deeds mean danger rather than honour, and a probable loss of social status (*No More Parades*, p. 186; *The Tree of Heaven*, pp. 393–4). When Tietjens declares 'I hate soldiering' (*No More Parades*, p. 27), what might be at stake is the representation of his feelings of estrangement and depreciation that result from his difficulty to adjust to brutality (*A Man Could Stand Up –*, p. 72). As in *A Man Could Stand Up –*, soldiering even amounts to desperation in *Anne Severn*: 'why did that dwarf behave in a smart and soldierly manner? Through despair?' (p. 95). The army is a mechanism in which there is no room for the specificities of the individual psyche: 'An army – especially in peace time! – is a very complex and nicely adjusted affair [. . .]. [A colonel's] refusal, precisely like a grain of sand in the works of a chronometer, may cause the most singular perturbations. It was so in this case' (p. 107). Here, one can first note the emphasis on 'case', which is central in Sinclair's fiction. Explicitly in her novels and implicitly in *Parade's End*, the questions raised by the soldiers' narratives remind one of Freudian case studies: for Ford and Sinclair, the soldier's mind is so complex an enigma that it challenges existing categories or theoretical frameworks and thus calls for new discourses. The word 'case' stands in sharp contrast with two other expressions describing the army: 'nicely adjusted affair' and 'chronometer', which leave no space for the unforeseen, while the texts suggest that the workings of the conscious and unconscious minds of soldiers do not fit in with the military machine. The focus on the soldiers' subjectivity conflicts with the denial of individuality, which is inherent to the war experience. In other words, war heroism, for Ford and Sinclair, also entails fighting against one's own army.

This is also at stake when Ford and Sinclair represent the soldiers' unjust physical and spiritual sacrifices:

> Heavy depression settled down more heavily upon him. The distrust of the home Cabinet, felt by then by the greater part of that army, became like physical pain. These immense sacrifices, this ocean of mental sufferings, were all undergone to further the private vanities of men who amidst these hugenesses of landscapes [. . .] appeared pigmies! (*No More Parades*, pp. 16–17)

Yet for Ford and Sinclair, sacrifices seem linked with different psychological issues. For Sinclair, sacrifice is a necessary step towards the sublimation of the libido while Ford is more critical and identifies sacrifice as

a cause of Tietjens' depression. In this war of a new kind, sacrificed soldiers become heroes just because they are cannon fodder on the Front:

> The Feudal Spirit was broken. Perhaps it would therefore be harmful to
> Trench Warfare. It used to be comfortable and cosy. [. . .]
>   At any rate, as at present arranged, dying was a lonely affair. (*A Man
> Could Stand Up –*, p. 127)

A similar shift from Victorian literary war heroism to a modern tragedy
of the absurd is echoed in Charlotte Redhead's reflections on fatigue and
loneliness in Sinclair's *The Romantic* (1920): 'could war tire you and
wear you down, and change you from yourself? In two weeks?',[22] which
can also be read in: 'the agonized waiting of men; the weight upon the
mind like a weight upon the brows' (*No More Parades*, p. 51). If these
last two extracts combine dark tones and gloomy concerns coalesce,
both are also part of a critique of classical war heroism. Charlotte's
questions betray her ignorance of John's past (John, in fact, has not
changed at all), while in *No More Parades* the wordplay on 'weight' and
'wait' stresses the 'unthinkableness' (p. 51) of the soldiers' situation.
    Interestingly, waiting is also given a particular role in the depiction of
the soldiers' experience in *The Tree of Heaven* (p. 80), in *The Romantic*,
in which the soldiers and stretcher-bearers have nothing to do but wait
for a rescue team (pp. 50, 52, 76), and in *A Man Could Stand Up –*.
Tietjens, for instance, declares: 'the waiting wrings your soul; but it does
not induce panic or the desire to run – at any rate to nearly the same
extent. Where, in any event, could you run to?' (p. 109). The dark tone
of the rhetorical question shows us how the mind, and its rationalisation
processes, is struggling for control over bodily sensations.[23] Through
their emphasis on the effects of waiting on a war zone, Ford and Sinclair
probe into the psychological factors of heroism: the soldier becomes a
hero because of the powers of his mind.

Heroic Women

Ford and Sinclair also show the way their soldiers see themselves robbed
of their own heroic potential, as war also witnesses the arrivals of new
heroes: women. In *Tasker Jevons*, Jevons is represented as doing nothing
but his mere duty, even if he risks his life – and he loses his writing
hand in order to save an entire regiment. By contrast, his wife's presence on the Front as a nurse is deemed exceptional and heroic: Viola is
the one who finds Jevons (p. 293), and compares herself to Joan of Arc
(p. 317); she is leading the way ('nobody's going to stop me', p. 288);

she is giving advice to the narrator ('you'd better take your things if you want to get out of here', p. 292) while giving the impression that she is there to protect him ('it looked as if the Special Correspondent would be smuggled through under Viola's protection', p. 288). She is systemati-cally depicted in positive yet aggressive ('her arrogance', p. 281) terms. For Ford's and Sinclair's soldiers, women often embody the continuity of civilian life – and its problems. Thus their presence on the Front, as nurses, stretcher-bearers or as mere visitors, upsets their possible peace fantasies as wartime isolation is now confronted to other temporalities.

The duality of the soldier's position is caused by the new role that war gives to women. Chivalry is a much-discussed topic in *Parade's End* and Sinclair's novels, before, during and after the war. For Jevons, war is a matter of protecting women; but ironically, chivalry is mostly associated with the character of Viola: '[she was] flinging herself out of the car and proposing to climb over the ruins of several houses and walk by herself, under shell-fire, to Zele, because she thought he was there' (p. 318). Women seem to rob the soldiers of their heroic pedestal: Viola's remark, 'nowadays women have chivalry' (pp. 316–17), echoes Sylvia's excla-mation: 'Damn his chivalry!' (*No More Parades*, p. 113). Significantly, Queenie Fielding, Colin Fielding's unfaithful wife in *Anne Severn*, is qualified as 'worse than war' (p. 117): she is a threat to the soldier's integrity. Female sexuality challenges traditional male heroism and high-lights the soldiers' weaknesses. If in *The Romantic* John Conway is char-acterised by his aggressiveness towards women, his platonic relationship with Charlotte Redhead and his paralysing fear of combat are analysed by Dr McClane as a sign of his impotence:

> The war upset him. [It] whipped up the naked savage in him. [. . .] He couldn't help *that*. He suffered from some physical disability. [. . .] It made him so that he couldn't live a man's life. He was afraid to enter a profession. He was afraid of women. (p. 142)

Contrasting male weakness, and especially the physical weaknesses of men with women's bodily strength, is a frequent strategy in Sinclair's texts. In that respect, Colin Fielding and his wife Queenie appear as a very typical Sinclairian couple. Her height, charisma and sense of authority are contrasted with his small physique, his feebleness, shyness and delicacy. Interestingly, Christopher and Sylvia offer a near reverse variation as Tiejtens is described as massive, but Sylvia's skills in manipulation help her get the upper hand. Both authors clearly show how the interaction and the contact with women on the Front deeply influence the soldier's state of mind. Such perspective is prolonged in Sinclair's text as Colin and Queenie Fielding seem to reach orgasm for the first time on the eve of his departure to France: 'And with her young, beautiful body pressed tight to him, with her mouth on his and her eyes shining close and big in the darkness, Colin would forget' (p. 109). This scene recalls Sylvia's strangely renewed passion for Tietjens 'before his coming out there again to France' (*No More Parades*, p. 71) as well as Tietjens' 'invitation' to Valentine (p. 75). The parallel between Tietjens and Colin can be furthered in the way they both suffer from shell shock and are hospitalised. They are also discredited as war heroes because of their respect for their unfaithful wives and their peculiar artistic skills.

The Battle of the Mind

With disturbed, fragmented minds and potential social discredit, Ford's and Sinclair's soldiers are ill-equipped for the trenches, which seem to be the major cause of their war trauma, as Uncle Morrie remarks in Sinclair's *The Tree of Heaven*:

> You people here don't know what war is. [. . .] It's dirt and funk and stinks and more funk all the time. It's lying out all night [. . .] and getting frozen, and waking up and finding you've got warm again because your neighbour's inside's been fired out on the top of you [. . .] and [his] flesh gives way like rotten fruit [. . .]. That's war. (p. 80)

A later passage in the novel compares the way the mind reacts in civilian and war contexts:

> At home your mind isn't adjusted to horrors. [. . .] Whereas out here every-thing's shifted in the queerest way. Your mind shifts. You funk your first and your second sight, say, of a bad stretcher case; but when it comes to the third and the fourth you don't funk at all; you're not shocked, you're not a bit surprised. It's all in the picture, and you're in the picture too. There's a sort of horrible harmony. (p. 365)

In this extract, what is highlighted is the way the soldier adapts and tries to make sense of his environment by resorting to the oxymoronic concept of 'horrible harmony'. Habit also helps soldiers, as Michael Harrison explains: 'when it comes to [. . .] the fourth you don't funk', echoing research in social psychology on desensitisation and condition-ing.[24]

When Tietjens declares 'you cannot force your mind' (*No More Parades*, p. 73), he confesses that his mind is overwhelmed by the com-plexity of the war experience. It can no longer choose its own patterns and becomes a mere subject to the intense reality of combat: 'solid noise that swept your brain off its feet. Something else took control of it. You became second in command of your own soul' (p. 77). For Michael Harrison, what takes over is an intense physical thrill, devoid of any form of spirituality: '[a] beastly sensation when you're half way between your parapet and theirs' (*The Tree of Heaven*, p. 363). The 'heroic impulse' is devoid of any spiritual or moral direction.

The soldier's mind seems also defeated when the characters lose track of time:

> The general said:
> 'It isn't Sunday, is it?'
> Tietjens said:
> 'No sir; Thursday, the seventeenth, I think, of January.... (*No More Parades*, p. 245)

Losing track of the calendar is two-fold. It can first convey the idea that the usual social landmarks are irrelevant to military life. This is further illustrated by the stretching of time, the lack of punctuality and the problems in communication with remote services, as they are represented in *Parade's End*. Yet the novel also suggests that when the general loses track of calendar organisation, he loses a crucial social skill along with it and heads towards confusion.

Mental capacities also appear ill-suited to help Tietjens react to other soldiers' shell-shock symptoms:

> There was no knowing. He said: 'Are you wounded?' [. . .] Tietjens could not see any blood flowing. The boy whispered: 'No, sir!' [. . .] Shell shock, very likely. There was no knowing what shell shock was or what it did to you. (*A Man Could Stand Up* –, p. 176)

The reader follows Tietjens' thought process: he first relies on his perceptions and then puts forward a hypothesis. Yet logical thinking seems to be of no avail as he fails to reach any solid conclusion. Such a situation echoes the early psychoanalytical cases that were often either unsolved or partially solved and challenged existing knowledge about the human psyche.[25] In such a context, experience alone is useless for Tietjens, who has been referred to as a mysterious case of war trauma earlier in the novel: 'Aren't there Institutions ... Military Sanatoria .... for cases precisely like that of this Captain Tietjens[?]' (p. 52).

The influence of Dr Charles Myers, a colleague of Sinclair's at the Medico-Psychological Clinic and one of the earliest describers of shell shock, is perceptible in Sinclair's and Ford's novels. Myers' seminal article 'A Contribution to the Study of Shell Shock' (1915) relies on three of his clinical cases, which Sinclair reworks so as to give her readers detailed and organised accounts of her protagonists' disorders.

Her clinical description of Colin's crises or John's fears gathers, in a very small number of pages, various mental and physical symptoms exposed by Myers, such as memory loss, depression, anxiety crises and panic attacks, nightmares, hallucinations, temporal paralyses, shakings, sleeping disorders or increased noise sensitivity.[26] Because of its external focalisation, *Anne Severn* strongly resembles clinical descriptions and diagnoses. Details are conveyed through lists that show the extent of Colin's suffering, as well as the various chains of events that trigger his crises. In *Parade's End*, on the contrary, shell shock is thoroughly linked with a reorganisation of time: it entails fragmentations, ellipses, analepses or prolepses and is often represented as *in situ* experiences, while Sinclair's texts provide a posteriori analytical anamneses. Symptoms of shell shock are described by Tietjens himself, who talks on several occasions about the evolution of his condition in rather banal comments such as '*I am very tired*' (*No More Parades*, p. 86) or with personal diagnoses: 'it was mental rather than physical' (A *Man Could Stand Up* –, p. 98).

By contrast, in Sinclair's fiction, symptoms are classified as different aspects of a complex psycho-physiological disorder and play a very different role. This is where Ford's modernity differs from Sinclair's. Her characters hardly voice their war neuroses as the psychological expertise is often left to the narrator. By contrast, *Parade's End* makes Tietjens present his own apprehension and perplexity through the impressionistic scattering of information. Sinclair provides us with actual lists of symptoms and calls to her reader's psychoanalytical skills while Ford often displays accurate intuition as a basis for literary experimentation. For Ford, psychological representation often goes through a specific use of internal monologue:

> What about the accursed obsession of O Nine Morgan that intermittently jumped on him? [. . .] And all the time a dreadful depression! A weight! In the hotel last night he had nearly fainted [. . .]. It was getting to be a serious matter! It might mean that there was a crack in his, Tietjens', brain. A lesion! If that was to go on . . . O Nine Morgan, dirty as he always was [. . .].
> (*No More Parades*, pp. 228–9)

This extract transforms physiological concerns into symptoms of obsession. Tietjens has displayed a morbid sense of projection: 'his mind was still with the dead' (p. 87) and has also been subject to recurring visual hallucinations (p. 85), but here readers see him fight against his own mind.

Aftermath

In *No More Parades*, Tietjens refuses to speak about his civilian life, which becomes more problematic as he considers his return: 'I can never go home. I have to go underground somewhere. If I went back to England there would be nothing for me but going underground by suicide' (p. 237). In *A Man Could Stand Up* –, survivor's guilt seems to meet terror and trauma, which makes returning to England difficult:

> Still! – He saw those grey spectral shapes that had surrounded and interpenetrated all his later days. The image came over him with the mood of repulsion at odd moments [. . .]; without suggestion there floated before his eyes the image, the landscape of greyish forms. (p. 198)

Here, the hallucinatory vision of the war is turned into a haunting nightmare and shows the new problems of modern war from which the soldier goes back 'a changed man [. . .] with a mind of a different specific gravity' (*No More Parades*, p. 73). As a survivor, criteria for judging the world are different and the transition into civilian life is often a hardship in itself: 'but could one wangle out of a hard into a soft job?' (p. 228). Tietjens' question actually points at the soldier's next fear: 'repose' (p. 135), the paradoxical readjustment to post-war life.

When we are told that he 'was astonished at the bitterness of his voice [. . .] and he was again astonished at the deference in his voice' (*No More Parades*, p. 228), he does not recognise himself any more. The self has become another entity and, where Sinclair's *Anne Severn* focuses on therapeutic cures and word association, *Parade's End* concentrates on darker concerns. Following the clinical cases she was acquainted with,[27] Sinclair portrays at great lengths the difficulty of recovery. Anne pays attention to placing Colin in familiar surroundings, she suggests memory training exercises, she cares for him with utter benevolence, she gives him fieldwork and entrusts him with gradual responsibility, she encourages him to play music again and, most importantly, guided by her own intuition, she sets off a form of talking cure. Some of these prospects can be found in *Some Do Not . . .* and *Last Post*, but unlike other war pieces such as *No Enemy* (1929), the tetralogy shows no improvement in the protagonist's condition. The novel highlights Tietjens' wounded pride as he suffers from memory loss in *Some Do Not . . .*. Besides, he is noticeably absent in the last volume. Absent from the text, the hero is also absent from his mind. Such an ending is also revealing of the Fordian strategy of suggestion and presentation: it is up to the reader to make the comparisons and freely ponder on all characters' states of mind and feelings, while Sinclair invites us, somewhat more directly, towards psychoanalytical criticism.

Ford's and Sinclair's war fiction thus represent new types of battles, which are neither won nor necessarily traditionally heroic. Sinclair stages the death of the romantic hero in *Tasker Jevons*, and in *Last Post*, Tietjens is still far from recovery. By concentrating on the battles of the soldier's mind, both authors actually highlight a new type of heroism, which is built on the still mysterious 'borderland powers'[28] of the unconscious, on the multiple links and conflicts between the physical and the psychological, as well as on the importance of the characters' personal history and antecedents. In concentrating on the soldier's unique individuality and personal patterns, Ford's and Sinclair's novels single out their soldiers as late nineteenth- or early twentieth-century patients undergoing psychotherapeutic cures, exploring the unchartered territory of war trauma. With common references and diverging methods, both manage to bring out the specific aspects of the First World War and the soldiers' war experience. But where Sinclair concentrates on the difficulty of recovery, Ford represents the ambiguous influence of war. Just like in Freud's case histories,[29] and unlike most successful Victorian literary war heroes, Ford's soldier does not meet closure and remains neither 'dead [nor] an open book' (*No More Parades*, p. 69), thereby forging a new type of war heroism.

Notes

1. Sinclair, *Journal of Impressions in Belgium*, p. 4.
2. Mackenzie, *Popular Imperialism and the Military, 1850–1950*, pp. 112–13. See also Paris, *Warrior Nation*, pp. 49–82, 233; MacDonald, *The Language of Empire*, p. 61.
3. Ford, *It Was the Nightingale*, p. 197.
4. Ford, *Some Do Not . . .*, ed. Max Saunders, p. 200. All further references are to this edition.
5. Ford, *No More Parades*, ed. Joseph Wiesenfarth, p. 11. All further references are to this edition.
6. See, for example, Sinclair, *Tasker Jevons*, p. 321; *The Tree of Heaven*, p. 374. All further references are to these editions.
7. Spielrein, 'Destruction as a Cause of Coming into Being', p. 182.
8. Ford, 'Arms and the Mind', *War Prose*, p. 38.
9. Sinclair, *A Defence of Idealism*, p. 379.
10. Ibid. p. 141.
11. Ford, 'Arms and the Mind', p. 43.
12. Spielrein, 'Destruction as a Cause of Coming into Being', p. 182.
13. See also: 'that was accidental, so it was not part of any psychological rhythm' (*No More Parades,* p. 135); Sinclair, *Way of Sublimation*, p. 94; 'Portrait of My Uncle', p. 37.

14. See, for example, Sinclair, *A Defence of Idealism*, p. 141; *A Journal of Impressions in Belgium*, pp. 13–14.
15. Mackenzie, *Popular Imperialism and the Military, 1850–1950*, p. 115.
16. Ford, *A Man Could Stand Up –*, ed. Sara Haslam, p. 68. All further references are to this edition.
17. Southborough, *Report of the War Office Committee of Enquiry into 'Shell-Shock'*, p. 149.
18. One can note similar scenes in Sinclair's fiction, the earliest occurrence being her short story 'Superseded' (1901), in which a doctor prescribes reading fiction, as part of a therapeutic cure, to a depressed elementary-school teacher.
19. Fragmentation is a key notion in Freud's description of the dynamics of dreams and Tietjens' and Tasker Jevons' (pp. 323–4) obsession with writing bears at times a similar oneiric quality.
20. Sharpe, 'Similar and Divergent Unconscious Determinants Underlying the Sublimations of Pure Art and Pure Science', p. 144.
21. Sinclair, *Far End*, p. 63.
22. Sinclair, *The Romantic*, p. 162.
23. This is in keeping with Sinclair's psychoanalytical approach to boredom in *The Three Sisters* (1914), in which ennui is depicted as an alienating, yet necessary, step before sublimation.
24. See, for example, Jones, 'A Laboratory Study of Fear', pp. 308–15.
25. See, for example, 'Notes Upon a Case of Obsessional Neurosis', in which Freud first addresses the notion of 'ambivalence', or 'From the History of an Infantile Neurosis' ('Little Hans'), in which he first discusses the Oedipus complex: Freud, *Three Case-Histories*.
26. Myers, 'A Contribution to the Study of Shell Shock', pp. 317–19. See also Sinclair, *Anne Severn*, p. 121.
27. Raitt, 'Early British Psychoanalysis and the Medico-Psychological Clinic', p. 74.
28. Sinclair, *A Defence of Idealism*, p. 268.
29. Showalter, *Hystories*, p. 95.

Chapter 10

Peace of Mind in *Parade's End*

Gene M. Moore

In the late summer of 1924 – between the publication of *Some Do Not . . .* and the writing of *No More Parades* – Ford Madox Ford observed:

> A great many novelists have treated of the late war in terms solely of the war: in terms of pip-squeaks, trench-coats, wire-aprons, shells, mud, dust, and sending the bayonet home with a grunt. For that reason interest in the late war is said to have died. But, had you taken part actually in those hostilities, you would know how infinitely little part the actual fighting itself took in your mentality.[1]

In the series of novels that would become *Parade's End*, Ford examines not so much the 'actual fighting' as the psychological effects of war on the mind, and explores the various strategies developed by men suffering stress to preserve their sanity and self-control under wartime conditions. In this context, Christopher Tietjens stands out as a prime example of the Good Soldier: he is an effective and capable officer who not only does his duty but manages without fail to help his fellow soldiers even when they are handicapped by alcohol, prejudice or fits of madness. Tietjens is severely tested by the trauma of war and the threat of insanity, yet he emerges from the test with his values strengthened and clarified. What is it in Tietjens' character or constitution that enables him to withstand the hell of Armageddon?

Ford was literally 'shell shocked' during the Battle of the Somme, when he was, as he described the moment to his daughter Katherine: 'blown up by a 4.2 & shaken into a nervous breakdown which has made me unbearable to myself & all my kind'.[2] He suffered a concussion, loosened teeth, and a severe but temporary loss of memory; but in his various accounts of this near-death experience, like Tietjens, he was always careful to distinguish its physical from its psychological effects, noting, for example: 'I have been lifted off my feet and dropped two yards away by the explosion of a shell and felt complete assurance of immunity.'[3] After the war, he acknowledged in a famous passage that: 'You may say that every one who had taken physical part in the war was then mad';[4] but while biographers generally assume that he suffered shell shock, he never explicitly accepted the diagnosis. Perhaps the closest he came was in a letter to C. F. G. Masterman, to whom he confided, that after thirty-six hours spent revising the proofs of a French translation of *Between St. Denis and St. George* (1915), 'indeed I collapsed & was made to see the M. O. [Medical Officer] who said I was suffering from specific shell-shock & ought to go to hospital. However, I wdn't. & got back here'.[5] Here, the specific cause of his collapse was not the shock of shells but the sustained concentration of reading proof against a deadline (although, as Alan Judd and Max Saunders have noted, the effects of stress are often apparent only in the aftermath of a traumatic event).[6] Ford complained in his wartime letters of exhaustion, of lungs 'charred up' by gas and bad weather, of fever and headaches, toothache and neuritis;[7] but in his letters and memoirs, shell shock is always something suffered by others. In any case, Ford's symptoms, and those of Tietjens, do not seem to match the 'fits, faints and paralyses' that came to be understood as typical of shell shock, which 'included withered, trembling arms, paralysed hands, stumbling gaits, tics, tremors and shakes, as well as numbed muteness, palpitations, sweaty hallucinations and nightmares'.[8] Although he remained short of breath, Ford's experience of the war seems even to have cured the agoraphobia and neurasthenia to which he was prone in his earlier years and left him relatively sane and confident of his powers. As Max Saunders has noted:

> Of course Ford's experience of shell-shock had pathological effects. But what is astonishing about *Parade's End* is not that it still bears the impress of that trauma, but that despite Ford's suffering he was able to produce a work so generous, humane, and sane.[9]

What are the mental attitudes or strategies that enable Christopher Tietjens to preserve his generosity, humanity, and sanity?

The Mind in Pieces

One of the unique features of *Parade's End* is its presentation of the mind not as unitary or stable, but as a system of interrelating and often non-communicating parts, in a manner that extends the notion of consciousness well beyond the Freudian economy of ego, id, and superego to include a wide range of minds or aspects of mind.[10] The word 'mind' in various forms occurs more than 300 times in the course of the tetralogy, often with qualifiers that include not only the 'conscious mind' and the 'unconscious mind' but also the 'surface mind', the 'uppermost mind', the 'under mind', the 'inner mind', and the 'subordinate mind'. The mind is not only a receptacle into which things can be placed, or something to be 'made up', but a being capable of agency, of having so to speak a mind of its own. Daydreaming of Tietjens, Valentine Wannop imagines herself being embraced by the 'arms of his mind' (*Some Do Not . . .*, p. 306). In Ford's world, minds can talk to themselves, and even sing; they can be pleased or fatigued; they can become clear, but they can also 'stop' without warning. There are times when Tietjens does not know what his mind will do and times when he is dismayed by his mind's behaviour. During a night-time attack, one's brain is no longer fully one's own:

> In the trench you could see nothing and noise rushed like black angels gone mad; solid noise that swept you off your feet. . . . Swept your brain off its feet. Someone else took control of it. You became second-in-command of your own soul.[11]

Throughout the tetralogy, he and many of the other characters are in a constant state of negotiation with their own minds, trying to understand them and keep them under control, and to find mental stability and peace.

Julian Barnes has noted the wide range of animals to which Tietjens is compared by others:

> In the course of the novel he is variously compared to a maddened horse, an ox, a swollen animal, a mad bullock, a lonely buffalo, a town bull, a raging stallion, a dying bulldog, a grey bear, a farmyard boar, a hog, and finally a dejected bulldog.[12]

But Barnes does not include in this list the animals to which Tietjens compares his own mind. When he is irritated by Colonel Levin's references to his marital situation, he compares his mind to a strong but recalcitrant horse: 'His mind had become a coffin-headed, leather-jawed charger, like Schomburg. Sitting on his mind was like sitting on Schomburg at a dull water-jump.'[13] While waiting for a German attack to begin, he compares his mind to a well-trained dog:

> He wished his mind would not go on and on figuring. It did it whilst you weren't looking. As a well-trained dog will do when you tell it to stay in one part of a room and it prefers another. It prefers to do figuring. Creeps from the rug by the door to the hearth-rug, its eyes on your unconscious face. . . . That was what your mind was like. Like a dog! (*A Man Could Stand Up –*, p. 78)

And when he finds himself compelled to think of Sylvia and the paternity of his son, he recalls these as 'moments when his mind was like a blind octopus, squirming in an agony of knife-cuts' (*No More Parades*, p. 73).

Tietjens' mind presents itself to him as a menagerie of creatures whose behaviour cannot always be predicted or controlled.

Along with the fragmentation of the mind into multiple entities not always at peace with one another, the novel also plays with the misunderstanding and confusion of proper names, as if the nominal identities of the characters were out of focus for one another and occasionally also for the reader. The name Wannop is confused with Wanostrocht; Private Smith's real name turns out to be Eisenstein; the Colonel in command whom Tietjens replaces, who dies of cancer on Armistice Day, is never given a surname; Marie Léonie is also known as Charlotte; and Christopher's putative son is named both Michael and Mark. Captain McKechnie is wrongly identified as Captain Mackenzie even by the narrator of the opening scene of *No More Parades*, and the mistaken name appears in this volume more often (fifty-two times) than his correct name (forty-seven times). Along with his struggle to control his multiple minds, Tietjens also struggles to determine and remember the exact names of people and things. In both cases, his mastery over his thoughts increases in the course of the novel. He recovers from amnesia to remember the names of Metternich and Bemerton; and if his multiple minds often behave in surprising ways, they also endow him with a remarkable capacity for multitasking, making it possible for him to do many different kinds of things at once.

Parade's End is often understood as a novel about recovery from war trauma or shell shock, but it is important to remember that the main sources of trauma in Tietjens' life – his wife's infidelity and his son's uncertain paternity – both predate the outbreak of war. The war in fact comes to Tietjens as a kind of relief from the stress of his situation, both personal and professional. At first he cannot imagine that England will be involved in the war. He recalls his visit to his sister on the Yorkshire moors with his boy as 'the last days of happiness he was to know', and daydreams of joining the French Foreign Legion as an alternative to life in his decadent, hypocritical society:

> It would be restful to serve, if only as a slave, people who saw clearly, coldly, straight: not obliquely and with hypocrisy only such things as should deviously conduce to the standard of comfort of hogs and to lecheries winked at. . . . He would rather sit for hours on a bench in a barrack-room polishing a badge in preparation for the cruellest of route marches of immense lengths under the Algerian sun. (*Some Do Not . . .*, p. 230)

His wish is fulfilled when he finds himself appreciating the restful comfort of an orderly room, even comparing it to 'A paradise! [. . .] *the paradise of the Other Ranks*':

He felt a yearning towards rooms in huts, warmed by coke-stoves and electrically lit, with acting lance-corporals bending over A.F.B.'s on a background of deal pigeon-holes filled with returns on buff and blue paper. You got quiet and engrossment there. It was a queer thing: the only place where he, Christopher Tietjens of Groby, could be absently satisfied was in some orderly room or other. (*No More Parades*, p. 55)

The war provides him with an orderly and honourable escape from his marital difficulties, and with a means of achieving peace and unity of mind even at the risk of imminent death. In the third novel of the tetralogy, Tietjens realises that even in the face of mortal danger one can find peace of mind:

If you are lying down under fire – flat under pretty smart fire – and you have only a paper bag in front of your head for cover you feel immeasurably safer than you do without it. You have a mind at rest. (*A Man Could Stand Up –*, p. 60)

The tetralogy is not so much the story of a war-damaged mind seeking recovery as the chronicle of a good man's efforts to find mental repose in a disordered world.

Tietjens of Groby

Luckily for his peace of mind, Tietjens is endowed with certain attributes that others lack. Although he is uncomfortable with his social position and ultimately rejects it, his status as a member of the landed gentry is initially a source of security and stability. In *Some Do Not . . .*, the very first thing we are told about Tietjens and his friend Vincent Macmaster is that 'they were of the English public official class' that 'administered the world' (pp. 3, 4); yet they are by no means of the same social class, and the narrative proceeds immediately to mark their differences. Tietjens is the 'youngest son of a Yorkshire country gentleman' and future lord of the manor, a casual Tory gentleman who feels not the slightest need to prove himself. The narrator tells us that 'Tietjens himself was entitled to the best – the best that first-class public offices and first-class people could afford. He was without ambition, but these things would come to him as they do in England' (p. 6). Macmaster, in contrast, is a socially insecure Scotsman of undistinguished parentage who constantly feels a need to prove himself. Luckily for Macmaster, Tietjens has a strong sense of social responsibility with regard to those who are not 'born', and is even grateful to Macmaster for the opportunity to be of service. The relationship between the two friends is described in carefully qualified terms: 'Tietjens had always accepted Macmaster [. . .]. So for Macmaster he had a very deep affection – even a gratitude. And Macmaster might be considered as returning these feelings' (p. 7). The rest of the tetralogy amply demonstrates the extent to which Macmaster is incapable of gratitude, a characteristic which Tietjens seems to associate with his being a Scotsman: 'With an English young man of the lower orders that [a gift of money for college expenses] would have left a sense of class obligation. With Macmaster it just didn't' (p. 8). 'Acceptance' is hardly an equal basis for friendship, and Macmaster is aware that Tietjens cannot accept him as an equal. When Tietjens confides to him that he cannot be certain that he is the father of his wife's child, Macmaster finds the admission 'appalling' and 'almost an insult' because: 'It was the sort of confidence a man didn't make to his equal, but only to solicitors, doctors, or the clergy who are not quite men' (p. 21).

As a member of the landed gentry, Tietjens embodies a code of conduct that involves responsibility for the land and for the lower classes, and a deep appreciation of the natural world of plants and animals. It also involves an ideal of fidelity and a silent refusal to protest against insult or injury. As Tietjens tells Macmaster: 'I stand for monogamy and chastity. And for no talking about it' (p. 24). The mental discipline of this code of rectitude and reticence stands Tietjens in good stead under conditions of war. Unlike many of the other characters in the novel, his conscience is relatively clean and he remains generally on good terms with himself. He has developed a capacity for self-control that is not only automatic but reinforced by conscious deliberation:

> In electing to be peculiarly English in habits and in as much of his temperament as he could control – for, though no man can choose the land of his birth or his ancestry, he can, if he have industry and determination, so watch over himself as materially to modify his automatic habits – Tietjens had quite advisedly and of set purpose adopted a habit of behaviour that he considered to be the best in the world for the normal life. (*Some Do Not . . .*, p. 220)

Tietjens knows that the 'repressions of the passionate drive them mad' (*No More Parades*, p. 15), and this gentlemanly code makes life particularly difficult for reticent Yorkshiremen who cannot easily give vent to their emotions: 'For the basis of Christopher Tietjens' emotional existence was a complete taciturnity – at any rate as to his emotions. As Tietjens saw the world, you didn't "talk." Perhaps you didn't even think about how you felt' (*Some Do Not . . .*, p. 8). The first three volumes of the tetralogy are, among other things, a chronicle of Tietjens' learning to think about his feelings and to manage the various 'minds' involved in this process.

In the context of his habitual 'self-suppression', the moments at which Tietjens and the other characters reveal their unconscious selves are particularly striking. The argument about monogamy and chastity in the opening chapter of *Some Do Not . . .* is launched by such an 'unconscious' outburst from Macmaster: 'Suddenly – and as if in a sort of unconscious losing of his head – Macmaster remarked: "You can't say the man wasn't a poet!"' (p. 21). Tietjens' own efforts to 'watch over himself' are put to the test by the two unresolved issues that he works hardest to repress. His stress is revealed in the opening chapter by the intensity of his attack on Macmaster's sentimental veneration of what Tietjens calls the 'lachrymose polygamy' (p. 24) of the Pre-Raphaelites, which is of course not only an argument about Rossetti but also a comment on Tietjens' own preoccupations with his wife and putative son. His first meeting with Valentine Wannop reveals to him the stress to which he has been subjected: 'He felt himself to be content for the first time in four months [that is, since Sylvia left him with Perowne]. His pulse beat calmly; the heat of the sun all over him appeared to be a beneficent flood' (p. 89). That evening, he decides to apply his mind in an effort to understand 'the conditions of his life with Sylvia'; and while 'one half of his mind' is occupied with a game of patience, he becomes lost in concentration so deeply that Macmaster's sudden entrance shatters his world:

> He nearly vomited: his brain reeled and the room fell about. [. . .] He had, he knew, carried the suppression of thought in his conscious mind so far that his unconscious self had taken command and had, for the time, paralysed both his body and his mind. (p. 101)

Such mental and physical paralysis anticipates the symptoms of shell shock, signalling that there are limits to how much stress the mind can bear before it shuts down. Yet these effects take place before the war, and never again in the course of the tetralogy will Tietjens so lose control of himself, despite the horrors of war and his being blown off his feet more than once. Paradoxically, the discipline and responsibility of service at the Front brings relief to Tietjens, clarifying his sense of himself and giving him a firm foundation for self-reconstruction. Stella Bowen described Ford as:

> the only intellectual I had met to whom army discipline provided a conscious release from the torments and indecisions of a super-sensitive brain. To obey orders was, for him, a positive holiday, and the pleasure he took in recounting rather bucolic anecdotes of the army was the measure of his need for escape from the intrigues and sophistications of Literary London.[14]

Army discipline focuses Tietjens' mind, as exemplified by the military-style account he writes on the night of Sylvia's visit to Rouen, which leads him to admit to himself the depth of his love for Valentine Wannop.

Tietjens as Therapist

The degree of Tietjens' self-control can be measured by his ability to help those in mental difficulty, even when they dislike him or outrank him. *No More Parades* opens in the confused chiaroscuro of a hut in a depot being bombed by a German aeroplane, where an argument occurs between Tietjens and a young Scotsman who is in many respects a more troubled military version of Macmaster, and who turns out to be Macmaster's nephew. Captain McKechnie is introduced as an angry, embittered young officer without self-control and 'just upon out of his mind' (p. 12). As against Tietjens' constitutional reticence, McKechnie finds relief in ranting: 'his mind [was] eased by having got off his chest a confounded lot of semi-nonsensical ravings' (p. 25). McKechnie's instability is obvious to everyone, but he is also a competent officer, and General Campion has placed him in Tietjens' particular care: 'Probably Campion imagined that they had no work to do in that unit: they might become an acting lunatic ward' (p. 18). Tietjens, himself depressed and worried by 'the worries of all these wet millions in mud-brown' (p. 17), accepts responsibility for McKechnie, realising that 'it was a military duty to bother himself about the mental equilibrium of this member of the lower classes' (p. 26).

In this first scene Tietjens helps McKechnie by engaging him in an argument where Tietjens shows himself to be even more cynical about the managers of the war than McKechnie is. In effect Tietjens performs an effective 'talking cure' at the end of which McKechnie is obliged to concede: 'I dare say you're right' (p. 27). At that moment, O Nine Morgan enters the hut and reports his own death in 'a high wooden voice: "'Ere's another bloomin' casualty' (p. 28). Tietjens will later be haunted by this moment (he refers to his condition afterwards as a 'complex'), but his mind's immediate reaction – although his 'thoughts seemed to have to shout to him between earthquake shocks' (p. 29) – is to cling to what might be called images of innocence. Morgan falls over a fellow soldier sitting in the lurid light of a brazier, yet to Tietjens, bizarrely and tenderly, the two soldiers resemble 'one girl that should be combing the hair of another recumbent before her'. The sight of Morgan's streaming blood then suggests to him 'fresh water bubbling up in sand' (pp. 28–9), an image recalling the bubbling fountain in the final chapter of *Some Do Not . . .* that 'could be trusted to keep on for ever' (p. 347), symbolising for Tietjens his love for Valentine Wannop. Tietjens' hands and clothing are bloodied from lifting Morgan's corpse off his fellow soldier, and when the soldier then offers him a bowl of water to wash himself, he notices that 'the water shone innocently, a half-moon of translucence wavering over the white bottom of the basin. [...] Tietjens placed his hands in the innocent water and watched light purple-scarlet mist diffuse itself over the pale half-moon' (p. 32). By way of reflection and metaphor, Morgan's blood thus achieves a kind of cosmic significance, becoming a stain upon the moon. The orchestration of leitmotifs in this scene reveals the importance of innocence as a mainstay under conditions of unbearable stress.[15]

In the third volume, Tietjens finds himself in a baggage car on his way to the Front in the company of the lunatic McKechnie and his wife's ex-lover Perowne, and is again called upon to provide a kind of therapy in the form of consolation for Major Perowne, who has a strong premonition that he is about to die. Tietjens later remembers 'the heavy, authoritative words he had used' to convince Perowne 'that Death supplied His own anaesthetics' (p. 93). The therapy apparently works, since Perowne is found dead the following night with a smile on his face.

These instances of Tietjens' ability and willingness to help others in mental distress, even when they are placed over him in the military hierarchy, are signs of his own relative mental stability. As Tietjens tells Colonel Levin: 'the thing is to be able to stick to the integrity of your character, whatever earthquake sets the house tumbling over your head. . . .' (*No More Parades*, p. 196).

Pastoralism and Peace

Among the many threads woven into the tetralogy is the leitmotif of George Herbert's church at Bemerton, near Salisbury, which gradually comes into focus for Tietjens as an image of the ideal life of peace and contentment. He daydreams of taking orders and of following in Herbert's footsteps, abandoning the nobility in favour of clerical life. In *A Man Could Stand Up –*, Tietjens can still remind himself of the prerogatives of his social standing – 'He was still Tietjens of Groby: no man could give him anything, no man could take anything from him' (p. 76) – yet in the course of the volume his mind finds itself increasingly obsessed with Valentine Wannop. When he suddenly imagines himself walking beside her on a country road – although he hates 'walking on roads!' (*Some Do Not . . .*, p. 136) – he abandons his dream of a country parsonage and realises that what he needs and craves is not the peace of

Bemerton but the sound of her voice: 'It would rest him to hear that' (*A Man Could Stand Up –*, p. 136).

The fourth volume of the tetralogy is a masterpiece of indirection in which contradictions are resolved and peace is established at the cost of extreme renunciations. Mark Tietjens' immobility and silence provide a fixed, Archimedean perspective from which to survey not only a glorious view of four counties but also the intolerable conditions of social life. Paradoxically, although he was never in combat, the form taken by Mark's withdrawal from the world closely resembles the paralysis and mutism characteristic of shell shock, and occurs for similar reasons. His act of renunciation is an implacable judgement of the administrative classes that ruled the world: 'the Governing Classes were no good';[16] 'public life had become so discreditable an affair that the only remedy was for the real governing classes to retire altogether from public pursuits' (p. 95). His silence is the ultimate expression of his native Yorkshire reticence, and marks his refusal to be implicated in a corrupt and dishonourable world. Yet like his brother's wartime discovery of solutions to problems that predate the war, the outcome of the war provides Mark with an opportunity to solve a problem into which he was born:

> at a very early age he had decided that he would chuck the country-gentleman business. He didn't see that he was the one to bother with those confounded, hard-headed beggars or with those confounded wind-swept moors and wet valley bottoms. One owed the blighters a duty, but one did not have to live among them or see that they aired their bedrooms. (p. 85)

Mark's career in the Department of Transport was thus an escape from 'the country-gentleman business'; and his ultimate retirement into the countryside marks the final step in his refusal to be the victim of his heritage.

Christopher, 'under the long strain of the war', has similarly 'outgrown alike the mentality and the traditions of his own family and his own race' (p. 103). He rejects the company of his social equals for reasons that recall his former friendship with Macmaster:

> If he had to go into partnership and be thrown into close contact with anyone at all he did not care much who it was as long as it was not either a bounder or a man of his own class and race. To be in close mental communion with either an English bounder or an Englishman of good family would, he was aware, be intolerable to him. (p. 102)

Groby has been abandoned to 'Papists' and American tenants, yet the two couples in the cottage are happy: Mark finds 'complete satisfaction' (p. 71) in his association with Marie Léonie; she wishes for nothing better than to care for him; and Tietjens finds peace of mind by renouncing his inheritance and making his own living with Valentine in his own way as a dealer in antique furniture. Of course, not everyone achieves peace of mind in the end. Sylvia recognises that her husband has found peace at last, and faces a bitter future: 'Her main bitterness was that they had this peace. She was cutting the painter, but they were going on in this peace; her world was waning' (p. 171).

As Paul Skinner aptly puts it: 'Tietjens does not make sense of the war; but the war, in large part, makes sense of Tietjens. [. . .] The release of long repressed feelings grants him "a mind entire", body and brain brought into harmony and productive balance.'[17] The tetralogy that began with a 'perfectly appointed railway carriage' (p. 3) in which two friends have an unresolved argument ends with an open view not only of four counties but of the starry skies above, and of nearness to God, made manifest in the sounds of 'cattle and sheep and horses and pigs crashing through all the hedges of the county': 'The cattle had been panicked because they had been sensible of the presence of the Almighty walking upon the firmament. . . .' (pp. 201–2). It also ends with the first words Mark has spoken since beginning his vow of silence, words which express rough compassion for Sylvia and bestow a blessing upon Valentine and Christopher and the son they are expecting.

Much has been said about the tetralogy as a novel of 'reconstruction'; but the reconstruction in question is not that of a mind shattered by war but clarified and purified by it, unified and focused by a transparent and simple lifestyle close to the land and its deep history. Ford believed that such basic values were capable of preventing future wars, and he would elaborate this idea in later works such as *Provence* (1935) and *Great Trade Route* (1937). *Parade's End* marks the end of parades, of ceremonies and fanfare, but it also signals the possibility of a more humane and intimate peace than the one declared by the treaty at Versailles. Ford's answer to Valentine's question – 'How are we ever to live?' (*Last Post*, p. 203) – is to live simply, frugally, and with an abiding awareness of the natural world. These are the values that sustain Tietjens in the war, and through them he finds his peace of mind.

Notes

1. Ford, *Joseph Conrad*, p. 192.
2. December 1916: quoted in Judd, *Ford Madox Ford*, pp. 295–6.
3. Ford, 'Arms and the Mind', *War Prose*, p. 41.
4. Ford, *It Was the Nightingale*, p. 63.
5. 13 September 1916: Ford, *Letters of Ford Madox Ford*, p. 76.

6. Judd, *Ford Madox Ford*, p. 297; Saunders, *Ford Madox Ford*, II, p. 23.
7. Ford, *Letters of Ford Madox Ford*, pp. 72–88.
8. Leese, *Shell Shock*, pp. 2–3.
9. Saunders, *Ford Madox Ford*, II, p. 237.
10. Freud's name is invoked only once in the tetralogy, when Sylvia tells Father Consett, 'I prefer to pin my faith to Mrs. Vanderdecken. And, of course, Freud': Ford, *Some Do Not . . .*, ed. Max Saunders, p. 49. All further references are to this edition.
11. Ford, *A Man Could Stand Up –*, ed. Joseph Wiesenfarth, p. 77. All further references are to this edition.
12. Barnes, 'Ford's Anglican Saint', p. 66.
13. Ford, *No More Parades*, ed. Sara Haslam, p. 192. All further references are to this edition.
14. Bowen, *Drawn from Life*, pp. 61–2.
15. The washing of hands also reveals Tietjens' guilt by recalling the gesture of Pontius Pilate: Matthew 27: 24. Tietjens feels that Morgan's blood is on his hands because he refused to grant him leave to save him from being beaten to death by his wife's lover, a prize-fighter.
16. Ford, *Last Post*, ed. Paul Skinner, p. 64. All further references are to this edition.
17. Skinner, 'The Painful Processes of Reconstruction', p. 71.

Notes on Contributors

Alexandra Becquet teaches English as a Second Language at the Université Paris 13. She received her PhD from the Université Sorbonne Nouvelle – Paris 3 in 2013 with a thesis on the intermediality of Ford's Impressionist aesthetics. Her essays include: 'Modernity, Shock and Cinema: The Visual Aesthetics of Ford Madox Ford's *Parade's End*' (in *Ford Madox Ford and Visual Culture*, Rodopi, 2009); 'Impressionist Confusion, Dissolving Landscapes: Ford Madox Ford's Great French Route and Trade' (in *Ford Madox Ford, France and Provence*, Rodopi, 2011); and 'Ford Madox Ford, compositeur: un regard "impressionniste" sur la Grande Guerre', published in the transdisciplinary volume *Mutations et adaptations : le XXème siècle* (Nouveau Monde éditions, 2009), which she co-edited. She is one of the contributors to the forthcoming *Ashgate Research Companion to Ford Madox Ford* and is revising her PhD thesis for publication with the Éditions Honoré Champion.

Leslie de Bont is a *professeure agrégée* (tenured lecturer) who teaches English in the Faculty of Psychology, Université de Nantes. She is also a PhD candidate at the Université Sorbonne Nouvelle – Paris 3: her thesis is titled '"Like Anecdotes from a case-book": dialogues entre discours théoriques et représentations du singulier dans les romans de May Sinclair'. She has given talks and published articles on Sinclair in French and English, including: 'From the Priest to the Therapist: Secrecy, Language and Technique in Ford's *A Call* and May Sinclair's *Anne Severn and the Fieldings*' (in *The Edwardian Ford Madox Ford*, Rodopi, 2013); and '"I was the only one who wasn't quite sane": être femme, épouse, mère et artiste dans *The Creators* (1910) de May Sinclair' (in *Cahiers Victoriens et Edouardiens*, 2014). She is also a translator and a member of the May Sinclair Society.

Ashley Chantler is Senior Lecturer in English at the University of Chester. He is the series editor of *Character Studies* (Continuum); author of *Heart of Darkness: Character Studies* (Continuum, 2008); and co-editor of *Translation Practices: Through Language to Culture* (Rodopi, 2009), *Studying English Literature* (Continuum 2010), and *Literature and Authenticity, 1780–1900* (Ashgate, 2011). His essays include: 'Ford's Pre-War Poetry and the "Rotting City"' (in *Ford Madox Ford and the City*, Rodopi, 2005); 'Ford and the Impressionist Lyric' (in *Ford Madox Ford and Visual Culture*, Rodopi, 2009); 'Editing Ford's Poetry' (in *Ford Madox Ford, Modernist Magazines and Editing*, Rodopi, 2010); 'Ford Madox Ford and the Troubadours' (in *Ford Madox Ford, France and Provence*, Rodopi, 2011); and 'Ford Madox Ford's Edwardian Poetry' (in *The Edwardian Ford Madox Ford*, Rodopi, 2013). With Rob Hawkes, he is co-editor of *Ford Madox Ford's Parade's End: The First World War, Culture, and Modernity* (Rodopi, 2014) and *Ford Madox Ford: An Introduction* (Ashgate, forthcoming).

Barbara Farnworth is a PhD student and instructor at the University of Rhode Island. Her thesis explores humour, gender, and psychology in nineteenth- and early twentieth-century British literature, and examines the works of authors such as Ford, Austen, Dickens, and Trollope.

Meghan Marie Hammond teaches at the University of Chicago. She is author of *Empathy and the Psychology of Literary Modernism* (Edinburgh University Press, 2014) and co-editor of *Rethinking Empathy Through Literature* (Routledge, 2014). Her published work includes essays on Ford, Ishiguro, James, and Melville. She is currently working on a second book project that examines the significance of the corpse in literary and visual culture.

Rob Hawkes is Senior Lecturer in English Studies at Teesside University. He is author of *Ford Madox Ford and the Misfit Moderns: Edwardian Fiction and the First World War* (Palgrave Macmillan, 2012). His essays include: 'Personalities of Paper: Characterisation in *A Call* and *The Good Soldier*' (in *Ford Madox Ford: Literary Networks and Cultural Transformations*, Rodopi, 2008); 'Visuality vs. Temporality: Plotting and Depiction in *The Fifth Queen* and *Ladies Whose Bright Eyes*' (in *Ford Madox Ford and Visual Culture*, Rodopi, 2009); and 'Trusting in Provence: Financial Crisis in *The Rash Act* and *Henry for Hugh*' (in *Ford Madox Ford, France and Provence*, Rodopi, 2011). With Ashley Chantler, he is co-editor of *Ford Madox Ford's Parade's End: The First*

World War, Culture, and Modernity (Rodopi, 2014) and *Ford Madox Ford: An Introduction* (Ashgate, forthcoming).

Charlotte Jones is a PhD student at University College London. Her thesis investigates realism in Edwardian literature, and considers the work of authors such as Ford, Bennett, Chesterton, Conrad, Sinclair, and Wells.

Sarah Kingston is a PhD candidate in the English Literature department at the University of Rhode Island. She is currently working on her thesis, which explores the relationship between insomnia and the production of identity in British and American modernist literature. Her research focuses on the work of authors including Ford, Fitzgerald, Forster, Frank, Nabokov, Richardson, Wells, and Woolf.

Gene M. Moore was Senior Lecturer in English and American Literature at the Universiteit van Amsterdam until his retirement in 2013. Along with various essays on Faulkner and Ford and a casebook on *Heart of Darkness* (Oxford University Press, 2005), his publications include: *Proust and Musil: The Novel as Research Instrument* (Garland, 1985); *Conrad's Cities* (Rodopi, 1992); *Conrad on Film* (Cambridge University Press, 1997); and the *Suspense* volume of the Cambridge Edition of the Works of Joseph Conrad (2011). With Owen Knowles, he co-authored the *Oxford Reader's Companion to Joseph Conrad* (2000), and co-edited, with Laurence Davies and others, the last two volumes of Conrad's *Collected Letters* (Cambridge University Press, 2007, 2008). He also catalogued the Hans van Marle Archive for Special Collections at Senate House, University of London.

Max Saunders is Director of the Arts and Humanities Research Institute, Professor of English and Co-Director of the Centre for Life-Writing Research at King's College London. He is author of *Ford Madox Ford: A Dual Life*, 2 vols (Oxford University Press, 1996) and *Self Impression: Life-Writing, Autobiografiction, and the Forms of Modern Literature* (Oxford University Press, 2010); the editor of Ford's *Selected Poems*, *War Prose*, *Some Do Not . . .*, and (with Richard Stang) *Critical Essays* (Carcanet Press, 1997, 1999, 2010, 2002), and of the Oxford World's Classics edition of *The Good Soldier* (2012). He has published essays on life writing, Impressionism, Ford, Aldington, Burgess, Conrad, Eliot, Forster, Freud, James, Joyce, Lawrence, Lehmann, Pound, Ruskin, Sinclair, and others. He is also general editor of International Ford Madox Ford Studies. He was awarded a Leverhulme Major Research

Fellowship from 2008–10 to research the To-Day and To-Morrow book series, and in 2013 an Advanced Grant from the ERC for a five-year collaborative project on Digital Life Writing.

Eve Sorum is Associate Professor of English at the University of Massachusetts Boston and the recipient of a 2013–14 Fulbright Fellowship. Her essays include: 'Mourning and Moving On: Life After War in Ford Madox Ford's *The Last Post*' (in *Modernism and Mourning*, Bucknell University Press, 2007); '"The Place on the Map": Geography and Meter in Hardy's Elegies' (in *Modernism/modernity*, 2009); 'Hardy's Geography of Narrative Empathy' (in *Studies in the Novel*, 2011); 'Dissolving Landscapes: Auden's Protean Nostalgia' (in *Modernism and Nostalgia: Bodies, Locations, Aesthetics*, Palgrave Macmillan, 2013); 'Poetry of the Great War' (in *A Companion to Modernist Poetry*, Wiley-Blackwell, 2014); and 'Psychology, Psychoanalysis, and the New Subjectivities of the Early Twentieth Century' (forthcoming in *The Cambridge Companion to The Waste Land*). She is currently working on a book about loss and modernist empathy.

Karolyn Steffens earned her doctorate from the University of Wisconsin-Madison in 2014. Her essays include: 'Communicating Trauma: Pat Barker's *Regeneration* Trilogy and W. H. R. Rivers's Psychoanalytic Method' (in the *Journal of Modern Literature*, 2014); and '"Often faulty . . . always lovable . . . sometimes great": Ford Madox Ford's Reception History', co-authored with Joseph Wiesenfarth for the *Ashgate Research Companion to Ford Madox Ford* (forthcoming). Her book project, *Modernist Affirmation: Twentieth-Century Fiction and the Discourse of Trauma*, investigates affirmative possibilities within both trauma and modernist studies through readings of Ford, Barker, Coetzee, McEwan, and Woolf.

Bibliography

Alberti, Leon Battista, *On Painting: A New Translation and Critical Edition*, trans. Rocco Sinisgalli (Cambridge: Cambridge University Press, [1435] 2011).

Aldington, Richard, *Death of a Hero* (London: Chatto & Windus, 1929).

Arasse, Daniel, *Histoires de peinture* (Paris: Gallimard, 2004).

Arnheim, Rudolf, *Art and Visual Perception: A Psychology of the Creative Eye: The New Version* (Berkeley: University of California Press, 1974).

Attridge, John, '"A Taboo on the Mention of Taboo": Taciturnity and Englishness in *Parade's End* and André Maurois' *Les Silences du Colonel Bramble*', in Ashley Chantler and Rob Hawkes (eds), *Ford Madox Ford's Parade's End: The First World War, Culture, and Modernity*, International Ford Madox Ford Studies 13 (Amsterdam: Rodopi, 2014), pp. 23–35.

Babington, Anthony, *Shell-Shock: A History of the Changing Attitudes to War Neurosis* (London: Leo Cooper, 1997).

Backès, Jean-Louis, *Musique et littérature: Essai de poétique comparée* (Paris: PUF, 1994).

Barnard, A. B., 'Habit', in Caroline Benedict Burrell and William Byron Forbush (eds), *The Mother's Book* (New York: University Society, 1919), pp. 99–101.

Barnes, Julian, Introduction to Ford Madox Ford, *Parade's End* (London: Penguin, 2012), pp. vii–xviii.

Barnes, Julian, 'Ford's Anglican Saint', *Through the Window: Seventeen Essays (and One Short Story)* (London: Vintage, 2012), pp. 64–76.

Becquet, Alexandra, 'Impressionist Confusion, Dissolving Landscape: Reconstructing Provence', in Dominique Lemarchal and Claire Davison-Pégon (eds), *Ford Madox Ford, France and Provence*, International Ford Madox Ford Studies 10 (Amsterdam: Rodopi, 2011), pp. 119–31.

Bell, Michael, 'The Metaphysics of Modernism', in Michael Levenson (ed.), *The Cambridge Companion to Modernism* (Cambridge: Cambridge University Press, 1999), pp. 9–32.

Bergson, Henri, *Matière et mémoire: Essai sur la relation du corps à l'esprit* (Paris: PUF, [1896] 2004).

Binnevald, Hans, *From Shell Shock to Combat Stress*, trans. John O'Kane (Amsterdam: Amsterdam University Press, 1997).

Bogacz, Ted, 'War Neurosis and Cultural Change in England 1914–22: The Work of the War Office Committee of Enquiry into "Shell-Shock"', *Journal of Contemporary History*, 24.2 (1989), pp. 227–56.

Bonikowski, Wyatt, *Shell Shock and the Modernist Imagination: The Death Drive in Post-World War One British Fiction* (Farnham: Ashgate, 2013).

Bordo, Susan, *Unbearable Weight: Feminism, Western Culture, and the Body* (Berkeley: University of California Press, 2003).

Bordogna, Francesca, 'Inner Division and Uncertain Contours: William James and the Politics of the Modern Self', *British Journal for the History of Science*, 40.4 (2007), pp. 505–36.

Boring, Edwin G., *A History of Experimental Psychology* (New York: Meredith, 1957).

Boulter, Jonathan, '"After . . . Armageddon": Trauma and History in Ford Madox Ford's *No Enemy*', in Joseph Wiesenfarth (ed.), *History and Representation in Ford Madox Ford's Writings*, International Ford Madox Ford Studies 3 (Amsterdam: Rodopi, 2004), pp. 77–90.

Bourke, Joanna, *Dismembering the Male: Men's Bodies, Britain and the Great War* (Chicago: University of Chicago Press, 1996).

Bowen, Stella, *Drawn from Life* (London: Collins, 1941).

Bradbury, Malcolm, 'The Denuded Place: War and Form in *Parade's End* and *U.S.A.*', in Holger Klein (ed.), *The First World War in Fiction: A Collection of Critical Essays* (London: Macmillan, 1976), pp. 193–209.

Brown, Dennis, 'Remains of the Day: Tietjens the Englishman', in Robert Hampson and Max Saunders (eds), *Ford Madox Ford's Modernity*, International Ford Madox Ford Studies 2 (Amsterdam: Rodopi, 2003), pp. 161–74.

Bryson, Norman, *Vision and Painting: The Logic of the Gaze* (New Haven, CT: Yale University Press, 1983).

Byrne, Romana, *Aesthetic Sexuality: A Literary History of Sadomasochism* (London: Bloomsbury, 2013).

Burgess, Anthony, 'Literature', in William Davis (ed.), *The Best of Everything* (London: Weidenfeld & Nicholson, 1980), pp. 95–101.

Caruth, Cathy, *Unclaimed Experience: Trauma, Narrative, and History* (Baltimore: Johns Hopkins University Press, 1996).

Cassell, Richard A., *Ford Madox Ford: A Study of His Novels* (Baltimore: Johns Hopkins Press, 1962).

Childs, Peter, *Modernism* (London: Routledge, 2000).

Cole, Sarah, *Modernism, Male Friendship, and the First World War* (Cambridge: Cambridge University Press, 2003).

Conroy, Mark, 'A Map of Tory Misreading in *Parade's End*', in Laura Colombino (ed.), *Ford Madox Ford and Visual Culture*, International Ford Madox Ford Studies 8 (Amsterdam: Rodopi, 2009), pp. 175–90.

Das, Santanu, *Touch and Intimacy in First World War Literature* (Cambridge: Cambridge University Press, 2005).

Deleuze, Gilles, and Felix Guattari, *A Thousand Plateaus: Capitalism and Schizophrenia*, trans. Brian Massumi (Minneapolis: University of Minnesota Press, 1987).

Erll, Astrid, 'The Great War Remembered: The Rhetoric of Collective Memory in Ford Madox Ford's *Parade's End* and Arnold Zweig's *Der Streit um den Sergeanten Grischa*', *Journal for the Study of British Cultures*, 10.1 (2003), pp. 49–75.

Eysteinsson, Astradur, *The Concept of Modernism* (Ithaca, NY: Cornell University Press, 1990).

Felman, Shoshana, and Dori Laub, *Testimony* (New York: Routledge, 1992).

Fernihough, Anne, 'Consciousness as a stream', in Morag Shiach (ed.), *The Cambridge Companion to the Modernist Novel* (Cambridge: Cambridge University Press, 2007), pp. 65–81.

Ford, Ford Madox, *Ancient Lights and Certain New Reflections: Being the Memories of a Young Man* (London: Chapman & Hall, 1911).

Ford, Ford Madox, *The Critical Attitude* (London: Duckworth, 1911).

Ford, Ford Madox, *Between St. Dennis and St. George: A Sketch of Three Civilisations* (London: Hodder & Stoughton, 1915).

Ford, Ford Madox, *When Blood Is Their Argument: An Analysis of Prussian Culture* (London: Hodder & Stoughton, 1915).

Ford, Ford Madox, 'Trois Jours de Permission', *Nation*, 19 (30 September 1916), 817–18.

Ford, Ford Madox, *On Heaven and Poems Written on Active Service* (London: John Lane, The Bodley Head; New York: John Lane, 1918).

Ford, Ford Madox, *The Marsden Case* (London: Duckworth, 1923).

Ford, Ford Madox, *Joseph Conrad: A Personal Remembrance* (London: Duckworth, 1924).

Ford, Ford Madox, 'Declined with Thanks', *New York Herald Tribune Books* (24 June 1928), pp. 1, 6.

Ford, Ford Madox, *Provence: From Minstrels to the Machine*, ed. John Coyle (Manchester: Carcanet Press, [1935] 2009).

Ford, Ford Madox, *Mightier Than the Sword* (London: George Allen & Unwin, 1938).

Ford, Ford Madox, *Critical Writings of Ford Madox Ford*, ed. Frank MacShane (Lincoln: University of Nebraska Press, 1964).

Ford, Ford Madox, *Letters of Ford Madox Ford*, ed. Richard M. Ludwig (Princeton: Princeton University Press, 1965).

Ford, Ford Madox, *The Correspondence of Ford Madox Ford and Stella Bowen*, ed. Sondra J. Stang and Karen Cochran (Bloomington: Indiana University Press, 1993).

Ford, Ford Madox, *Return to Yesterday*, ed. Bill Hutchings (Manchester: Carcanet Press, [1931] 1999).

Ford, Ford Madox, *War Prose*, ed. Max Saunders (Manchester: Carcanet Press, 1999).

Ford, Ford Madox, *Critical Essays*, ed. Max Saunders and Richard Stang (Manchester: Carcanet Press, 2002), pp. 208–17.

Ford, Ford Madox, *No Enemy: A Tale of Reconstruction*, ed. Paul Skinner (Manchester: Carcanet Press, [1929] 2002).

Ford, Ford Madox, *It Was the Nightingale,* ed. John Coyle (Manchester: Carcanet Press, [1933] 2007).

Ford, Ford Madox, *Some Do Not . . .*, ed. Max Saunders (Manchester: Carcanet Press, [1924] 2010).

Ford, Ford Madox, *No More Parades*, ed. Joseph Wiesenfarth (Manchester: Carcanet Press, [1925] 2011).

Ford, Ford Madox, *A Man Could Stand Up –*, ed. Sara Haslam (Manchester: Carcanet Press, [1926] 2011).

Ford, Ford Madox, *Last Post*, ed. Paul Skinner (Manchester: Carcanet Press, [1928] 2011).

Ford, Ford Madox, *The Good Soldier*, 2nd edn, ed. Martin Stannard (New York: Norton, [1915] 2012).

Foucault, Michel, *Discipline and Punish: The Birth of the Prison*, trans. Alan Sheridan (New York: Vintage, 1995).

Freud, Sigmund, *Reflections on War and Death*, trans. A. A. Brill and Alfred Kuttner (New York: Moffat, 1918).

Freud, Sigmund, *Three Essays on the Theory of Sexuality*, *The Standard Edition of the Complete Psychological Works of Sigmund Freud*, vol. VII, ed. James Strachey (London: The Hogarth Press, 1953), pp. 125–230.

Freud, Sigmund, 'The Psychotherapy of Hysteria', *The Standard Edition of the Complete Psychological Works of Sigmund Freud*, vol. II, ed. James Strachey (London: The Hogarth Press, 1955), pp. 253–306.

Freud, Sigmund, 'Remembering, Repeating and Working-Through', *The Standard Edition of the Complete Psychological Works of Sigmund Freud*, vol. XII, ed. James Strachey (London: The Hogarth Press, 1958), pp. 147–56.

Freud, Sigmund, *Beyond the Pleasure Principle*, trans. James Strachey (New York: Norton, [1920] 1961).

Freud, Sigmund, 'Beyond the Pleasure Principle', *The Essentials of Psycho-Analysis*, trans. James Strachey (London: Penguin, [1922] 1991), pp. 218–68.

Freud, Sigmund, *Three Case-Histories* (New York: Simon and Schuster, [1909–18] 2008).

Freud, Sigmund, and Joseph Breuer, *Studies on Hysteria*, trans. Nicola Luckhurst (Harmondsworth: Penguin, [1895] 2004).

Freud, Sigmund, Sandor Ferenczi and Karl Abraham, *Sur les névroses de guerre*, trans. Olivier Mannoni, Ilse Barande, Judith Dupont and Myriam Viliker (Paris: Éditions Payot and Rivages, [1919] 2010).

Fussell, Paul, *The Great War and Modern Memory* (Oxford: Oxford University Press, 1975).

Gathorne-Hardy, Jonathan, *The Old School Tie: The Phenomenon of the English Public School* (New York: Viking Press, 1978).

Gay, Peter, *Freud: A Life for Our Time* (New York: Norton, 1998).

Gay, Peter (ed.), *The Freud Reader* (New York: Norton, 1989).

Gordon, Ambrose, *The Invisible Tent: The War Novels of Ford Madox Ford* (Austin: University of Texas Press, 1964).

Gould, Gerald, 'Sex Obsession', *Observer*, 6 April 1924, p. 9.

Gould, Gerald, 'The English Novel of Today', *Observer*, 1 June 1924, p. 9.

Greene, Graham, *Ways of Escape* (London: The Bodley Head, 1980).

Hammond, Meghan Marie, *Empathy and the Psychology of Literary Modernism* (Edinburgh: Edinburgh University Press, 2014).

Harvey, David Dow, *Ford Madox Ford: 1873–1939: A Bibliography of Works and Criticism* (Princeton: Princeton University Press, 1962).

Haslam, Sara, *Fragmenting Modernism: Ford Madox Ford, the Novel and the Great War* (Manchester: Manchester University Press, 2002).

Haslam, Sara, 'From Conversation to Humiliation: *Parade's End* and the Eighteenth Century', in Ashley Chantler and Rob Hawkes (eds), *Ford Madox Ford's Parade's End: The First World War, Culture, and Modernity*, International Ford Madox Ford Studies 13 (Amsterdam: Rodopi, 2014), pp. 37–52.

Hawkes, Rob, *Ford Madox Ford and the Misfit Moderns: Edwardian Fiction and the First World War* (Basingstoke: Palgrave Macmillan, 2012).

Heldman, James M., 'The Last Victorian Novel: Technique and Theme in *Parade's End*', *Twentieth Century Literature*, 18:4 (October 1972), pp. 271–84.

Henighan, T. J., 'Tietjens Transformed: A Reading of *Parade's End*', *English Literature in Transition, 1880–1920*, 15.2 (1972), pp. 144–57.

Hoffmann, Charles G., *Ford Madox Ford* (New York: Twayne, 1967).

Hunt, Morton, *The Story of Psychology* (New York: Doubleday, 1994).

Hume, David, *A Treatise of Human Nature*, ed. Ernest C. Mossner (London: Penguin, [1739] 1969).

Hynes, Samuel, 'The Genre of *No Enemy*', *Antaeus*, 56 (1986), 125–42.

Jain, Anurag, 'When Propaganda Is Your Argument: Ford and First World War Propaganda', in Dennis Brown and Jenny Plastow (eds), *Ford Madox Ford and Englishness*, International Ford Madox Ford Studies 5 (Amsterdam: Rodopi, 2006), pp. 163–75.

James, Henry, 'Robert Louis Stevenson', *Partial Portraits* (London: Macmillan, [1888] 1919).

James, William, *The Principles of Psychology*, 2 vols (New York: Dover, [1890] 1950).

James, William, *Habit* (New York: Henry Holt, 1914).

James, William, *Essays in Psychology* (Cambridge, MA: Harvard University Press, 1984).

Jones, Mary Cover, 'A Laboratory Study of Fear: The Case of Peter', *Pedagogical Seminary*, 31 (1924), pp. 308–15.

Judd, Alan, *Ford Madox Ford* (Hammersmith: HarperCollins, 1991).

Keen, Suzanne, *Empathy and the Novel* (New York: Oxford University Press, 2007).

Kingsbury, Celia Malone, *The Peculiar Sanity of War: Hysteria in the Literature of World War One* (Texas: Texas University Press, 2002).

LaCapra, Dominick, *Writing History, Writing Trauma* (Baltimore: Johns Hopkins University Press, 2001).

Lee, Vernon, 'Anthropomorphic Aesthetics', in Vernon Lee and C. Anstruther-Thomson, *Beauty and Ugliness and Other Studies in Psychological Aesthetics* (London: John Lane, 1912), pp. 1–44.

Lee, Vernon, *The Beautiful: An Introduction to Psychological Aesthetics* (Cambridge: Cambridge University Press, 1913).

Leese, Peter, *Shell Shock: Traumatic Neurosis and the British Soldiers of the First World War* (Basingstoke: Palgrave Macmillan, 2002).

Léger, Fernand, 'Couleur dans le monde', *Fonctions de la peinture* (Paris: Gallimard, [1937] 2004), pp. 205–25.

Lerner, Paul, 'Psychiatry and Casualties of War in Germany, 1914–18', *Journal of Contemporary History*, 35.1 (2000), pp. 13–28.

Lodge, Oliver, 'On the Subliminal Self and on the Book *Human Personality*', *The Survival of Man*, expanded edition (New York: George H. Doran, 1920).

Loeffler, Toby Henry, 'The "Backbone of England": History, Memory, Landscape, and the Fordian Reconstruction of Englishness', *Texas Studies in Literature and Language*, 53.1 (2011), pp. 1–25.

Macauley, Robie, 'The Good Ford', *Kenyon Review*, 11 (1949), pp. 269–88.

McCarthy, Jeffrey Mathes, '"The Foul System": The Great War and Instrumental Rationality in *Parade's End*', *Studies in the Novel*, 41.2 (2009), pp. 178–200.

MacCurdy, John, *War Neuroses* (Cambridge: Cambridge University Press, 1918).

MacDonald, Robert, *The Language of Empire: Myths and Metaphors of Popular Imperialism* (Manchester: Manchester University Press, 1994).

MacFarlane, A. W., *Insomnia and Its Therapeutics* (New York: William Wood, 1891).

Mackenzie, John (ed.), *Popular Imperialism and the Military, 1850–1950* (Manchester: Manchester University Press, 1992).

Marinetti, Filippo Tommaso, 'Imagination sans fils et les mots en liberté: manifeste futuriste' (1913), in Giovanni Lista (ed.), *Futurisme: Manifestes-documents-proclamations* (Lausanne: L'Âge d'Homme, 1973), pp. 142–6.

Marin, Louis, *De la représentation* (Évreux: Seuil/Gallimard, 1994).

Martin, Meredith, 'Therapeutic Measures: The Hydra and Wilfred Owen at Craiglockhart War Hospital', *Modernism/Modernity*, 14.1 (2007), pp. 35–54.

Matz, Jesse, *Literary Impressionism and Modernist Aesthetics* (Cambridge: Cambridge University Press, 2001).

Meisel, Perry, 'Psychology', in David Bradshaw and Kevin J. H. Dettmar (eds), *A Companion to Modernist Literature and Culture* (Chichester: Wiley-Blackwell, 2006), pp. 79–91.

Meyer, Eric, 'Ford's War and (Post)Modern Memory: *Parade's End* and National Allegory', *Criticism*, 32.1 (1990), pp. 81–99.

Mitchell, Silas Weir, *Fat and Blood: An Essay on the Treatment of Certain Forms of Neurasthenia and Hysteria* (London: J. B. Lippincott, 1885).

Mizener, Arthur, *The Saddest Story: A Biography of Ford Madox Ford* (New York: World Publishing, 1971).

Moses, Michael Valdez, 'Disorientalism: Conrad and the Imperial Origins of Modernist Aesthetics', in Richard Begam and Michael Valdez Moses (eds), *Modernism and Colonialism* (Durham, NC: Duke University Press, 2007), pp. 43–69.

Myers, Charles, 'A Contribution to the Study of Shell Shock', *Lancet* (February 1915), pp. 316–20.

Myers, Charles, *Shell Shock in France 1914–1918* (Cambridge: Cambridge University Press, 1940).

Naumburg, Edward, Jr., 'A Collector Looks at Ford Again', in Sondra J. Stang (ed.), *The Presence of Ford Madox Ford: A Memorial Volume of Essays, Poems, and Memoirs* (Philadelphia: University of Pennsylvania Press, 1981).

Ngai, Sianne, *Ugly Feelings* (Cambridge, MA: Harvard University Press, 2005).

Norris, Margot, *Writing War in the Twentieth Century* (Charlottesville: University of Virginia Press, 2000).

O'Malley, Seamus, '*The Return of the Soldier* and *Parade's End*: Ford's Reworking of West's Pastoral', in Paul Skinner (ed.), *Ford Madox Ford's Literary Contacts*, International Ford Madox Ford Studies 6 (Amsterdam: Rodopi, 2007), pp. 155–64.

O'Malley, Seamus, 'How Much Mud Does A Man Need? Land and Liquidity in *Parade's End*', in Ashley Chantler and Rob Hawkes (eds), *Ford Madox Ford's Parade's End: The First World War, Culture, and Modernity*, International Ford Madox Ford Studies 13 (Amsterdam: Rodopi, 2014), pp. 119–28.

Owen, Wilfred, 'Mental Cases', *The Works of Wilfred Owen*, ed. Douglas Kerr (Ware: Wordsworth Poetry Library, 1994).

Paris, Michael, *Warrior Nation: Images of War in British Popular Culture, 1850–2000* (London: Reaktion, 2000).

Pick, Daniel, *War Machine: The Rationalisation of Slaughter in the Modern Age* (New Haven: Yale University Press, 1993).

Piette, Adam, 'War and Division in *Parade's End*', in Ashley Chantler and Rob Hawkes (eds), *Ford Madox Ford's Parade's End: The First World War, Culture, and Modernity*, International Ford Madox Ford Studies 13 (Amsterdam: Rodopi, 2014), pp. 141–52.

Pinkerton, Steve, 'Trauma and Cure in Rebecca West's *The Return of the Soldier*', *Journal of Modern Literature*, 32.1 (2008), pp. 1–12.

Pividori, Cristina, 'Eros and Thanatos Revisited: The Poetics of Trauma in Rebecca West's *The Return of the Soldier*', *Journal of the Spanish Association of Anglo-American Studies*, 32.2 (2010), pp. 89–104.

Rabinbach, Anson, *The Human Motor: Energy, Fatigue, and the Origins of Modernity* (New York: Basic, 1990).

Raitt, Suzanne, 'Early British Psychoanalysis and the Medico-Psychological Clinic', *History Workshop Journal*, 58 (2004), pp. 63–85.

Rankin, Guthrie, 'Broken Sleep', *British Medical Journal*, 2.3004 (27 July 1918), pp. 77–8.

Reid, Fiona, *Broken Men: Shell Shock, Treatment and Recovery in Britain 1914–30* (London: Continuum, 2012).

Rimbaud, Arthur, 'Parade', *Collected Poems*, trans. Martin Sorrell (Oxford: Oxford University Press, 2001).

Rivers, W. H. R., 'The Repression of War Experience', *Lancet* (February 1918), pp. 173–7.

Rivers, W. H. R., *Instinct and the Unconscious* (Cambridge: Cambridge University Press, 1920).

Roth, John K., *Freedom and the Moral Life: The Ethics of William James* (Philadelphia: Westminster Press, 1969).

Ryan, Judith, *The Vanishing Subject: Early Psychology and Literary Modernism* (Chicago: University of Chicago Press, 1991).

Sandler, Joseph, Alex Holder, Christopher Care and Anna Ursula Dreher, *Freud's Models of the Mind* (Madison, CT: International Universities Press, 1997).

Sassoon, Siegfried, *Memoirs of an Infantry Officer*, *The Complete Memoirs of George Sherston* (London: Faber and Faber, 1972), pp. 285–516.

Saunders, Max, *Ford Madox Ford: A Dual Life*, 2 vols (Oxford: Oxford University Press, 1996).

Saunders, Max, 'Ford Madox Ford: Further Bibliographies', *English Literature in Transition 1880–1920*, 43.2 (2000), pp. 131–205.

Saunders, Max, 'From Pre-Raphaelism to Impressionism', in Laura Colombino (ed.), *Ford Madox Ford and Visual Culture*, International Ford Madox Ford Studies 8 (Amsterdam: Rodopi, 2009), pp. 51–70.

Schwenger, Peter, *At the Borders of Sleep: On Liminal Literature* (Minneapolis: University of Minnesota Press, 2012).

Sharpe, Ella, 'Similar and Divergent Unconscious Determinants Underlying the Sublimations of Pure Art and Pure Science' [1938], *Collected Papers on Psychoanalysis* (London: Hogarth Press, 1950), pp. 137–54.

Shephard, Ben, *A War of Nerves: Soldiers and Psychiatrists 1914–1994* (London: Jonathan Cape, 2000).

Sherry, Vincent, *The Great War and the Language of Modernism* (New York: Oxford University Press, 2003).

Shildrick, Margrit, '"You are there, like my skin": Reconfiguring Relational Economies', in Sara Ahmed and Jackie Stacey (eds), *Thinking Through the Skin* (London: Routledge, 2001), pp. 160–73.

Showalter, Elaine, *The Female Malady: Women, Madness, and English Culture, 1830–1980* (New York: Penguin, 1985).

Showalter, Elaine, *Hystories: Hysterical Epidemics and Modern Media* (New York: Columbia University Press, 1997).

Sinclair, May, *A Journal of Impressions in Belgium* (London: Macmillan, 1915).

Sinclair, May, *Way of Sublimation* (c. 1915), Rare Book and Manuscript Library, University of Pennsylvania, Box 23.

Sinclair, May, *A Defence of Idealism* (London: Macmillan, 1917).

Sinclair, May, 'The Novels of Dorothy Richardson', *Little Review*, 4.12 (April 1918), pp. 3–11.

Sinclair, May, *Far End* (London: Hutchinson, 1926).

Sinclair, May, 'Portrait of My Uncle', *Tales Told by Simpson* (London: Macmillan, 1930), pp. 29–48.

Sinclair, May, *The Romantic* (Charleston, SC: Bibliobazaar, [1920] 2006).

Sinclair, May, *The Tree of Heaven* (Whitefish, MT: Kessinger, [1916] 2009).

Sinclair, May, 'Superseded', *Two Sides of a Question* (Whitefish, MT: Kessinger, [1910] 2009), pp. 203–332.

Sinclair, May, *The Three Sisters* (Whitefish, MT: Kessinger, [1914] 2010).

Sinclair, May, *Tasker Jevons: The Real Story* (Charleston, SC: Bibliobazaar, [1917] 2010).

Sinclair, May, *Anne Severn and the Fieldings* (Charleston, SC: Bibliobazaar, [1922] 2010).

Skinner, Paul, Introduction to Ford, *No Enemy: A Tale of Reconstruction*, ed. Paul Skinner (Manchester: Carcanet Press, [1929] 2002), pp. vii–xxiii.

Skinner, Paul, 'The Painful Process of Reconstruction: History in *No Enemy* and *Last Post*', in Joseph Wiesenfarth (ed.), *History and Representation in Ford Madox Ford's Writings*, International Ford Madox Ford Studies 3 (Amsterdam: Rodopi, 2004), pp. 65–75.

Smith, Adam, *The Theory of Moral Sentiments* (London: A. Millar, [1759] 1761).

Snitow, Ann Barr, *Ford Madox Ford and the Voice of Uncertainty* (Baton Rouge: Louisiana State University Press, 1984).

Sorum, Eve, 'Mourning and Moving On: Life After War in Ford Madox Ford's *The Last Post*', in Patricia Rae (ed.), *Modernism and Mourning* (Lewisberg, PA: Bucknell University Press, 2007), pp. 154–67.

Southborough, Lord, *Report of the War Office Committee of Enquiry Into 'Shell-Shock'* (London: HMSO, 1922).

Spielrein, Sabina, 'Destruction as a Cause of Coming into Being', *Journal of Analytical Psychology*, 39, ([1912] 1994), pp. 155–86.

Stang, Sondra J., *Ford Madox Ford* (New York: Ungar, 1977).

Stein, Edith, *On the Problem of Empathy*, trans. Waltraut Stein, 3rd rev. edn (Washington: ICS, [1759] 1761).

Stevenson, Randall, *Modernist Fiction*, rev. edn (Harlow: Prentice Hall, 1998).

Strauss, Harold, *Ford Madox Ford. Parade's End: The Story of an Old Book Newly Made* (New York: Knopf, 1950).

Stryker, Laurinda, 'Mental Cases: British Shellshock and the Politics of Interpretation', in Gail Braybon (ed.), *Evidence, History and the Great War: Historians and the Impact of 1914–18* (Oxford: Berghahn, 2003), pp. 154–71.

Summers-Bremner, Eluned, *Insomnia: A Cultural History* (London: Reaktion, 2008).

Tal, Kalí, *Worlds of Hurt* (Cambridge: Cambridge University Press, 1996).

Tatar, Maria, *Lustmord: Sexual Murder in Weimar Germany* (Princeton: Princeton University Press, 1997).

Tate, Trudi, *Modernism, History, and the First World War* (Manchester: Manchester University Press, 1998).

Trotter, David, 'Edwardian Sex Novels', *Critical Quarterly*, 31.1 (1989), pp. 92–106.

Trotter, David, *The English Novel in History: 1895–1920* (London: Routledge, 1993).

Vandevelde, Tom, '"Are You Going to Mind the Noise?": Mapping the Soundscape of *Parade's End*', in Ashley Chantler and Rob Hawkes (eds), *Ford Madox Ford's Parade's End: The First World War, Culture, and Modernity*, International Ford Madox Ford Studies 13 (Amsterdam: Rodopi, 2014), pp. 53–66.

West, Rebecca, and G. E. Hutchinson, 'On *The Return of the Soldier*', *Yale University Library Gazette*, 57.1–2 (1982), pp. 66–71.

West, Rebecca, *The Return of the Soldier* (London: Penguin, [1918] 1998).

West, Rebecca, *Selected Letters of Rebecca West*, ed. Bonnie Kime Scott (London: Yale University Press, 2000).

Woolf, Virginia, 'Modern Fiction', *Collected Essays*, 4 vols (London: Hogarth Press, 1966–7), II, pp. 103–10.

Woolf, Virginia, *Moments of Being*, ed. Jeanne Schulkind (San Diego: Harcourt Brace, [1976] 1985).

Woolf, Virginia, *Jacob's Room*, ed. Sue Roe (London: Penguin, [1922] 1992).

Woolf, Virginia, *Mrs Dalloway*, ed. Stella McNichol (London: Penguin, [1925] 2000).

Woolf, Virginia, *To the Lighthouse*, ed. Stella McNichol (London: Penguin, [1927] 2000).

Worringer, Wilhelm, *Abstraction and Empathy: A Contribution to the Psychology of Style*, trans. Michael Bullock (Chicago: Ivan R. Dee, [1908] 1997).

Wrenn, Angus, 'Wagner's *Ring* Cycle and *Parade's End*', in Ashley Chantler and Rob Hawkes (eds), *Ford Madox Ford's Parade's End: The First World War, Culture, and Modernity*, International Ford Madox Ford Studies 13 (Amsterdam: Rodopi, 2014), pp. 67–80.

Young, Kenneth, *Ford Madox Ford*, rev. edn (Harlow: Longmans, Green, 1970).

Index